LALA AMARNATH

THE MAKING OF A LEGEND

THE MAKING
OF A LEGEND

LALA
AMARNATH

LIFE AND TIMES

RAJENDER AMARNATH

Published in Great Britain by
SportsBooks Limited
1 Evelyn Court
Malvern Road
Cheltenham
GL50 2JR

A catalogue record for this book is available from
the British Library.

ISBN 9781899807 55 0

Printed and bound in England by
Cromwell Press.

CONTENTS

TO

SHARDA & KARAN

ACKNOWLEDGEMENTS

IT WOULDN'T be an understatement to say that this book would have been incomplete but for the affectionate contribution of my mother Kailash Kumari and other members of the family, especially Kamla, Tommy and Jimmy. Mum retrieved some rare documents for this book. There were other members of the family who recounted details from Papa's childhood. Undoubtedly, the credit for completing this book also goes to my wife Sharda for encouraging me to write it and my son Karan who spent innumerable days and nights patiently keying in the manuscript into the computer.

As a youngster, I had heard many stories about my father and Patiala from the people of that era. I was fortunate to have possessed K. Natwar Singh's *The Magnificent Maharaja*, Wally Hammond's *Cricket My World*, Vijay Hazare's *Cricket Replayed*, Sir Donald Bradman's *Farewell to Cricket*, J C Mitra's *Indian Sports Flashback*, Mukhatir Bhatti's *Pakistan in Test Cricket* and *Wisden* to shed light on my father's cricketing exploits. *The Cricketer* magazine very kindly sent me details of the 1946 England tour by the Indian team. The staff at the Nehru Library helped me trace newspapers from the early 1930s. I would also like to place on record my thanks to P R Mansingh, K Jagannadha Rao, Anandji Dossa, Rajneesh Gupta and many of my friends who contributed towards completing this book.

PROLOGUE

PAPA'S MEMORY was unbelievable, his observations impeccable. He remembered the minutest details of his career with amazing precision. I would constantly plead with him to share the vast storehouse of his memory, spanning several decades of glorious cricket and stories from that period. Papa's perpetual refrain was "I'll do it soon." His health was deteriorating and I convinced him to narrate everything on tape so that we could string his recollections together as his autobiography. He was all set to do that when a freak accident at home left him with a broken hip-bone and delayed the recording. Later, the untimely demise of his favourite son-in-law, Suresh Chander Sharma, broke his heart and he never recovered from the shock.

As the domestic help was forbidden from handling either the precious Belgian whisky or wine crystalware, from the time I was very young I was often entrusted with the responsibility of entertaining his guests, unofficially assuming the role of a barman. Maharajas, Nawabs, film personalities, politicians, industrialists and, of course, cricketers would frequent our home. There was never a dull moment, with Papa holding centre stage, unfolding one anecdote after another. Raja Bhalindra Singh, son of Maharaja Bhupinder Singh of Patiala, remained his closest friend till his death. Both would nurse their drinks till well past midnight, remembering good old Patiala days with Papa recounting his experiences with the Maharaja of Patiala.

Most anecdotes in this book have their genesis in those late evening sessions at home, when I would catch each word while the audience would be regaled. I would invariably jot down these interesting anecdotes to share them with my brothers Surender and Mohinder when they returned from tours. Although I had listened to those stories, not even in my wildest dreams did I imagine writing Papa's biography. I know he would have done a stupendously better job than I could ever hope to. After all, he had lived it all. A chance suggestion by my wife Sharda one evening spurred me to attempt my hand at writing this biography. Fortunately, with my mother remembering everything and the majority of the paper clippings and his old photographs secure at home, my job became that much easier.

Having spent more time with him than any of my siblings, I reckon I knew him better than them. He was never overawed by anyone in his life. It was always the other way round. Often, his dominant personality made even his superiors squirm in his presence. Let me cite one example. On one occasion, the general manager of the Indian Railways was inaugurating an athletic meet. Since all arrangements fell under his jurisdiction, he wanted to impress everyone present, including Papa. Repeatedly, he would enquire about the food served to the athletes. Papa evaded the question by simply nodding his head, offering no comments. Presuming it to be in the affirmative, the general manager requested Papa to comment without fear. "So be it," Papa said. "The food served to the athletes is so bad that even my dogs wouldn't touch that." Everyone, including the general manager, was left speechless by this remark.

After retiring from the Railways in the mid-1960s, Papa continued to occupy the Railway bungalow for another decade in his capacity as sports advisor on the recommendation of the then minister for Railways, Gulzarilal Nanda. The minister offered him a lucrative package but Papa refused to accept money. To him, his dignity was far more important than money and he accepted an honorarium of rupee one as salary along with the accommodation. Unfortunately, when the minister's portfolio changed, jealous officers got down to finding ways to evict Papa from the premises. This forced him to take the Railways to court, where he won a favourable verdict. He finally vacated the premises when Madhu Dandavate, Railway minister in the Janata Party government, agreed to waive off all dues and release his funds. Unfortunately, the funds never reached him.

Papa was often projected as an angry man and a fighter to the core but few people knew that he was, in fact, very soft deep down and forgave people in due course of time. For example, on the Indian team's tour of England in 1946, Britton Jones offered him his hand of friendship. Now, Jones was the manager of the

Indian team that had infamously sent Papa back from the tour of England in 1936. Instead of declining, Papa shook hands with him in public, winning the hearts of even his critics.

His large-heartedness was often taken advantage of but being a firm believer in destiny he took it all in his stride. After his father's death, we went to the village to take charge of our ancestral properties, including some farmland which would have seen the family through the financial crisis it was in at that time. In the village, an old woman begged him not to sell the shop where her son had worked for my grandfather. Unable to bear her tears, he gifted her the shop with all the merchandise in it.

As soon as the village heard of this benevolent gesture, many peasants started to pour in with similar requests. Papa then told the village sarpanch to distribute all his father's land to those landless peasants who had tilled it for him. For one with such varied qualities and different moods, Papa was basically a simple man. He never forgot people who, and places which, helped him to achieve what he had. Throughout his life, the Bombay Gymkhana, where he became the first Indian to score a Test century, remained his Mecca. Whenever he drove past this ground, he would take off his hat as a token of respect. "What I am today, it is due to this place," he would always say.

As a family man, Papa was quite different at home. He tried to spend whatever little time he had with his family. Despite carrying a reputation of being short-tempered, he was kind and gentle with his four daughters. But none of us brothers was spared when it came to cricket. We were forced out of our cozy beds in the extremely cold Delhi winters so that we could get acclimatised to English weather conditions. He created every possible playing condition at home to ensure that we were habituated to playing in them. He was a guide, philosopher, friend and guru combined in one. Both Surender and Mohinder owed their international careers to him — he was our Dronacharya.

Rajender Amarnath
Gurgaon, Haryana

ONE

EARLY LIFE & LAHORE

TOWARDS THE dawn of the twentieth century, British-ruled India was fragmented into many principalities, each governed according to its ruler's whims and fancies. Kapurthala, a prominent state in northern India was probably the only one where French influence was the most predominant. British presence was visible too but in token measure — that too only because of its paramount status as the ruler of the country. Thus, cricket was confined mainly to areas where the British resided or had their club cricket grounds. Most of the subjects in Kapurthala state looked upon cricket as unsuitable to their way of life and nature. This outlook, however, was to undergo a sea change and Kapurthala was to find a place in the annals of world cricket.

Amarnath was born on September 11, 1911 into a Brahmin family of a businessman father, Nanak Chand. The elders in Nanak Chand's family frowned at his vocation — business — since he did not sustain the established tradition of spreading knowledge of the scriptures as practised by their ancestors for centuries. The family originally hailed from Talban area in Punjab and its ancestors came from the lineage of *Aathwanshi* (group of eight families) Bharadwaj Brahmins. They were revered as Guru Devs (literary and spiritual teachers) in many villages where people came for their blessings. Much to their discomfort, the enterprising Nanak Chand soon became a leading money-lender, with quite a profitable business. With plenty of money at his disposal, he bought large tracts of farmland and got local peasants to till it. He also invested his profits intelligently in large commercial properties and rented them to the local businessmen for an extra yield.

When Amarnath was born, the joyous occasion was celebrated for days together as he was the first son born among all the family, both from his father's and mother's side. As was the Hindu custom, a pundit was called to draw the newborn's horoscope and make predictions. The pundit prophesied that the child would travel around the world and rub shoulders with Maharajas all his life. All laughed and dismissed it as the usual way of soothsayers who exaggerated the events for a better reward. The newborn was initially named Lal Chand by his father but his doting mother, Saraswati found the name quite outdated and unsuitable for her son. She renamed her son "Amarnath," "Amar" meaning immortal and "Nath", lord.

According to his father Nanak Chand, Amarnath was a very protected child due to the fear of his being poisoned by his relations. His indulgent mother made sure that he was not deprived of any thing. She tasted everything first before allowing her baby to eat anything which was offered. In the evenings, Amarnath was regularly taken out by his mother to the park to play with other children. On one such occasion, while he was on his way to the park, little Amarnath saw some Englishmen playing cricket and was instantly drawn towards the game. He promptly demanded a cricket bat from his mother. The loving mother searched high and low in Kapurthala but could not find a single shop that sold cricket bats. Eager to oblige her son, she hit upon a brilliant idea. She went to the local carpenter and asked him to make a small bat, which cost one paisa. When this bat was presented to Amarnath, he jumped with joy and clung on to his mother's neck in excitement. With this prized possession, Amarnath did not lose much time in collecting a number of boys of the area and start playing cricket.

It was always Amarnath who batted first, as the bat belonged to him and the others hardly got an opportunity to use the willow, as he never got out. At times, when the rubber ball was torn to shreds and Amarnath's appetite remained unsatiated, he would ask his friends to throw pebbles, which he would hit lustily with a horizontal bat. Amarnath recalled causing quite a few injuries to the ladies and old people passing by. His boisterous brigade would create such a commotion while playing cricket that many a complaint inevitably began to reach Nanak Chand. Infuriated, he burnt Amarnath's bat one day. It broke the young boy's heart and he rushed to his mother for consolation.

When Nanak Chand left for work the following day, Amarnath's mother gave her son one paisa to get a new bat made by the carpenter. This routine continued for some time till his father realised that the boy was now grown up enough to be sent to school. Amarnath was enrolled at Randhir High School in the hope that he would concentrate on his studies. This move solved two problems for Nanak Chand. First, Amarnath was spending time in school. More important, no fresh complaints reached him from the neighbours. The distance between his home and school gave Amarnath little time to play cricket with his friends. Since the sport was not played at school, he was forced to play hockey like other boys. Finding this game rough and not to his liking, he was not keen on pursuing it. Moreover, Amarnath was constantly getting hit on the knuckles causing him minor injuries and also leading to a lot of heated exchange of words.

On his way to school, Amarnath would watch the State Army doing morning drills mainly comprising running and exercising. Since his heart did not lie in hockey, he started emulating the Army by running and exercising on his own. "I loved and enjoyed going for long runs very early in my youth," he would say later in life. On Sundays, the Europeans played cricket at their club and an enthralled Amarnath watched their matches for hours on end, always dreaming of wearing the same beautiful flannel dress and solar hat. The days passed without any scolding at home or in school. In due course, Amarnath chanced upon a local club called SSS and played organised cricket for the first time in his life.

Everything seemed to be going fine and all seemed hunky-dory when at the tender age of ten, Amarnath faced his life's biggest heartbreak. The death of his mother caused a big vacuum in his life. Since Nanak Chand neither remarried nor took time away from his business, Amarnath started to find life very lonely and hard. Finding him becoming a recluse, Amarnath's paternal grandparents Milkey Ram and Malavi decided to take him with them to their native place — Lahore.

This move brought about an incredible change in Amarnath's life. Apart from being strategically located, Lahore was also the centre of education and culture since the days of the great Mughals and later, as the capital of Maharaja Ranjit Singh. In the early twentieth century, Lahore was called the Paris of the East. It had wide boulevards, beautiful gardens with fountains, the ever bustling Anarkali Bazaar, majestic Red Fort, the cool River Ravi. Furthermore, there were sprawling parks in which cricket would be played and the Minto Park was especially reserved for this game. For the young lad, it was like stepping into the magical world of dreams.

Maharaja Bhupinder Singh's passion for cricket and his desire that the princes of Patiala be coached well, saw him bring a number of English and Australian professional cricketers to India. Whenever they travelled to Lahore, Amarnath would be present at the Minto Park, standing behind the nets for hours and observing them very closely. On returning home, he would practise in front of a mirror. He realised very early in his life the advantage of using the feet to the slow bowlers. Where other batsmen struggled against spinners, he relished the very sight of them.

Watching his grandson's love for, and obsession with, cricket, Milkey Ram encouraged him to go and play wherever an opportunity arose. Amarnath was once again enjoying the same love and care, which he had missed in the months after his mother's death. His grandparents ensured that he did not feel neglected at any stage. All his requirements were taken care of. Probably, over-pampering spoilt Amarnath early in his childhood.

The Hindu Arya Samaj was very active, too, although Lahore mainly comprised a large Muslim population. Both communities were equally aggressive in all spheres of life, including sports. Club rivalries often spilled over to the streets after a game, resulting in many an unnecessary scuffle and injury. Mostly it was the losing team, which waited outside the ground to settle scores! The Punjabi language, particularly of the strain spoken in Lahore, always carried few seemingly abusive expletives in each sentence, without anyone being conscious of their connotations. Sometimes, the epithets were used even in a casual exchange of pleasantries. During this period, there was a general perception that all those who inhaled the fresh air of Lahore behaved like ferocious tigers, whether in sports or in politics. No Lahori would back off from a problem under any circumstance and would face it unflinchingly without thinking of the consequences.

Those years in Lahore moulded and formed Amarnath's character and personality. These factors, combined with the prevailing circumstances, made him aggressive (a style prevalent then) and persuasive on the field and even in his personal life. Off the field, Amarnath learnt the art to impress all with his command over Urdu, which he had learned and mastered at school.

Although he did not talk much about his childhood, Amarnath would share some anecdotes if he were in an exceptionally good mood. "At Kapurthala, apart from Urdu and English, French was also encouraged in the schools due to its influence on the royalty," he recalled. "Though French was seemingly encouraged, it remained confined mostly to the books, either due to non-availability of a French teacher or due to the lackadaisical attitude of the students towards the subject. In school, when I opted for French, many eyebrows were raised, some even taunting me. 'Are you planning to go to Paris?' they asked, but I was adamant. The state of Kapurthala granted me a scholarship of five rupees to pursue the studies of this language. Ironically, money came but not much of French!"

Yet, cricket was always an obsession and was beginning to take precedence over everything else. At the slightest opportunity, he would be playing cricket. When he was about seven, he was desperate to go and play cricket with his friends each evening. "Once," Amarnath said in his inimitable style, "a lady from the neighbourhood handed me her small child and I had to take care of the baby till she had finished her conversation with my mother. I missed the game that day. The next evening, as I was about to leave to play with my friends, the lady came and made me baby- sit again. This frustrating routine continued for a few more days depriving me of the opportunity of playing my favourite sport. I had to quickly devise a plan to get out of this situation once and for all. One day, before the lady could hand over the child to me I myself sought her, thereby surprising her. Taking the child with me to the park, I sat on an ant-hill.

Within minutes, hundreds of tiny brown ants were all over us, biting us. The baby screamed out loud in pain but I held my agony. I carried the wailing child to her mother, looking terribly guilty for causing the little innocent soul such discomfort and pain! Next day, when the lady tried to hand over her baby, the poor little child clung on, stubbornly refusing to let go of her mother and come to me. I was now a free boy, able to enjoy my cricket once again."

After completing his matriculation at Lahore, Amarnath was enrolled at Aligarh to pursue his further studies but destiny had something else in store for him. Within a short time, Amarnath was recalled to Lahore by his club to play some important matches. From here, he went to Amritsar and various other places but could never return to Aligarh. Amarnath's biggest regret was that he could not pursue his studies further due to his preoccupation with cricket.

If Bombay was considered the epicentre of cricket south of the Aravalli ranges, then Lahore produced many outstanding cricketers from the northern part of India till Partition robbed her of this nursery. Cricket was played hard, with no quarter asked and none given on the field. In this environment, Amarnath learnt a bitter experience, which opened his eyes and taught him that nothing comes easy in life. He saw people with connections unscrupulously taking advantage of the situation irrespective of their calibre and capabilities. Amarnath was the up and coming youngster for the Hindus in Lahore. This qualification came to naught when he was selected for the Hindu team as a wicket-keeper batsman to play in a local tournament in the early 1930s but could not keep wickets. Prof. Vishwanath, a teacher in the Government College, insisted on keeping wickets. None of the members of the team could do anything other than accept the Professor's diktat due to his influence. This episode left a lasting impression on the young cricketer, who decided to work extra hard to become indispensable as wicket-keeper batsman to his side.

Amarnath was constantly practising — at times for hours on his own, hitting the ball hard in the nets. Despite all the dedication, hard work and early lessons, he strongly felt the need for someone to guide and help him with his game. Without a proper coach, his faults continued to haunt him. Lahore, being the nursery of cricket, gave all aspiring cricketers plenty of opportunity to excel in local tournaments. It was here, while playing in one such game that luck smiled upon him. 'Master' Roop Lal, an elderly Railway employee while passing through the park, saw a young wicket-keeper standing up to a pace bowler and whipping the bails in a flash on the leg-side. Intrigued, the keen eyes of the Master coach kept rooted to the ground to see if the young lad performed as well with the bat. Amarnath did not disappoint him. If his movements were swift while keeping wickets, his nimble feet made batting look so easy and lucrative. After the game was over, Master approached Amarnath and asked if he would be keen to play at a higher level. For Amarnath, this meant playing with the goras (the English) and the Maharajas. He was thrilled at the prospect of going to the big cities around the country and even travelling to England.

After getting through with the trials successfully and on Master's recommendation, Amarnath was enrolled with a club called Crescent Cricket Club (CCC) in Lahore. "I had to perform better than all the other players, as I was the only Hindu playing for the predominantly Muslim club," he recalled. Progress began under the watchful eyes of Master Roop Lal who gave him a simple coaching lesson. He told Amarnath, "If the ball is pitched up to you, then your left foot should reach the ball and you should hit the ball as hard as possible. If the ball is pitched short, then your right leg should always be in line, enabling you to get behind the ball. In case the ball bounces above the waist, use the horizontal bat to either cut or pull the ball with full force." Amarnath found these words simple, yet most effective. The experience at CCC made him very tough and aggressive at a young age. The experience taught him that cricket was a big world with small space, where only the fittest survived. And, he wanted to be one of them.

With his never-say-die attitude, Amarnath was not the kind to be left out so easily. He soon proved his potential in Lahore with consistent performances. Word spread of his impressive display. On one of his trips to Lahore, Frank Tarrant, an Australian coach employed with Patiala, watched Amarnath during a local tournament. He was so impressed with Amarnath's approach and style of cricket that he wrote a letter to the Board of Control for Cricket in India, saying, "This young boy's brilliance behind the stumps is awesome and batting so authoritative that any team would like him to be on their side." With India due to make a historic trip to England in 1932, Tarrant was trying to help the selectors but the reply was not up to his expectations. The Board said that since they had not watched Amarnath in action, they could not say much. In other words, it was a polite refusal to include him in the list of the probables. Though Amarnath missed the tour, he was not disheartened. On the contrary, he was elated at the very thought that his name was being proposed for the All India team.

If Amarnath was on the verge of playing for India and was an asset to his team in Lahore, he was also a threat to his opponents, particularly the Muslims while representing the Hindus in some local matches. Once, he had a tiff with the members of the Muslim team a day before a game. In his usual boastful manner, Amarnath declared that he would destroy the Muslim attack single-handedly and win the match for his team. Tempers in such matches rose high, even leading to scuffles in the stands. The Muslims, realising the importance of the match and Amarnath's capabilities, decided to remove the threat before the match. That evening, Amarnath was strolling in the Anarkali Bazaar with his friends, when suddenly a group of supporters of the Muslim team attacked them with *lathis* shouting, "Break Amarnath's bones!" Since he was the fulcrum of the Hindu team, his friends fell on him, covering him and taking blows on their own bodies, till reinforcements in the form of Hindu supporters came to their rescue.

Far from breaking Amarnath's resolve, the incident made him more determined to perform under stress. Minto Park was the heart and soul of Lahore cricket and everyone interested in this game flocked to the ground to witness the best of cricket. The ground had a tradition of displaying full information of the next match on a large board outside the main entrance including the names of the teams and its members. Once Amarnath became a celebrity after his Test century against the MCC in Bombay, only his name would be written on the big board to allow people to know that he was playing the following day and, invariably, the result was a large gathering.

In December 1932, a team from Ceylon (as Sri Lanka was known) was touring Punjab to play a couple of matches. Amarnath was expecting a big break against the visiting team but politics got the better of his luck. When the All India team was announced to play Ceylon, he was named 13th man, which meant watching the game from the dressing room. Hoping for a better deal from the local team, Amarnath waited anxiously for its announcement. When the news came, it rubbed salt into his wounds. Amarnath was named 12th man for the local team. Frustrated and baffled, he couldn't understand this treatment. If he was good enough to be part of the All India team, then surely he deserved a place in the local side's XI, he thought. Disenchanted and annoyed at this treatment, Amarnath declined even that invitation. Many felt he had acted in haste, possibly harming his chances of playing higher grade of cricket but he was adamant. To show his disapproval, he did not go to the ground to witness the match despite several messages and reminders, some even threatening. Instead, he went to the nets to concentrate on his mission — to represent India at all cost and prove everyone wrong for neglecting him.

If one opportunity bypassed him, another came his way soon. A big moment in the history of Indian cricket arrived when MCC (Marylebone Cricket Club) accepted the Indian Board's invitation for an official tour of India in 1933 under the captaincy of Douglas Jardine. As the historic day approached, a series of events jeopardised the tour. "First, MCC received a telegram from the Indian Board, stating in bold and measured terms that the selection of MCC side as has been announced was a disgusting insult to 'India and Indian cricket'. Unless, more stars are added to the list, the tour would be cancelled as a protest," wrote Wally Hammond in *Cricket My World*. "Thunderstruck, MCC officials looked over the list of the selected and found that six to eight of most famous players were supported by others very nearly as good. In fact, the side was completely representative and might have given even Australia 'a jolly good struggle'. Cables began to burn and even political circles were consulted in case any serious trouble arose at this critical time in India's history. Fortunately, the bubble was pricked and it was later found that a clerk with no authority at all sent the cable on behalf of the board." It was surprising and hard to believe that such a faux pas could be made with Anthony de Mello functioning as the Board secretary.

With the misunderstanding removed, the tour proceeded

as scheduled with MCC's first match against CB Rubie's XI at Karachi. The next important fixture was at Lahore against the Northern India team. This was the opportunity Amarnath had been anxiously waiting for and hoped that better sense would prevail in the selection of the team. He knew the importance of this match and had laboured hard to prepare for it. The good news came when *Associate Press'* Lahore correspondent Mr. Wagle used his influence as did Tarrant and secured Amarnath a berth in the side. The match was a disaster for the home side, which collapsed in both the innings. The saving grace for Amarnath was that he managed to score 26 from a meagre total of 50-odd runs scored by his side in the second innings. Maharaja Bhupinder Singh of Patiala was not impressed by this display of the Northern India team or by Amarnath whom Tarrant had described as a future India star.

After wrapping up this game, MCC concentrated on another battle, this time against the Maharaja of Patiala's team in Amritsar. Tarrant prevailed upon the Maharaja to include Amarnath in the Southern Punjab team on the basis of his birth qualification. Maharaja Bhupinder Singh was known for his hospitality and to keep this tradition intact, he got a new pavilion constructed at the Lawrence ground (now called the Gandhi ground) for the comfort of both teams. The entire ground was covered with colourful *shamianas* (tents). When the Maharaja walked along with the MCC captain for the toss, the crowd broke into a continuous applause, knowing the historical importance of this match.

"There was great enthusiasm amongst the large sporting public of the holy city of Amritsar to witness the first appearance of the MCC against Southern Punjab," wrote the *Bombay Chronicle*. The home side won the toss and batted first on what seemed to be an ideal batting pitch. Nobby Clark and Morris Nichols opened the tourist attack and generated tremendous speed off the strip to reduce Southern Punjab to 12 for three wickets. Wazir, Qamaruddin and Prithviraj were all cooling their heels in the pavilion. This was not the start the 8,000-odd strong local supporters had come to witness. The Maharaja too expected a better show from his reliable and experienced players.

Amarnath had made three when he faced a tense moment. There was a loud appeal for caught behind the wicket by Levett and the close-in fielders but the umpire negated it. This umpire was none other than Frank Tarrant, who along with his son Lawrence, was officiating this match. After the over, the MCC captain Jardine walked up to Amarnath and asked him if he had played the ball. Amarnath responded, "There was definitely a sound." Hearing this Jardine retorted, "The bloody sound could have been heard clearly even in Sydney." It was a none too subtle reference to the Australian umpires officiating the game.

This kiss of life changed the complexion of the match. The young man did not look back. Along with Yuvraj Yadvindra Singh, Amarnath tore the menacing attack to shreds. If the Lahore boy entertained the vociferously cheering large supporters with his swashbuckling strokes around the ground, then the young prince added flavour to the proceedings with his delightful cover-drives and astonishing lofted shots. With every stroke of Amarnath's that bisected the fieldsmen, the crowd cheered lustily. The clapping became louder in the newly-constructed pavilion when Yadvindra Singh was on strike. Elated, the proud father Maharaja Bhupinder Singh clapped with a broad smile to set in motion a similar response from the hundreds of enthusiastic followers.

The repair work had started in the form of a counter attack, which released the pressure off the two batsmen. Amarnath cut and pulled anything short in length and drove the spinners in front of the wicket with power-packed strokes. Finding the home side in a strong position, the crowd cheered continuously at all their strokes, even if they were intercepted by the alert MCC fielders.

After lunch, Yadvindra (66) lost his wicket to a quick delivery from Clark but the rocking boat had been steadied. At the other end, Amarnath continued to counter and dominate the fierce MCC attack in his usual style. This display amazed everyone and they could hardly believe that it was only his second first-class game. Unmindful of the wickets tumbling at the other end, Amarnath continued to punish the slow bowlers. He often danced four to five feet down the wicket to drive the spinners through the covers or lift them over the heads of the fielders to the fence.

When Amarnath was in his 90s, the Maharaja himself walked in to bat to the thunderous applause from the gallery. In the company of His Excellency, running singles was a risk and stealing a run completely out of the question. Patiently, the young lad waited till he drove Langridge to the mid-off boundary to reach a well-deserved century. The applause rose to a crescendo and the Maharaja himself came across the pitch to pat Amarnath on his shoulder in appreciation. Hardly had the euphoria calmed down when the excited Amarnath fell victim to Clark. The Maharaja stayed on the crease for sometime, swinging the willow to reach 22 runs, before his luck too ran out when he tried to squeeze a single only to find himself short of the crease. "Thank God," remembered the non-striker Nazir, "it was Maharaja's call and not mine!" At tea, the score read 210 for six wickets.

The start after the recess was delayed as the teams were entertained to tea by Municipal Commissioner Khan Saheb Hissam-u-din. Normally, the timings of the match and the recess were shuffled to suit the Maharaja's mood and this tradition was followed at any given time without any protest. Every influential person in the city, whether Hindu, Muslim or Sikh, lost no opportunity to get involved in the match in some way or the other. The deputy commissioner and other English officers, understanding the importance of these communities after a great deal of deliberation, managed to accommodate them. These manoeuvres were primarily to be seen in the company of the English and the Maharaja to raise their stature and respect in the eyes of the local people. As the Maharaja was known to enjoy fancy dress, even a fancy dress dance was arranged but only a select few were invited from the home team. The English team was out in full strength to enjoy the evening. The ambience was carnival-like. All those who could not make it to the fancy dress dance were invited to Pearl Talkies for a private show. "Though watching a show at the 'Talkies' in itself meant that you were special, I declined as I was tired and wanted to concentrate on cricket," Amarnath recalled.

The home side was bowled out for 264 the following day and the MCC innings commenced at 11.30. The wicket was still playing true. The visitors' strong line-up made their intentions loud and clear that they had come to India on serious business. The fielders were sent on a leatherhunt. The Maharaja found the proceedings unfruitful and boring, as the tourists accumulated runs at will. With his bowlers making no impact on them, he retired to the pavilion midway through the innings. At the end of the day, MCC had piled up a huge score of 324 for four when the game was called off at 5 p.m. None of the bowlers including the great Mohammed Nissar was able to stop the run flow.

The third day's play started forty-five minutes behind schedule on account of Armistice Day Service. The Yuvraj led the team in the absence of his father who had gone to the Golden Temple in the morning and had not returned at the time of the start of play. The home side bowlers continued to suffer till MCC declared at 480 for eight. The match ended in a draw when Wazir Ali and Prithviraj were associated in a century partnership in the second innings. For Amarnath, success in this match brought him into the limelight and opened the door for a possible chance to play for India. He was hailed as a bright prospect for India and Tarrant was a happy man, because his observation was coming true.

Having proved his potential, Amarnath was invited to play for Patiala at the Baradari ground. This was his first visit to this part of the world and he was quite an attraction after his last match. With Lady Luck smiling brightly, he scored another quick 56 runs in 46 minutes to impress H D Kanga, member of the Selection Committee. Kanga invited Amarnath to attend the All India trials in Bombay. "The journey to Bombay via Delhi was enjoyable but long. I could hardly sleep. Every time the thought of representing India crossed my mind, I would get butterflies in my stomach," Amarnath recalled.

On November 25, 1933, two teams assembled at the Esplanade maidan for the trials. Wazir Ali led one side which consisted of Dilawar Hussain, Shahabudin, Baqa Jilani, Nazir Ali, Amir Elahi to name a few of the heavyweights. C K Nayudu led the other side comprising Yuvraj Patiala, M J Gopalan, Mushtaq Ali, C S Nayudu, Amarnath, etc. The first two trials did not spot any hidden talent, though Yuvraj and Amarnath were tipped to represent India. Vijay Merchant was a big flop in these matches but the selectors wanted to include him at any cost. Contrary to expectations, Amarnath too did not score many runs and A L Hosie, one of the selectors, asked him the reason for these failures. Amarnath told him that he was not an opening batsman and he had been told to open the innings like other wicket-keepers. "Allow me to bat at number three and then judge," said

Amarnath. "Okay," replied Hosie. Another trial was held to finalise the All India team for the first Test. The trials were held at the Bombay Gymkhana ground where Amarnath scored 50 and an unbeaten 78 to secure a place for the inaugural Test. "It was the greatest moment of my life when Hosie congratulated me on my selection and asked me to go to the Army and Navy store to let the tailor take measurements for my blazer and cap. The walk from the ground to the store and then to the hotel was like a dream but it wasn't. It was reality!"

The All India team was led by C K Nayudu and included Navle, Jai, Amarnath, Merchant, Ramji, Amar Singh, Jamshedji, Wazir Ali, Colah and Mohammed Nissar. Many felt bad for Lall Singh for not being considered for the home series despite playing for India in 1932 in England. It was not that the selectors did not pick him. If the Indian Board had earlier given MCC sleepless nights, it was their turn to face unpleasant but harsh reality. Douglas Jardine objected to Lall Singh's inclusion on the grounds that the Sikh was stationed at Malaya (Malaysia) and hadn't completed his residential qualification in India to play for the country. The Indian Board tried their best to impress upon Jardine but he was in no mood to accommodate them. The rules were clearly defined and the Imperial Cricket Council (as ICC was known then) decided to back the English captain. Poor Lall Singh had to sit out and watch the game in disbelief. This episode demonstrated the uncompromising attitude and the strong will-power of the English captain. Despite this, the cricket crazy people of Bombay waited anxiously for the author of the infamous Bodyline tactics in the recently-concluded Ashes series in Australia. The question on everyone's mind was whether Jardine would perform an encore in India or not.

TWO

THE MAKING OF A LEGEND

DECEMBER 15, 1933 was the historic day on which the governor of Bombay, Lord Brabourne, was introduced to both teams at the Gymkhana ground. After this formality, the great grand personality of Indian cricket, C K Nayudu, walked in with Douglas Jardine for the toss. The Indian captain won the toss and elected to bat first on what looked like a good batting strip. "Never had Bombay turned out in such large numbers for a cricket festival, as they did on Friday for the opening Test match between India and England," wrote the *Bombay Chronicle*. "The estimated 50,000 people crowded the stands and every vantage point from which a view could be obtained."

The atmosphere was both electric and tense when Wazir Ali and Navle walked in to take strike. The Indian batsmen were born entertainers and loved enthralling crowds with their strokeplay but lacked patience when the bowling was tight and accurate. This weakness turned out to be a major stumbling block for the home side as the professional England team exploited this to its advantage. The Indians soon found the tourist attack difficult to negotiate due to self-created problems. Despite being well set and cruising, the home side lost wickets at crucial junctures due to unwarranted attacking shots.

In the first innings, Wazir Ali, Amarnath and C K Nayudu all got out playing across the line. The Indian batsmen had thrown away the advantage of the toss and managed a moderate score of 219. Amarnath was the top scorer with 38 but the rest simply gifted their wickets away.

When the home side fielded, C K Nayudu arranged an attacking field like the English, for both his opening bowlers Nissar and Amar Singh. This tactic misfired because the conditions had changed. Unmindful, the Indian captain continued with his aggressive approach despite runs flowing without restraint. The English batsmen feasted on this non-penetrative bowling and found large gaps. To make matters worse, the Indian close-in fielders dropped crucial chances. The tourists flourished and they amassed 438 runs.

Mohammed Nissar bowled with hostility to pick up five wickets and troubled every batsman, except Hedley Verity who scored a well-compiled century. It was rather sad that Amar Singh did not see eye-to-eye with his captain due to personal reasons. To embarras C K Nayudu, he bowled with shoes that had rubber soles. It did not affect the captain but Amar Singh's bowling and reputation suffered. This rivalry within the Indian camp robbed her of effectiveness as well as any chance of doing well against the tourists.

With a huge deficit, Wazir Ali and Navle were expected to give India a decent start but that was not to be. Both the openers were back in the pavilion with only 21 runs on the board. The crowd had witnessed Amarnath's short but classic batting display in the first innings and hoped for a better show. "The advent of Amarnath, the dashing Patiala youngster, raised fresh hopes in the hearts of India's supporters," reported the *Bombay Chronicle*. "In the company of his captain, he pulled India out of the deep trouble. The Patiala colt went on merrily and to the crowd's delight punished all English bowlers to his heart's content. His was the correct policy to adopt because he showed that English bowling was not as formidable as it looked. Amarnath's vigour and exuberance heartened the remaining Indian batsmen to retrieve the poor show of the first innings."

With each passing over, Amarnath grew in confidence and Clark, Nichols and Verity looked so simple to handle. The short rising deliveries were cut or hit to the square-leg boundary. Spinners came on to receive special treatment from his Gunn & Moore non-jar bat. He raced to his first 50 with the help of

11 fours, two twos and two singles. It was as if destiny had reserved this day especially for the bubbling youngster. Even the
fast-scoring Nayudu was left far behind. By the time the first
hour had passed, Amarnath had scored 70.

The real drama unfolded after tea when he and Nayudu
pounced on the English bowlers. The singles and boundaries
came at will for both the batsmen. With a view to check the
flow of runs, Jardine re-arranged his field and adopted defensive
methods. At one stage, the pace bowlers were bowling to Amarnath without a slip and other fielders spread to deep point,
square and fine-leg boundaries to intercept his cut or pull shots
but without success.

The news of such tremendous batting spread like wild fire
and thousands poured into the already packed ground. Amarnath galloped from 70 to 90 with a few more hits over the
ropes. Sensing history in the making, the crowd became ecstatic,
loudly cheering each stroke from his flashing blade. They were
enjoying the young Indian's supremacy over an attack that had
looked menacing earlier. The glorious moment arrived when
Amarnath reached his century in only 117 minutes. Describing his century, one newspaper wrote, "His daring tactics were
rewarded time and again by shots that reached the fence with
the twinkle of an eye-lid, no less than eighteen times." "It was
an innings full of power and pleasure," remembered another.
Even Jardine walked up to Amarnath and congratulated the
youngster for becoming the first Indian to score a century on
debut or otherwise. He applauded the hundred and reportedly,
confessed: "I just couldn't place a field for him" — or words to
that effect. Years afterwards, Jardine confirmed the truth of that
press report, adding "On that day he, (Amarnath) did what he
pleased."

Amarnath remembered every moment of it and described it
with pride. "When I completed the single to reach my century,
C K Nayudu touched his bat at the crease and walked down
the pitch to shake hands and congratulate me. Since the ball
was still in play, the throw landed in the wicket-keeper's gloves
with C K out of the crease. The wicket-keeper Elliott looked at his
captain for his approval to run the Indian skipper out but the
English captain disapproved with a gesture. It was a wonderful
display of true sporting spirit!"

There was pandemonium on the ground as thousands rushed towards the middle to garland their new hero. Such was the rush of the exuberant spectators across the field to congratulate the centurion that Jardine and the umpire had to restrain them. The sound of clapping was so deafening that even the public announcement system was drowned in the noise. While play was held up, the Army band kept playing various tunes including 'God save the King'.

When play resumed, C K Nayudu told Amarnath to apply the brakes and refrain from playing shots. This advice confused him, as he did not know the defensive game. To keep the skipper happy, Amarnath would jump out to the spinners and then remembering the instructions, block the half-volleys or push the full-toss. In the fifteen minutes to the close, Amarnath added only two runs to his century — he regretted having followed the instructions while remembering this innings later in his life. The third-wicket partnership yielded 138 with Amarnath remaining unbeaten at 102 and C K Nayudu 44 at the end of the third day. At the draw of stumps, the police had to rush in to the ground to save Amarnath from the large crowd that rushed in from all directions to shake hands with him. For once in his lifetime, C K Nayudu had been overshadowed in all aspects of batting by a youngster and he appreciated it.

When Amarnath walked back to the pavilion, Bombay's elite mobbed him. "I was unable to move an inch as hundreds of hands reached out to me with gifts. Charged with patriotic fervour and pride, ladies offered their precious ornaments to me, businessmen gave cash, and royalty, their Rolex watches and gold medals. The Maharaja of Chote Udaipur presented his gold cigarette case, and later took me on a lap of the ground where people showered me with gold and silver coins. While some reached me, others were caught midway by the excited crowd. (As coincidence would have it, some four decades later, Amarnath's eldest son Surender married the Maharaja's grand-daughter).

"When I reached Taj Mahal hotel, a large crowd was waiting for me at the entrance. It took me almost 15 minutes to find my way into the lobby. Messages had flooded my room, starting with the governor and mayor of Bombay and many other distinguished personalities. On the bed lay a dozen-odd gold Rolex watches and other gifts. But through all this surreal frenzy, my biggest satisfaction was having played for India and now for becoming the first Indian to score a century," Amarnath was to recall many years later. In the evening, a small function was organised privately where a silver salver signed by the Maharajas of Porbander and Dhangadra, the Thakore Sahebs of Palitana and Limbdi was presented to Amarnath as a memento for the excellent innings. At another function, Amarnath was presented a gold cup by the Poddars. As if this was not enough, members and friends of P J Hindu Gymkhana presented him with a large silver cup weighing a couple of kilograms! "There were so many functions arranged for me that at times I was literally dragged from one place to another to keep up with the appointments," he remembered.

The unknown boy from Lahore's Minto Park was a celebrity and Amarnath had become a household name. The pundit's prophecy had, indeed, come true!

The following day, the stands were jampacked as the crowds flocked to watch India's new cricket hero who had flogged the English bowlers to all parts of the field. Amarnath began in his usual flamboyant style by driving Verity to two successive fours. At the other end, C K Nayudu was playing brilliant cricket, reminiscent of his old self. With India hosting 200, a big total to match the tourists seemed possible. But after he made 118 and the team had reached 207, Amarnath hooked Clark and was brilliantly caught by Nichols who dived full length at the boundary. With it all hope of the resistance lasting longer vanished. After Nayudu's departure and some resistance by Merchant, the rest failed to put up any fight and India lost the match by nine wickets.

"After the Test match, I was packing my bags when Dulan Mehta, the young daughter of a famous Bombay jeweller, entered my room with a bag full of diamond jewellery and asked me if I would elope with her. I knew the consequences and the adverse publicity it would draw. Somehow, I convinced her to wait till we finished the series but deep in my heart I knew she was not suitable for me," Amarnath said. Casting aside all matrimonial offers, Amarnath returned to Lahore by the *Frontier Mail*. "The station was overflowing with hundreds of people and I was lifted from one shoulder to another. I was so scared that

I would be dropped any moment. Thank God, someone had brought a motorcar and I was safely tucked in."

Soon, Amarnath's success, and the popularity that came along with it, became a big problem for him. Before the second Test in Calcutta, Amarnath declined an invitation from the governor to play a match for his team in Calcutta since he had made some other commitments. This refusal landed him in big trouble later on. The English tour was like an irresistible show everyone wanted to be associated with. Most of the royalty had given their assent to stage a match in their domain but didn't have a team to field. This problem was solved by taking the services of players from all over the country by luring them with tempting rewards. With so many fixtures arranged, the same faces were seen in action. If Nawab Moin-ud-Dowla sought his presence in a game against MCC in Secunderabad, so did Vizianagram in Banaras. Amarnath was covering the length and breadth of the country to keep up with such engagements. No doubt, by playing these matches, he was fully rewarded by the royalty but the over-exposure harmed him, leaving him with insufficient rest in the run up to the subsequent Tests.

The Indian team reached Calcutta a couple of days early for combined practice. Since the main bowlers were not feeling too well, Amarnath picked up the ball to bowl at the nets. The wicket was slightly soft, helping his medium pace, and he troubled all those who faced him. C K Nayudu watched the plight of his front-line batsmen from behind the nets. Unable to bear it any longer, he padded up and walked in to face Amarnath. "I bowled straight towards the off-stump but the ball swerved to shatter Nayudu's wicket. I couldn't believe it. Nor, could the captain. The session ended amidst much laughter and joy," Amarnath said.

A communiqué was issued by the Bengal government declaring the first day (5 January) of the second Test between India and England as a public holiday. The English bureaucrats living in India had also started behaving like the native king and this order was nothing short of the Maharaja's! Though the stands were filled to their capacity, the second Test did not go well for the Indians. The success of the English at Bombay had elevated their confidence and this was evident in their batting. Jardine led the side from the front with another half-century as his team scored a massive 403.

During the English innings, something interesting happened. Despite the fact that Amarnath was drafted into the side as a wicket-keeper batsman, he did not keep wickets in Bombay, Navle did. In Calcutta, Dilawar Hussain filled the spot. Amarnath was fielding at mid-off when after a few overs, C K Nayudu tossed the ball to him. Holding the red cherry and looking at the skipper, he asked, "Who should I give the ball to, skipper?" C K responded, "You bowl." Amarnath bowled one over in which two boundaries were scored off the first two deliveries, but on the fourth ball a catch was dropped by the keeper. This was the only over he bowled. While batting, the home side pooled in their resources and fought hard to hold fort and draw the game to keep the series alive.

The third Test in Madras became vital for both sides. If India was to win, it would enhance her stature in international cricket but her chances receded when Nissar pulled out with a fitness problem. The English team's reputation was also at stake and Jardine was not the kind who would take even the slightest of chances. Like a general at war, he inspected the spikes and even the laces of each cricketer's shoes. Before the game, he was seen issuing orders to his team, which stood in a single file like troops on a mission.

In this Test also, England proved their superiority in all departments of the game. First, they put up a score of 335, thanks to Jardine, Bakewell and Walters' half-centuries. Amar Singh, who had been struggling in the previous matches and had been written off as a spent force by many critics, came up with a fine bowling performance. This match also converted Amarnath into an opening bowler due to Nissar's absence. The Indian batting once again faltered. In the initial part of the Indian innings, the pace bowlers bowled with hostility, while the spinners, surprisingly, caused the maximum damage. With the wicket responding to spin, Verity wrecked the Indian line-up with a seven-wicket haul. The Indian team managed only 145 runs.

With a substantial lead at their disposal, England went for quick runs and set India a target of 452 to win — an unachievable task. In the second innings, Dilawar Hussain took plenty of blows on his body from the fierce deliveries of Clark and Nichols. Watching his partner withstanding such blows and still not budging, Naomal too gathered courage and offered stiff resistance. Unfortunately, Naomal misread the bounce and pace of the tall left-arm fast bowler Clark and tried desperately to sway away from the line but it was too late. He was struck on the skull and fell to the ground. All the fielders rushed to him, as images of Oldfield (one of Larwood's victims in the Bodyline series of 1932) flashed across everyone's mind. In his anxiety, Dilawar Hussain also rushed to his partner and queried in Urdu, *"Arre Naomal, jawab de, tu zinda hai ya mar gaya* (Hey Naomal! Are you dead or alive?)" Naomal survived the blow but the *'Dead men never reply'* became the joke of the series!

The young Yuvraj of Patiala, Yadvindra Singh, playing his debut Test fared well. He scored an entertaining 60. The only other batsmen to perform were Amar Singh (48) and Amarnath (29 not out), coming down the order but the rest failed to put up any resistance. Amarnath remembered this match not so much for his batting but for his long spell with the new ball which made him India's opening bowler in the years to come. He bid good-bye to wicket-keeping and packed his stumper's gloves in the closet forever as a reminder of his past.

India lost the series to a more professional English team, which taught the Indians a couple of things. One of them was fielding. To keep the wicket-keeper and the fielders on their toes and to ensure the accuracy of the throws, every fielder was required to throw the ball to the wicket-keeper irrespective of whether there was any chance of a run or not but without wasting time. This is an approach that modern day cricketers have adopted as well.

JACK RYDER'S AUSTRALIAN TOUR 1935–36

The Board depended heavily on patrons, particularly Patiala, for finances. Maharaja Bhupinder Singh had come to its rescue earlier but on his own terms. The success of the Yuvraj in the last Test at Madras gave the Maharaja hope that his talented son could become captain of the Indian team. With no further official Test engagements in sight, he decided to fill this vacuum by arranging an unofficial tour. Frank Tarrant was sent to Australia to organise the tour and pick the best possible side. The entire expense towards sea passage, board and lodging, the players' allowances, kits, etc., was borne by Patiala.

There was no doubt it raised the Maharaja's stature in cricketing circles but it also made him poorer by thousands of pounds sterling. The tourists covered the length and breadth of the country, playing attractive and hard cricket. As anticipated, Yuvraj Yadvindra Singh was nominated India's captain but this move created a controversy. Selector H D Kanga resigned in protest as he felt there were better players available to lead India and 'birthright' alone could not become the criteria for this post. The Bombay Cricket Association even moved a motion to this effect. Players from the north were unhappy with this controversy, which left a bad taste. They knew of Yuvraj's talent and capability but many in Bombay did not.

The first 'Test' was played in Bombay. Much was expected from the strong Indian batting but it failed to live up to its reputation and was skittled out for 163. Only the captain faced the attack with some degree of authority to score 40. If Frederick Mair troubled the Indians with his spin bowling, then Nissar ripped through the Australian batting with six wickets as the tourists made 268. Nissar's analysis would have been even better had crucial chances been accepted. Jack Ryder played a marvellous innings and scored a century to put his side in a commanding position. The home side, with the exception of Amarnath who scored 41, faltered to make an identical 163 in the second innings as well. Chasing a moderate target, the Australians won the match by nine wickets. This loss, and the controversy affected Yuvraj, and he relinquished captaincy.

Unfortunately, a majority of the cricketers at that time did not play as a unit. They owed allegiance to their respective Maharaja or religion, resulting in a house divided against itself. When C K Nayudu (Holkar) was nominated captain, Amar Singh (Nawanagar) expressed unhappiness as relations between the rulers of Holkar and Nawanagar were at their lowest ebb.

The 'Test' in Calcutta was marred by rain, which made batting a nightmare for all. The tourists rode on their experience of having played in similar conditions. It was a match where the ball dominated the show. On a soggy wicket, the Indians were dismissed for 48 in the first innings and 127 in the second. Amarnath suffered a blow on his jaw from a ball, which rose sharply from a good length. The Australians also suffered at the hands of Nissar (six for 35) to be bundled out for 99. With a substantial lead at their disposal and the wicket becoming slightly easy after rolling and drying, Ryder's team cruised to a nine-wicket victory.

This defeat brought Wazir Ali to the captain's chair and he proved successful. The Nissar-Amar Singh combination proved too hot for the tourists and they lost the next two 'Tests' in the low-scoring matches. Amarnath had to pull out from these remaining two 'Tests' due to an ankle injury. The tour was a grand success and helped the Board raise its dwindling finances.

THREE

SENT HOME FROM TOUR OF ENGLAND

I T IS imperative that we delve a little into the background of the Indian team's tour of England in 1936, which is now remembered most for the controversy that rocked it.

In October 1931, Lord Wellingdon took over the viceroy's office from Lord Irwin. Till this time, Maharaja Bhupinder Singh had been calling the shots in the Board but with the advent of the new viceroy, the situation changed. Lord Wellingdon was not only interested in cricket but also took a keen interest in the affairs of the game. At this stage, India was preparing for her first official tour of England. At a meeting, Vizianagram offered the Board a substantial amount to take care of the tour expenses and also to establish himself in the Indian Board. This gesture of benevolence by a petty zamindar of Banaras, infuriated the Maharaja who considered this an affront to his stature. He made an offer none dare match, least of all Vizianagram. Maharaja Bhupinder Singh guaranteed to bear the expenses of not only the entire tour but also a month-long trial for fifty players in Patiala. This offer by the Maharaja and his strong desire to control the Board and cricket did not please the new viceroy, who wanted to be an integral part of the show and not a mere spectator. Clever as he was, he saw in young Vizianagram an ever-obliging subject and an ideal pawn to counter the Maharaja and his influence in cricket.

By now, cricket had gained popularity, thanks to the patronage of the Maharajas and the Nawabs. Realising this, it was but natural that the royalty would be at the helm of affairs. Whether it was for the good or bad of this game, did not matter. Sycophancy and ill advice made them take it for granted that to lead the national team was their birthright and not necessarily an honour, a post of pride. After all, they were instrumental in promoting the noble game!

Having pumped in a large amount of money into this venture, as expected, the Maharaja of Patiala was named captain of the All India team for its maiden official tour in 1932 (in 1911, he had captained the Indian team on an unofficial tour of England), assisted by Prince Ghanshyamsinhji of Limbdi as his deputy. Surprisingly, and perhaps with the influence of Wellingdon, Vizianagram found his name in the team as sub-deputy captain. Being third on the rung, he cited poor health and opted out of the tour. To keep the selectors and the establishment from reacting adversely, Vizianagram offered his services to the team in any capacity other than playing. Maharaja Bhupinder Singh also couldn't make the trip as the powers-that-be in London politely conveyed to him that he was too old to lead and that he had incurred heavy debts on his last trip. This directive shattered his dream of leading the first Indian team on an official tour and he resigned. The Maharaja of Porbander finally made it to the top.

With an eye on the 1936 tour of England, both the Maharaja of Patiala and Vizianagram started playing their cards judiciously. The latter was secretive but Maharaja Patiala was less discreet and did everything in his usual extravagant style. He wanted his son Yadvindra to achieve what he couldn't and felt strongly about it. It was no secret that the Australians had toured India due to Patiala's initiative and benevolence. Unable to match Patiala in any way, Vizianagram decided to take advantage of the cold relationship between the Maharaja and the viceroy. Opportunity came his way when Maharaja Bhupinder Singh sailed for England to attend the King Emperor's silver jubilee celebrations in London. His absence from India gave Vizianagram and his friends a chance to manipulate. He decided to celebrate the King's silver jubilee by organising a tournament at the Roshanara garden in Delhi to demonstrate his devotion both to the king and the viceroy. Having secured accolades from Lord Wellingdon for his services, Vizianagram effectively cultivated a personal relationship with Lady Wellingdon and Major Britton Jones, the former ADC and now a trusted servant and comptroller of the house of Lord Wellingdon, which came in handy later on. The icing on the cake was when he presented Delhi with the Wellingdon pavilion as a token of his love and appreciation.

The series against the Australians did not resolve the captaincy problem as three cricketers did this job. Since the Yuvraj of Patiala had led India against the Australians and also played in an official Test against England, Maharaja Patiala expected support from the majority of state associations. But this did not happen, probably due to the strained relations between him and Lord Wellingdon. There was another lobby, which wanted a cricketer to lead India and their choice was the Nawab of Pataudi, who had not played much cricket in England after the Bodyline series. He seemed keen to lead India on this tour to prove a thing or two to the gentlemen in the Long Room at Lord's. Just when everything looked set, he declared himself unavailable, citing personal and state reasons. This last minute withdrawal from the contest left only C K Nayudu and Vizianagram in the fray. Though Nayudu had better credentials both as a cricketer and captain, he lacked the royalty tag, considered so important at that period.

Wily as a fox, Vizianagram used his resources and connections to ensure maximum support in the Board for his candidature and secured ten votes. It was surprising that a player with no experience in first-class cricket or talent secured the coveted post of the captain despite resistance from Bombay, Gujarat, Central India, Southern Punjab and Northern India. Once again, birth got preference over performance and calibre. Poor Wazir Ali's record of leading the Indians to two 'Test' wins against the Australians found place only in the record books. Major Britton Jones was named manager. A lot was expected from the strong All India team, which included Nayudu, Wazir Ali, Amar Singh, Nissar, Mushtaq Ali, Vijay Merchant, Amarnath and many other great players of the era. Unfortunately, the team was already divided before it set sail for England. Nayudu and his friends were on one side, supported by Maharaja Bhupinder Singh, and Vizianagram on the other, with support from the anti-Patiala lobby.

The team left for England in early April. Amarnath found the journey exciting and enjoyable, as it was his first overseas tour. He was looking forward to proving his worth and establishing himself as the leading all-rounder of the team. He knew that the only other player capable of competing with him was his friend Amar Singh and he looked forward to this healthy competition. Much of the time on the ship was spent in discussing cricket and keeping fit through various exercises. Amarnath loved to show off his skipping skills and on several occasions he braved strong winds on the deck to skip the rope.

Back in 1933, English players on the Indian tour had told Amarnath a lot about England, especially the beautiful and picturesque county grounds. Now, his dream was coming true. The very thought of playing at the majestic Lord's, the Mecca of cricket, gave him goose pimples. With every passing day, he and the other members of the team regularly enquired from the steward or the captain of the ship the exact time and date of their arrival at England. The closer they got to their destination, the more exciting it got.

The ship anchored at Marseilles, the last port before London. The captain of the Indian team disembarked as he had already decided to travel to London overland, but his thirty-six personal pieces of luggage and two servants continued the journey along with the rest of the party. Since there was enough time available at Marseilles before the ship sailed for England, Amarnath and some of his friends took permission from S M Hadi, the treasurer of the team, to visit the city. Amarnath's knowledge of French — which he had picked up at school — was expected to come in handy. Nonetheless, he carried a pocket-size English-to-French translation mini-book.

Amarnath and his friends were enthralled by the sights in the beautiful city and they returned to the port well within time. In broken French, Amarnath enquired the fare from the taxi driver, which came to a few francs. Since no one had small change, a hundred franc note was offered with the hope that the balance would be returned. They cracked jokes making gestures with their hands. Unable to understand, the cab driver presumed the balance amount was being offered to him as his tip. Happily, he saluted the Indians and mumbled something. Since they could not grasp what was being said, they started laughing. Their laughter froze when they realised the cab was moving away. Amarnath sprinted, caught up with the cab and demanded the balance from the driver but he wouldn't budge. Finally, a policeman came to the Indians' rescue and they got their money back. Apparently, the cab driver had mistaken Amarnath and his friends for royals from India. This incident became a friendly joke of the tour and they were termed as *nakli Maharajas* (fake Maharajas)!

The Indians reached London, minus their captain and manager who arrived later. Till then Major Richets, ADC to Vizianagram officiated as acting manager in place of Major Jones. The team was greeted by an exceptionally cold and wet English weather. Due to the cold climate and wet conditions, the wickets remained soggy or damp, thereby robbing the tourists of any serious practice. To compensate for that, all the players enjoyed the warm and cozy halls in which many receptions were held to welcome them. At the luncheon reception in London, chaired by Lord Hailsham, the Lord Chancellor, speeches were made to please everyone's ears. In his speech, the Lord Chancellor compared the touring captain with K S Ranjitsinhji in many ways. He recalled the tremendous abilities and popularity that made Ranjitsinhji 'Ranji' in England and hoped that the same would happen with Vizianagram, who would then be known as Vizzy. In reply, Vizzy too showered lavish praise on the Empire in general, and Lord Wellingdon in particular, for helping not only the game of cricket to flourish but also its governance under his rule. Such remarks of mutual admiration were repeated at most functions, keeping the master and the subject happy.

The Indians found the conditions too harsh and uncomfortable. This kind of weather was last on their minds and many were not accustomed to it. After a couple of days of rest, the first game against Worcestershire began under cold and windy conditions. The match was keenly contested but the Indians suffered a three-wicket defeat. Vizianagram made frequent bowling changes when the situation demanded none. He tried to copy Douglas Jardine, R E S Wyatt and Bill Woodfull, who were known to follow this policy. At a crucial stage in the game, he removed Nissar when the bowler was on top, having captured three wickets in his first five overs and had the home side reeling at 67 for seven wickets. This move sealed his team's fate and it lost the match when victory was in sight.

"The Indian captain ought to remember that Jardine, Wyatt and Woodfull are not the only captains who have made frequent bowling changes, Nayudu who had earlier captained the Indian side did the same thing. But there was this difference," wrote R C Robertson-Glasgow in the *Morning Post*. "All these men of experience made the necessary changes in the bowling only at a psychological and right moment. It is difficult to point one instance against them when they have changed a bowler to give advantage to batsmen, as has been done on so many occasions by the Indian captain."

The free-flowing Indian batsmen found the ball not coming on to the bat on the soft English wickets, resulting in their downfall. Attributing this defeat to a long lay-off, they prepared for an easier encounter against Oxford University, presumably a cakewalk for the strong Indians. But much to their dismay, Oxford held them to a draw, raising quite a few questions about the tourists' capabilities.

After pulling up their socks and making some adjustments in their technique, the Indian batsmen fared better against Somerset. Merchant scored the first century of the tour and Nayudu chipped in with a half-century to put on a good score but the rest failed. The home side fared well as it was acquainted with such wickets. Somerset cruised to a 10-wicket victory. A lot was expected from Amarnath but he was not staying long enough in the middle, despite displaying glimpses of his talent during his brief innings.

With two defeats in three matches, the tour couldn't have commenced on a worse note. The bowling looked better than the batting but the result was unsatisfactory. The Indians were desperate for a better performance to lift their sagging morale. Amarnath was also anxious to get a big score to re-establish his reputation as a premier batsman. Good fortune smiled on him against Northamptonshire and he scored a dazzling century reminiscent of his innings in Bombay when all the bowlers were at his mercy. Finally, the Indians managed to put up a big total (405 for nine), giving their bowlers a fair chance to bowl the opponents out with an attacking field. Amar Singh and

Nissar made life miserable for the home team, capturing seven wickets between themselves. Amarnath too followed well with his medium pace taking two wickets. Though this match ended in a draw, it signalled Amarnath's return to form. By this time, the Indians had got acclimatised as well and were enjoying the English conditions.

The only worrying factor was Vizzy's incomprehensible captaincy. By choosing to place the field on his own and making frequent bowling changes, he robbed India of a certain victory. With little knowledge of captaincy, let alone its intricacies, he made one blunder after another. In the match against MCC at Lord's, Vizzy persisted with Shute Banerjee for a long spell despite the bowler showing signs of fatigue and proving expensive.

To add to India's woes, Vizzy came on to bowl himself to the English batsman Human, who had struggled to reach 97 while the frontline bowlers waited for another spell. Since Vizzy had never bowled regularly, the first delivery was truly a classic, landing halfway down the track. Human could not have asked for a better opportunity to add to his hard work. He dispatched the long hop for a six to reach his century. Immediately, the batsman walked up to Vizzy and said, "Thank you". In response, the Indian captain cheered him for the fine effort! "It was hard to understand whether our captain was playing for India or against," Amarnath recalled. No Englishman had been so generous to the Indian team throughout the tour as Vizzy was to the home players.

Word quickly spread that the touring captain was distributing gifts to his rival skippers to win their sympathy. He gifted them gold guineas irrespective of who won the toss. On one occasion, a county captain complained that he had no choice but to bowl a few long hops for Vizzy to hit because the Indian captain had gifted him a gold watch at the time of the toss. When the crowd booed the bowler, the captain promptly removed him from the attack and brought his main bowler back. Before long, Vizzy was on his way back to the pavilion. "We feel sorry for him but at the same time we cannot feed lollipops to him (Vizzy) throughout the innings," lamented the others.

The tour progressed with mixed luck for the team. With the Test match not too far, every player was aspiring to produce his best performance and cement his place in the side. Amarnath touched his peak form against Essex at Brentwood. Even in this match it was a familiar story. The Indian frontline collapsed once more with the scoreboard reading 29 for four. Very soon, the situation worsened when the cream of the batting, D D Hindlekar (0), Mushtaq Ali (1), C K Nayudu (2), L P Jai (5), P E Palia (6), Vizzy (4), and Amir Elahi (0) was back in the pavilion. The end of the Indian innings looked imminent with only Amarnath at the crease.

When the seventh wicket fell at 97, Amarnath was the lone ranger, fighting a losing battle. With Shute Banerjee for company, he realised the futility of holding fort with defensive tactics. He launched a blistering counter-attack against the menacing bowling. So severe was he in his attack that when the Indian innings terminated at 184, his contribution was 130 made in 145 minutes with 18 fours. Fresh from his batting exploits, he made the Essex batsmen dance to his tune while bowling. In his 30 overs, he captured four wickets for 54 runs. Despite his all-round display, the home side gained a substantial lead of 167 runs, thanks to the centuries by Cutmore and Smith.

The Indians' second innings did not fare any better than the first. Amarnath was back in the middle at the score of 16. The procession of the batsmen to the dressing room started immediately, with wickets tumbling for no apparent reason. By tea, defeat looked certain, as the scoreboard depicted none too happy a picture — 110 for seven — with Banerjee at the other end. After the break, Amarnath decided again that attack was the best form of defence and he soon completed his half-century in 95 minutes. At no stage did he play any false stroke or look uncomfortable against the accurate attack. The next 50 came in 75 minutes to make him the first to achieve the feat of scoring a century in each innings for India. Of course, Duleep Sinhji had achieved this feat in England in 1929–30 but he never played for India. It was a milestone in the annals of Indian cricket and a feather in Amarnath's cap. The century consumed 170 minutes and was studded with delightful cover drives, elegant late cuts and powerful hook shots. All this proved futile, as Essex required only 61 runs to win and achieved it for the loss of two wickets, both falling to Amarnath. It was Amarnath's best match of the tour, aggregating 237 runs and capturing six wickets to finally prove his true ability as the team's leading all-rounder.

The flip-flop performance of the team attracted media attention with several articles probing the causes. No doubt, unnecessary shuffling of the batting order was one of the reasons but the captaincy raised many eyebrows. The Indian captain was so obsessed with his appearance on the field that he changed into a fresh set of bosky flannels and silk shirt in every session. J B Fry described his costume as cool as Himalayan snow, a subtle remark on his spotless outfit. Though the team moved in the ground as one unit, the players' feelings for one another were miles away. It was a house divided, with each player looking for an opportunity to pull the other down. With each defeat, both the English and the Indian press started making digs at Vizzy's captaincy, making him more and more bitter with certain players. Perhaps, the press expected a little too much from the ordinary player that Vizzy was. To camouflage his failures, he started blaming a certain group — which did not enjoy his hospitality — for tarnishing the team's as well as his own image. Suspicious and frustrated, he created his own group. To keep their master happy, these players openly sang a rhyme: *"Bahar se kala, andar se kaala, bara badmash hai yeh Indorewala,* (Black on the outside, black within, this man from Indore is a rogue)." It was a reference to C K Nayudu's complexion and his supposed misdeeds. To complicate matters, Vizzy adopted the divide-and-rule policy of the British to further his gains.

Within a short time, the atmosphere reeked of distrust. It was a tour where every player felt threatened on the slightest pretext or a failure. Wild stories were planted against one another to gain the sympathy of the captain or the manager. This was a tour where the players watched their back more often as none was sure who would stab a knife in his back. The players exchanged few words in the dressing room for fear of being misquoted and when the game was over, they moved in small groups to have their dinner. Trust in each other had evaporated to such an extent that they did not believe in taking singles for the fear of being run out. Once, in a county match, a senior player of the opposite camp called Merchant for an easy single but Merchant refused to acknowledge his call till the striker yelled loudly, "Don't worry Vijay, I won't get you run out." If the players behaved in such an obnoxious manner, the captain too did not lag behind in conspiracy. He told Mushtaq Ali to get

Merchant run out but fortunately for the team and Merchant, the upright Holkar player did not oblige his captain.

With each passing day, the channels of communication between the captain and the players kept becoming narrower. In the match against Middlesex, Vizzy gave Amarnath a chance to bowl but set his own field. The first two deliveries were driven to the fence. When the third ball was dispatched to the boundary as well, Vizzy retrieved the ball and walked up to him and said, "Do you know who is batting? Patsy Hendren, the great Patsy." Vizzy then handed the ball to him. Of course, Amarnath had known all along that he was bowling to a great English batsman. But he wondered why the captain was putting psychological pressure on him instead of encouraging him.

Putting this pressure aside, Amarnath continued to bowl in the manner he knew best. He mixed his late in-swing with the lethal leg-cutters, which most batsmen found tempting as it was pitched on the leg and middle stumps. Attempting to whip the delivery to the leg side, some of the batsmen found the off-stump knocked back while others were caught in the slips. Amarnath bowled 26 overs with his usual zest and captured six wickets for 29 runs, 12 of which had come off his first three deliveries. By now, he was enjoying cricket as the premier all-rounder of the team. Unfortunately, this success did not go down too well with some of his teammates, who felt their place in the team was being threatened.

After a few days, a messenger went to Amarnath's room and told him that the skipper wished to speak to him privately in his room. When he met Vizzy, the captain was in a jolly good mood. He expressed satisfaction with Amarnath's performance. During the course of the conversation, Vizzy offered to use his resources to help him in getting a contract to play as a professional cricketer in the Lancashire League the following year. There was, however, a string attached. Amarnath was told not to speak with C K Nayudu and his mates and to avoid their company. Amarnath was startled by Vizzy's intrigue. He agreed not to dine with the group but could not promise to avoid dialogue with C K Nayudu, Jai and Palia as they were his seniors. Moreover, avoiding conversation would make him look rude, he explained. Looking disturbed and uncomfortable, Vizzy said, "Yes, yes, I can understand." After a little pause, Vizzy got up and the meeting ended abruptly. With nothing more to discuss, Amarnath wished his skipper good night and returned to his room, perturbed.

The team travelled to the land of Bert Sutcliffe and Len Hutton to face Yorkshire. The outing did not bring any joy to the batsmen as they struggled on a wet wicket and in damp conditions. The Indians were bowled out for 85. This time, neither Amarnath nor the tail enders managed to put up a decent score. If the Yorkshire pace bowlers made the tourists' life miserable, Nissar returned the compliment to the home side. Mitchell, Hutton, Sellars all fell to the mighty Nissar in the first few overs, beaten by sheer pace. Though Maurice Leyland and Sutcliffe tried to stop the landslide, Nissar was unplayable.

The familiar story of inconsistent captaincy was repeated and vital chances floored which helped Yorkshire, as later on, batsmen fought hard in a manner similar to that of the Roses match. This spirit enabled them to secure a first innings lead. To assist Yorkshire, the Indian captain committed several blunders, including not bowling Amarnath at all until Nissar, Banerjee, Nayudu and Baqa Jilani were tried. By then everything was lost. The Indians did not fare any better in the second innings and went down to another defeat.

Within two months, the team looked just a shadow of the united All India group which had left the Indian shores amid high expectations. A big mistake had been committed when an undeserving candidate was offered the responsibility. He handled the team recklessly, affecting the performance and morale of the majority and causing unnecessary defeats. The batting order, bowling changes and field placements were all at his mercy. "Even such a staunch supporter of his as Sewell, a correspondent with whom Vizzy discussed all matters, did not mince words," recalled Amarnath. "He stated that the best thing for the Indian captain would be to sit outside the ring and watch the proceedings. He lacks experience and judgment, which have deprived the team of victory. Where Nayudu won with ease, he has failed." There was disenchantment and discontentment in the rank and file but none dared challenge or speak out his mind for fear of an unpleasant dressing down. The manager Major Jones hardly exchanged any words with the team members and none was sure of his reactions. With no one to turn to for guidance, the team was like a simmering volcano, waiting for a little spark.

To complicate the already delicate relationship among the members, some stories started appearing in the newspapers that players wanted C K Nayudu or Wazir Ali instead of Vizzy to lead the team. All this added fuel to fire and suspicion prevailed wholesale in the dressing room. For instance, at Cambridge, during the photo session, the treasurer of the team S M Hadi was made to sit in the front row while a senior player like Jai was given the back row. To humiliate certain players, Hadi was named 12th man in some matches when the regular members of the side were available. This move not only deprived the reserve players of a much-needed opportunity to have a feel of cricket but also caused a lot of bitterness among them. They wondered if it was correct for a team official to perform his duty at their expense.

Essentially a happy-go-lucky person, Amarnath was also the most outspoken member of the team. Having been brought up in a place like Lahore and having served the Maharaja of Patiala, he never hid his feelings and spoke without malice. Being the team's most successful player, the manager and captain had ensured he played every game but Amarnath was not happy with the captain for consistently changing his batting order. During the game against Essex, he injured his shin and yet no rest was given to allow it to heal. Later, in the match against Cambridge, he sprained his back, aggravated by the cold weather. The captain and the manager insisted that he play the next match in which he had to bowl as well — resulting in his injury becoming worse and the pain unbearable. In the hope of getting a favourable response from his captain and expecting the manager to give him a break, Amarnath told them his problem but what came his way shocked him.

Before the Durham fixture, the manager summoned him to the captain's room. Instead of sympathising with him, the manager along with Vizzy accused him of not being serious and making excuses. Taken aback, Amarnath told them there appeared to have been some misunderstanding. "I am here to play cricket and not to holiday. But my injury has not healed fully," he pleaded as he tried to convince them. "Although we parted as friends, something bothered me when I left the captain's room. Being an optimist, I brushed aside this incident also and looked forward to the rest of the tour," Amarnath was to recall many years later.

The match against Minor Counties was especially important as he had struggled with form due to injuries. With the weather playing spoilsport and performance not up to expectation, Amarnath wanted desperately to score runs to boost his confidence. The Indians won the toss and batted first. The captain asked him to be ready as he was to bat at number four or five. At the same time, Mushtaq Ali was asked to pad up as well. When Hindlekar got out, Mushtaq went in and played out the day to remain not out along with Merchant. The following day, when Mushtaq got out after a fruitful partnership, Vizzy sent in Amar Singh to bat with Amarnath waiting padded up. He waited patiently till another wicket fell. He got up to pick his bat when he saw C S Nayudu marching towards the ground. Unable to control himself, he went up to the captain and asked if he still wanted him to keep his pads on. "Yes, keep them on, you'll be sent in," Vizzy replied curtly. Confused at this treatment, he kept quiet but was beginning to rage with anger.

Amarnath had his pads on all afternoon as well and, yet, at the fall of the fourth wicket, Wazir Ali was ordered to go ahead of him, frustrating him further. Such moves clearly demonstrated that the captain was playing everything but cricket. By now, Amarnath's sore back had become stiff and painful from sitting and waiting for his turn to bat. The shadows had lengthened and Amarnath presumed there would be a night-watchman padded. It was at such a moment that Wazir Ali got out. Vizzy looked at Amarnath and said, "Your turn." Reluctantly, Amarnath went in and played out time, remaining one not out. Furious at the treatment by the captain, he returned to the dressing room an annoyed man. Removing his gloves and then pads, he threw them one after another into his kit bag in one corner of the room. In typical Lahori Punjabi, he then mumbled aloud *"xxx xxx, aasi vi bari cricket khel li hai char saal tonh, asi koi bevkoof nahi haan, saano sab pata hai!* (I have played enough cricket in the last four years and I'm no fool, I know what is transpiring!)" The treasurer, Hadi, then walked up to an unhappy Amarnath and asked him if his sore back needed a massage. "I don't need any bloody massage," Amarnath shot back. Vizzy was sitting and watching everything but, like his colleagues from the southern or western parts of India, could not understand any Punjabi. Yet, he asked Amarnath if he was talking to him. "I am not talking to anybody, in particular, nor do I wish to speak to anyone," he replied. Many years later, Amarnath told me in private "That is all that transpired in the dressing room before the players dispersed to the hotel."

That evening, there was a conference attended by the supporters of Vizzy in his room. Since the majority of the players did not understand Punjabi, a distorted version of the incident reached the manager who had not been present in the dressing room. After the day's play, Major Jones asked Amarnath to meet him in his room. Changing into fresh clothes, he reached the manager's room. Without wasting any time, Jones produced a letter signed by several players, prominent being those from Vizzy's camp and a couple of others. They had demanded strict action against Amarnath for his behaviour in the dressing room. This came as a shock to him and he tried to reason with the Englishman. He told him that he felt sorry for getting excited on that occasion and was ready to apologise if he had hurt someone's feelings. He also promised to control his emotions and behaviour. No amount of persuasion had any effect on the fastidious manager, who it seemed had already made up his mind. Amarnath was to be sent back home on disciplinary grounds!

The dye had been cast. The reason was not cricket alone but much more than met the eye. The English used this incident as a tool to thwart the efforts of the Congress which was then agitating against the British rule and demanding *Swaraj* (independence). They argued, if eleven Indian cricketers could not stay together and play in peace and harmony, how would the Congress rule over millions having diverse cultures and religions? Inadvertently, Amarnath became a pawn and the sacrificial lamb in a political conflict.

When word of the decision reached seniors like Nayudu, Palia, Ramaswamy and Wazir Ali, they got together and approached Vizzy. They impressed upon him to change the earlier decision of sending Amarnath home. After a long dialogue, the captain agreed to change his decision on condition that a guarantee be given to him that similar incidents would not be repeated. The seniors gave the undertaking on Amarnath's behalf. Having received the assurance, Vizzy agreed to speak to the manager. Later in the day, the bad news was re-confirmed. Still he hoped.

In the evening, Amarnath was in Wazir Ali's room when Jones entered the room and told him, "I want you to vacate the hotel room by tomorrow afternoon." This ultimatum humiliated the upright Patiala lad no end but he was in no position to retaliate. He decided to delay his departure by not packing his baggage. In the afternoon, two members of the hotel staff went to clear the room and found everything scattered. Instructions were to evict Amarnath from the hotel. The hotel staff packed his belongings and cleared the room. He was then put on the boat train for Southampton to board the first available ship to India.

Events, there on, became unreal. Amarnath could not believe all that was happening to him, around him. "Climbing the twenty-odd steps on the ramp to *Kaiser-I-Hind*, my legs felt like lead and a few seconds' distance took a lot of time. I was sure my cricketing career was over and my ambitions could not be realised. Everything seemed like a bad dream," he recalled. The journey was tumultuous and seemed unending. Each morning as Amarnath opened his eyes, he hoped it was just a nightmare and that he would soon come out of it.

Unknown to him, news of this infamous incident had reached Indian shores. The public was outraged. The press and former cricketers came out openly in Amarnath's support, stating that not only was the method of punishment wrong but also too harsh for the offence. They argued that if he had broken any disciplinary code, he was liable to punishment, which could have been in the form of reprimanding or dropping him from the team in some subsequent matches but did not warrant sending back the team's leading all-rounder with the sole idea of humiliating him. Fingers began to be pointed at the Board for not appointing any vice-captain or a tour committee, allowing the captain and the manager to take unfettered advantage of their privileged position.

"The prestige of Indian cricket has suffered beyond reparation. The gate money has gone down so low that the tourists may not get the promised bonus after their return," reported the London correspondent of the *Bombay Chronicle*. In London, Indian students protested and demanded the removal of Maj Jones for his unsavoury role. They even wrote to Vizzy to recall Amarnath to England. The punishment was meant to send a strong signal to those who did not toe the captain and the manager's line. The signal backfired. Everything turned topsy-turvy. The seniors got together and proposed the name of C K Nayudu as captain and Wazir Ali as his deputy to Vizzy and Britton Jones. They also demanded that henceforth, seniors be consulted in the selection of the final XI and due respect be given to them. These demands amounted to an open rebellion. Vizzy refused to relinquish his post but knowing the strength of this group, acceded to the other demands of the seniors.

Gradually, the clouds of conspiracy began to clear. It came to light that Maj Jones had planned, and executed this decision on his own without consulting the Board. "Amarnath was a victim of a pre-arranged decision of an army man and a third-rate cricketer. Strange was the combination of Maj Jones and Maharaj Kumar whose class was rarely credited with a strict disciplined life. The only common thing that tied the two men together was a lack of vision. And, can a man without vision captain the All India XI without difficulty, though he could not find a place in a quadrangular tournament even in his own community (Hindus)," wrote the *Bombay Chronicle* on June 24, 1936.

The telegram to the Board president, Nawab of Bhopal, reached India at a time when Amarnath had already spent three days on board *Kaiser-I-Hind*. With each passing day, provocative statements started appearing in the English dailies. One such statement came from none other than Lord Wellingdon, former viceroy of India, at a dinner hosted by Surrey County Cricket Club in honour of the visiting team. During his speech, he defended the manager and gave him a clean chit for taking such a decision to discipline an Indian, even if he had not consulted either the Board or its president. The tone and tenor of his speech at the club reflected arrogance and was a reminder as to who actually ruled India. Vizzy received a pat on his back from Lord Wellingdon for supporting the manager.

When Amarnath got to know of Lord Wellingdon's remarks, he was reminded of an event which had taken place not too long ago when the latter was viceroy. While playing a match for the viceroy's team, Amarnath had batted at a crucial period and saved the match, when everything had seemed lost. At that moment an overjoyed Lord Wellingdon had walked halfway down the ground to congratulate him and said, "My boy, you have saved my honour." He also asked Amarnath where he was working.

"Patiala," Amarnath told him.

Lord Wellingdon's eyes opened wide since Patiala was a name he was allergic to. "Are you happy there?" he enquired.

"Yes sir, I am very happy there," Amarnath responded.

Wellingdon did not quite like it and sarcastically announced to all around, "This bloke says he is happy in Patiala. Are you sure, my boy?"

"Yes sir!"

"This is the first person I have met in private who says he is happy at Patiala."

Amarnath had not understood the implications of that conversation when it actually took place but it sank in now.

In London, on June 30, Vizzy hosted a fabulous dinner in honour of Marquees of Wellingdon to demonstrate his loyalty to them. He described the former viceroy as the greatest ever to reach the shores of India and Lady Wellingdon as "a fairy Godmother who kept a warm corner in her heart for Indian cricket." This sycophancy was duly rewarded within two weeks. On the recommendation of Lord Wellingdon, the King Emperor of England knighted the Indian captain at Buckingham Palace on July 15, 1936 for his invaluable services to the crown. An unknown zamindar from Banaras was now Sir Maharajkumar of Vizianagram.

Since Vizzy was busy attending his investiture in London, he was unable to play the next match. As a result, C K Nayudu was asked to lead the team against the powerful Lancashire squad. Vizzy's absence had a salutary effect as it afforded Nayudu a chance to secure victory. For the first time since 1909 when Noble's Australians beat them, Lancashire ended up on the losing side at the Aigburth ground. Victory was sweet, as it came at a time when Lancashire had every chance to win the game on the third day. Besides captaining his side with sound judgement, Nayudu bowled very well. The change in leadership brought about the desired results from the Indian team and this victory proved that it was not the players who were to blame for the poor show but inexperienced captaincy.

Yet, with the main all-rounder packed home in disgrace by the captain and the manager, the fragile batting and bowling suffered beyond repair. The Indians were bundled out for a meagre score of 147 and 93 in the first Test match to give England a nine-wicket victory. This result, and the poor performance on the tour, put a serious question mark on India's future as the ICC seriously wondered whether it would be wise to give the Indians three-match series in future.

The defeat was attributed to spineless batting and poor fielding, especially the catching which made even schoolboys in the enclosures laugh heartily. Moaned a critic: "The only time Indians looked motivated and showed enthusiasm to run swiftly on the field was at the end of the game when each tried to outrun the other in their pursuit to grab stumps as souvenirs. In this race to possess stumps, both C K and C S Nayudu, Nissar and Palia were the winners from the Indian side while the other two stumps were with the English batsmen. If only the same spirit was shown while batting or bowling, the outcome could have been different."

Meanwhile, back home in India, the Board President Nawab of Bhopal was trying to retrieve the situation by sending urgent cables to both the manager and the captain to stop Amarnath at Marseilles. He said if Amarnath had tendered an unconditional apology, then he should be allowed to return to the team. But both Vizzy and Maj Jones, enjoying the patronage of the king and Lord Wellingdon, refused to budge. Now the Board faced a ticklish question, which needed immediate attention and settlement. When Amarnath left India, his contract with the Indian Board stated that he would be required to serve the interests of Indian cricket. This, he had fulfilled by scoring the most runs (625) and stood second in capturing most wickets (32). Also, both the manager and the captain had admitted to the press that they had not consulted the Indian Board or its president before sacking Amarnath. But the authority and prestige of the Board had already suffered great damage. During the emergency meeting of the Board, these points were discussed and a decision was reached that in future, the powers of the manager and the captain would be restricted to avoid repetition of such an episode.

On the evening of July 9, 1936, the ship *Kaiser-I-Hind* docked outside the Bombay port. The news of Amarnath's arrival had already been leaked to the public by the local newspaper. Thousands came to the Mole station with hundreds of bouquets and garlands to accord their hero a grand reception. "Representatives of his Crescent Cricket Club, Lahore, had travelled the distance to Bombay to receive the centurion. Besides them, representatives of the Hindu and other Gymkhanas in the city were present. The Punjab Sewa Dal, the Kalba Devi Gumasta Mandal and the National Cricket Club had brought their followers and members in full strength. Frank Tarrant, Amarnath's godfather, came with his wife and son Lawrence to greet his *chela* (pupil)," wrote the *Bombay Chronicle*.

The Nawab of Bhopal especially sent Board Secretary Anthony de Mello to Bombay to receive Amarnath but he looked visibly shaken and uncomfortable at the sight of such a large gathering. Expecting trouble, Superintendent of Police Clyes was deputed to control the crowd at Mole station. At that moment, someone from the crowd noticed de Mello talking in whispers with the police superintendent and word spread that there was something fishy going on. When Amarnath was brought in a small mail boat to the Mole station, thousands cheered him loudly but the police cordon kept the crowds away from him.

De Mello was the first to enter the boat and Amarnath came out a few minutes later. Neither the press nor Amarnath's admirers got a chance to either talk to him or offer him the bouquets. Although a couple of enthusiasts did manage to get past the tight police cordon and garland their hero, the others were not so lucky. Even Tarrant was not allowed to meet him. No interviews were given as per the wishes and instructions of the Nawab of Bhopal. While the crowd was waiting, Amarnath was spirited away through the back gate into a waiting car. Amarnath's mysterious disappearance agitated the crowd and the waiting journalists and almost led to ugly scenes. They surrounded de Mello, who was left behind in the confusion, and demanded to know the location to which Amarnath was being taken away. Despite being surrounded by the menacing crowds, de Mello flippantly replied that their hero had left for his native place, Patiala. At that moment, an angry Tarrant walked up to de Mello and sarcastically said, "You did a good piece of work." His tone and piercing glance made de Mello nervous. Questions were thrown at the Board secretary but the wily fox ducked each question. Unable to wade his way out, he stated that Amarnath was leaving Bombay by the *Frontier Mail*. When one admirer suggested to another that all stations should be watched, de Mello cheekily added, "Watch the motorways and the airways!" The unnecessary exchange of words ignited the already volatile situation and the agitated crowd started shouting, "Shame, Shame!" Fortunately for him, the police sergeant on duty rescued him and his car in one piece.

Amarnath was really moved by the reception but felt frustrated at not being allowed to meet his friends, colleagues or fans. "I spotted Frank and his family in the large crowd and wanted to thank them for making the long journey. I couldn't exchange any words or shake their hands, which depressed me. I noticed tears in the eyes of Mrs Tarrant and felt bad as she treated me like her son. I couldn't do anything to comfort her," he remembered while narrating the events of that day.

With no clue available, the journalists and well-wishers searched all possible venues where Amarnath could have been taken. In small batches they moved towards Victoria Terminus and Bombay Central station to locate him but in vain. Even the Taj Mahal Hotel was not spared in their pursuit but the authorities there were least helpful. After two and a half hours of fruitless search, some journalists spotted de Mello dining at Brandons. After a lot of cajoling, he agreed to take the journalists to meet Amarnath at the Taj Mahal hotel where he was put up.

The meeting was both cordial and brief. Though Amarnath looked tired after his long journey, he was cheerful. In an interview he said, "Taking all things into consideration, I am glad to be back in India. I did my best in England as the results and averages will show. I look forward to do my best for Indian cricket for many more years. The incident has been an unhappy one. After I collect myself, I am placing the entire matter in the hands of the Board. I feel confident that they will give my case the consideration it deserves. I would like to add in this respect that by giving my case the best consideration, the Board would be saving India's and its own prestige. The voyage was, of course, not a happy one; but friends on board did their best to make me happy and forget the incident." The journalists handed him telegrams from his well-wishers they had received in their offices.

The following day all the newspapers carried his pictures along with conflicting stories about the episode. Some suggested that a committee would give its report pertaining to this episode only after the tour was over while others simply said that it might end with the committee terming the entire episode as unfortunate. The idea of setting up an impartial tribunal headed by Duleep Sinhji was also mooted. There was a general agreement among the public and journalists that in the interest of Indian cricket, a thorough investigation ought to be carried out without any fear or favour. All facts should be brought to light for the benefit of everyone. And then in all that hullabaloo, the *Associate Press* dropped a bombshell that Amarnath was going back to London in a few days to be available for the second Test.

By now, Amarnath had almost become a legend in the English sports circles. News that he was returning to England was received with great relief as no decent sportsman, however inclined he may be to stand in defence of discipline, could visualise ruining the cricketing career of such a promising all-rounder from India. Yet, a correspondent, friendly with the captain, stated, "It cannot be supposed that his (Amarnath's) return would be wholly popular with all members of the team, though, as sportsmen, they will sink any personal objection they may have, if it is for the good of the team, that a cricketer, however good a player he may be, can be fit to play in a Test match within 48 hours of arrival after a long journey by air." When some of Amarnath's team-mates read this statement, they could not help but laugh. After all, C S Nayudu had flown from India and he did not feel any strain from his long journey. He was fit and played the match the moment he arrived at Croyden.

"This fear of a backlash proved wrong when the Indian players travelling from Blackpool to Liverpool were conveyed the good news of his possible return," wrote the *Bombay Chronicle*. There was joy among all the members of the team, except the manager. Amarnath would be received by them with open arms, was the patient reply from all. Some of these players were also those who had signed the statement supporting the captain's contention that he had breached the discipline. They stated that had they known the penalty to which he would be subjected, they would have thought twice before putting their signature to any readymade document.

If the press in India circulated various probabilities, then the *Bombay Chronicle* correspondent reporting the tour did not lag behind. In one of the dispatches he wrote, "While both the Board in India and the authorities in England seem to be anxious to get Amarnath back to England at the earliest possible time, a new point of controversy has arisen, which might sway the decision one way or the other. The demand by Britton Jones that Amarnath should publicly apologise for what happened. He did not stop here. He suggested a specific form of an apology that has to be published."

"This is carrying things too far," said a well-known cricketer, when his attention was drawn to the stipulation. Cricket circles in Bombay and other places were surprised at the attitude of the manager. Quite a few expected that both Vizzy and Maj Jones would resign in protest at the decision of the Board and its president but both of them, for reasons best known to them, decided to welcome Amarnath back. Vizzy was even prepared to let bygones be bygones. There was definitely something more to it than met the eye. Were these two really keen to forget and forgive or were they just biding time?

After a day's rest, Amarnath left for Bhopal with his notes to counter the charges made by the manager and the captain against him. The meeting with the Nawab of Bhopal lasted a couple of hours, with the Board president giving him a patient hearing. Knowing the Nawab's nature and the events, many in Bhopal were quite confident that justice would be meted to the cricketer. It was an open secret that the Nawab of Bhopal was not in favour of the drastic action against the Patiala cricketer. Amarnath then presented his case and narrated the series of events to clear the Board president's doubts.

LALA AMARNATH'S DEFENCE

Following is the text of Amarnath's defence before the Nawab of Bhopal:

"We were quite happy when we left Bombay. At Eden, I met

the Private Secretary to the Maharaja of Kapurthala who asked me about the captain. I told him that the captain was a nice person and was quite popular with members of the team. The Private Secretary then told me that for some unknown reasons the captain was annoyed with me and he suggested I should clear up any misunderstanding that might exist. I did so and was quite friendly with him. The days on the boat passed happily. At Marseilles, the captain left the team and went to London overland.

"At Gravesend, where we played our first match, the captain was very nice to all of us and also at Worcester. While we were at our hotel prior to our match with Oxford University on May 5, the captain's servant came to call me. I went to the captain who straightaway asked me to join his side and not to mix up with C K Nayudu and several others with whom I generally mixed around. Up to this time, I was not aware of any party feeling amongst the players. Our group consisted of C K Nayudu, M J Gopalan, Mushtaq Ali, C Ramaswamy and myself. We generally gathered together. I told the captain that C K Nayudu was a friend of mine but I was not part of any particular group except that we generally went about together. I agreed to do what the captain thought best but I said that I did not like to hurt the feelings of anyone. After this, C K Nayudu suddenly stopped talking to me for which I could not assign any reason.

"At Northamptonshire, I made a century and the captain congratulated me. I generally went in his car to the field. During the match with MCC at Lord's (May 16, 18, 19) he was quite pleasant. Up to this time, I generally opened the bowling and batted at number 3 or 5. In the match against Leicester (May 20, 21, 22), I was bowling from the pavilion end and asked the captain to remove the third man and place him between covers and point. Instead of acceding to my request, the captain said curtly "Don't waste time. Carry on." I kept on bowling and was changed after two overs. I then fielded in the countryside.

"After the match was finished, I was discussing the game and said that I had never saw a captain refusing to assist a bowler so curtly. When the captain was dressed, he called out to me and taking me aside asked me why I had shown my anger on the field. I said that I was not angry but was hurt to think that he refused to let me place a fielder so curtly. To this Vizzy said, that he was captain of the team and he could do whatever he liked. I admitted this fact that he was captain but stated that we are all friends and did not expect the captain to be unreasonably curt or rude. After all, I was doing my best for the team. To this, Vizzy said "I am entitled to do whatever I like." The conversation was now getting heated as both of us tried to prove a point. Stung by such a lopsided justification by Vizzy the argument became intense. I (Amarnath) replied that he could not insult the players because we are not professionals, rather amateurs who are not paid to play cricket.

"The captain then threatened to report the matter to the manager, which he did without wasting any time. Britton Jones then called and asked me for an explanation. I reported to him the entire conversation with the captain. Hearing everything, the manager smilingly remarked that he knew what was going on and asked me, for his sake, to say sorry to the captain and shake hands. I did that promptly. Happy with the settlement, the manager then told me that he understood that I was anxious to join one of the clubs in Lancashire League and even promised to assist me in getting permission of the Indian Board and also to do his best in England.

"While playing against Middlesex at Lords (May 23, 25, 26) I was kept in the countryside (outfield) all the time and put to bowl fourth change. Whenever I was asked to bowl, I took a wicket and was taken off. My analysis in the match was six wickets for 29 runs. Nothing of any significance happened to affect my relationship with the captain or the manager.

"Against Essex at Brentwood (May 27, 28, 29), I scored two centuries and everyone congratulated me, as also the captain, who however remarked that I could have scored more if I had not tried to score off every ball and force the game all the time with the last wicket. I took the score from 103 to 130. In this match, I hurt my shin badly and had to retire for 10 minutes and later took the field after putting plaster (a sort of a sticking bandage) and fielded wherever I was placed.

"While practising in the nets prior to the match against Cambridge (May 30, June 1 and 2) I sprained my back very badly. The pain was so severe that I cried in agony and was frightened that something serious might have happened. There was no play due to rain and I went to bed, where I remained for four hours. Being in such a pathetic condition I requested to be left out, but the manager insisted that I should play. To examine me, he brought a doctor to the hotel, who put a plaster and asked me to try and bowl in the room. I tried but the pain was excruciating. Not satisfied, the manager then told me to try my action in the open field, as it would be a lot easier and less painful there.

"I went to the ground while the first pair was batting. My turn came to bat 10 minutes before lunch and I was out first ball. When we fielded, I was made to bowl second change with my back tightly strapped. On delivering the very first ball, I felt a sharp pain and could not bowl at all. I informed the captain and he told me to go to the pavilion. He also accompanied me and spoke to the manager. To keep my back warm, I put on my coat and stayed on to watch the match. After an hour with Cambridge still batting, the manager asked me how I was feeling. I replied that the pain was still bad. The manager then sent for a doctor who once again put the plaster all over my back. Without enquiring about my condition any further, the manager sent me out with a chit for the captain and also instructing me to tell him that I could bowl and field. I did as I was told. After reading the chit and listening to me, he said it was the manager's look out and walked away. After 45 minutes, he put me on to bowl but after bowling four to five overs the pain increased considerably and was unendurable. Unable to continue, I was sent to the countryside to field. Later on I came to bowl with the new ball and managed to claim two wickets.

"At lunch, I was talking to Amir Elahi, Baqa Jilani and others in the vernacular. After lunch, the manager asked me to go upstairs and see him. He had in his hand two letters, one addressed to the ruler of Bhopal and the other to the Maharaja of Patiala. These he exhibited threateningly to me and saying that he would post them and also send me back to India, as my behaviour was not proper and language foul. It was obvious that those letters contained some complaints about me. I said that if the manager wanted to send me back to India, he could do so as he had the power and I could be sent off the next day. To this, the manager replied that he wanted to give me another chance. I said "There was no occasion for me to beg for another chance as I had not consciously offended anyone." He then accused me of presuming that I was indispensable to the side and attributed my alleged improper behaviour to this presumption. He also impressed upon me that I was not indispensable. I admitted that my cricket had its limitations and I was not foolish enough to think that the team could not do without me. There was no more conversation with Britton Jones after this.

"When we went to play against Yorkshire (June 6, 8 and 9) my shin had an open bruise and the pain in my back had not completely disappeared. Under these circumstances, I could not possibly play and I informed the manager accordingly. Once again the manager insisted on my playing. In this match too, I was made to run about all over the outfield. There were no more arguments after this.

"At the station on our way to Durham, the manager accused me of running after women. I was startled by this new accusation. Ever since I arrived in England, I was always in bed by 10.30 p.m. on match days and by 11.30 p.m. on off days. I gave no occasion for anyone to reprimand me for late nights. I told the manager that I had come to England to play cricket, which I like much more than women. Unable to pin me down, the manager then said that he had seen me with women. To this I replied, that he could not have seen me misbehaving disgracefully or in a compromising way on any occasion. He was not in a position to make any such remarks. With all allegations refuted, Britton Jones said that he believed me and with it ended this episode.

"On the way before we began our match at Durham (June 10) the Manager called me and took me to a room where Vizzy was sitting alone and asked me to play the match and play for the team. I told them that both knew I always played for the side. Then the manager remarked that the captain and I should be friends. I said that I had nothing against the captain and remarked that the captain should not make unkind remarks about me to the others. If he was displeased with me in any way, he might speak to me directly. I said I would welcome a reprimand and scolding directly from the captain or the manager or even from the senior members of the team because I realise the spirit of such an attitude. I was always aggrieved when I heard outsiders remarking that I was constantly treading on the corns of those in authority and wilfully getting into their bad books. The captain was very pleased with my efforts to make the Durham match a draw and said, 'You did very well indeed.'

"Owing to rain there was not much play against the Notts. The captain promised to send me at number 5. By the time we played the Minor Counties at Lord's (June 17, 18, 19). I was quite fit again. I bowled and fielded as I was directed to do. When our first pair went in to bat, I was told to be No. 4 or 5 but Amar Singh went at No. 4. Then I went to the captain and asked him when I was to go in. He replied that he didn't know when he would send me in to bat. Two others followed Amar Singh and 10 minutes before the close of play, I was sent in No. 7. In the meanwhile when one of the players asked the captain why I was sent in so late, he replied that he wanted

*The debutant: Lala Amaranth padded up before his first
Test at the Bombay Gymkhana in 1933.*

Maharaja Bhupinder Singh of Patiala.

Lala Amarnath attacking in England in 1936.

Sent home from England in 1936: Lala Amarnath boards the Kaiser-I-Hind.

Lala Amarnath carries the bouquets offered after breaking the double century record of A L Hosie by scoring 241 in the Pentangular tournament at the Brabourne Stadium, Bombay, in 1938.

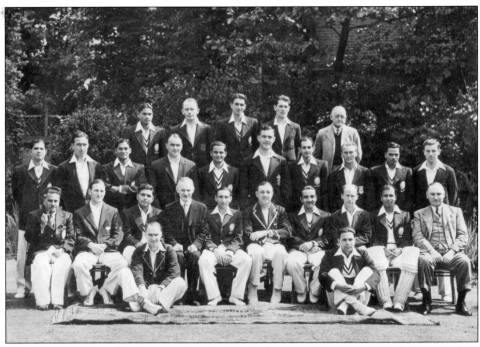

The Indian and England teams in 1946. Lala Amarnath is seated third from the left. The Nawab of Pataudi and Wally Hammond are seated fifth and sixth.

The All India team in England in 1946. Seated (left to right): Banerjee, Merchant, Pataudi (capt), Amarnath and Mushtaq Ali.

"Captain Amarnath" in Patiala army uniform, England 1946.

All India team before departure to England in 1946. Standing (left to right): two officials, Banerjee, Rusi Modi, Mushtaq Ali, Merchant, Pataudi, Amarnath, P Gupta (manager), Hazare, deMello, Sohoni. Squatting (left to right): Sarwate, Mankad and Gul Mohammad

Bowling in England 1946.

Lala Amarnath strolling in London, 1946, with Rusi Modi.

*Bowling in Manchester again. The photograph is proof that dogs
do not always chase balls.*

Mushtaq Ali and Vijay Merchant going out to bat in England in 1946.

The first Indian team to visit Australia in 1947/48. The captain, Lala Amarnath is seated in the middle of the second row.

The all-conquering Australians faced by India.
Don Bradman is seated in the middle.

Lala Amarnath with air hostess Hillary Johnson and the captain in Perth.

Rai Singh, Hazare, Lala Amarnath and Rangachari.

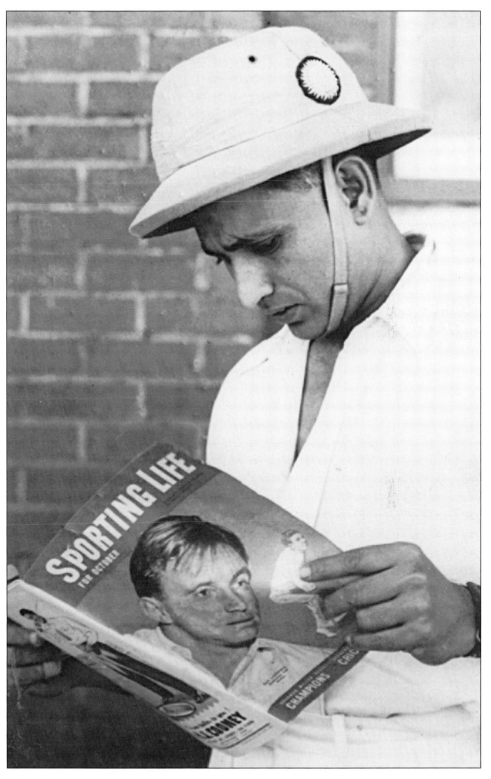

The introduction of the solar hat in Australia 1947/48.

Lala Amarnath and Don Bradman at Sydney 1947/48.

Left: testing the Syndey pitch with Don Bradman in 1947/48.

Below: charging Australian fast bowler Keith Miller.

The Indian team arrives in Tasmania. Lala Amarnath is flanked by Mankad (left) and Adhikari in the second row.

Lala Amarnath examining the Australian ball with Hazare and Phadkar and an Australian official.

faster scorers. I played out the time and came back to the pavilion rather excited. While undressing, I threw about my pads, gloves etc. near my bag in the corner. I felt quite disgusted and talked to several players in Punjabi. What I said was slang and it meant that I had not wasted four years uselessly but learnt cricket. Similar slang has always been used without meaning any offence among Punjabi players. The captain asked me, 'Are you talking to me.' I replied I was not talking to anyone. Then Hadi asked if I required any massage. I replied I did not want any bloody massage. In the evening, there was a conference in the captain's room.

"After this match, Amar Singh suggested to me that I should apologise to the captain for my behaviour in the dressing room on the previous day and do so in writing. I said that I had done nothing to offend the captain for which I should send a written apology. The manager asked me to see him at 6 pm that day. He produced a statement signed by several players and asked me for (an) explanation. I said that although I was excited and gave vent to my feelings, I had not insulted anyone in particular. I did throw my things about but that should not have hurt anybody. Then, the manager said, 'All right, I am sending you back to India next week.'

"An hour later, when I was in Wazir Ali's room, the manager asked me to vacate the hotel by 10.30 the next day and leave by *Kaiser-I-Hind*. I was rather surprised at the attitude of the manager and realising he meant to keep his threat, I asked him for another chance to prove my sincerity to the team but he replied that he could not alter his decision.

"Some of the players — Nissar, Nayudu, Wazir Ali, Ramaswamy, Amir Elahi and Hindlekar went to the captain and pleaded to persuade the manager not to take such an extreme step and the captain agreed. He asked these players to obtain from me a written guarantee of good behaviour for the rest of the tour, which I gave at once. Then the captain asked me to see him at 8 a.m the following day. Next day, the captain and I went to the manager's room but I did not go inside. The captain came out after a few minutes and asked me to go to Wazir Ali's room and took Wazir Ali to his room. A little later, Wazir Ali returned and informed me that the manager's decision could not be changed and brought back my written guarantee of good behaviour.

"I left for India by *Kaiser-I-Hind*."

THE BEAUMONT COMMITTEE

The Nawab of Bhopal circulated the manager and the captain's chargesheet against Amarnath along with his reply among the Board members. Soon the Nawab received the views of several members of the Board who concurred with him on sending Amarnath back to England. Unable to influence any member of the Board while in England, Maj Jones started creating difficulties for the Board president, insisting on a specific apology by Amarnath. This incensed the Nawab of Bhopal who appeared to be against any such demand. He felt that acceding to such a demand would amount to justifying the actions of the both captain and the manager. At the same time, the Board wanted to make it clear that it would not encourage indiscipline in the side but the method of punishment was incorrect. Amarnath was reprimanded for the minor incident at Lord's and, it would appear, he was prepared to express his regret. Many associations felt it was a grave mistake to send back Amarnath from England when the team was failing miserably, courtesy bad management and worse captaincy. News of the decision to send Amarnath back to England was leaked to the media which flashed it with big headlines all over the country.

Since the decision had been confidential, the Nawab of Bhopal's private secretary pronounced this report by the *Associate Press* as "both premature and unauthorised. No decision has been taken so far in this connection either by the Board or its President. Amarnath's case is under consideration by the Board and any decision that may be taken by the proper authorities will, if necessary, be announced in due course to the public. HH (the Nawab of Bhopal) hopes that no attention will be paid to unauthorised publication of news in this connection."

At the same time, an interesting development took place in England. C K Nayudu and Wazir Ali became 'chums' and were ready to play under one another's captaincy for the sake of Indian cricket. Another story circulated in cricket circles was that in case the manager resigned in protest then the team treasurer, S M Hadi would take on the added responsibility of manager. The triumph of public opinion in England in favour of Amarnath, despite Lord Wellingdon and other big guns, the reported decision of the Nawab of Bhopal to reinstate Amarnath without consulting Vizzy, etc., was the hottest topic of discussion in cricket circles. It was considered a well-deserved rebuke to the captain. With such confusing news in circulation, Vizzy told *Reuters* in an interview, "I have heard nothing from India on the subject. Until I receive an official intimation from the Board, I cannot make any comment." Despite putting up a brave front while expressing ignorance, Vizzy looked visibly shaken by the chain of events.

Besides the Amarnath incident, the Board members were not very comfortable with the team's performance. Knowing that the composition of the team was not correct, they were anxious to find a way out by which India could regain lost prestige in the field of cricket before the team returned to India. The Amarnath incident was godsend and they took this opportunity to set matters right.

Various aspects were discussed including the repercussions of Amarnath being sent back to England. What would happen to the captain and the manager? The Board seemed fully aware of the consequences of its decision in favour of sending Amarnath back. In case the captain and the manager did not accept the Board's decision and continued to carry on in their usual capacities, the only course left was to ask them to resign. It appeared that the Board had already prepared itself to meet that contingency.

If Bhopal, and twelve of the seventeen associations were in favour of sending Amarnath immediately to England by Danish Air Mail to be in time for the second Test, Vizzy and Maj Jones were not sitting idle either. In England, Vizzy's status had risen after he was conferred the knighthood. He was not ready to jeopardise his position and be ridiculed not only by the players but also the press upon Amarnath's arrival. The manager too felt threatened by a similar prospect. Due to his proximity with the Wellingdons, Vizzy then used Maj Jones to lay his case before his godmother, Lady Wellingdon, and her husband, the ex-viceroy of India who had connections at the highest level in the government. Lady Wellingdon did not disappoint them as she played a prominent role after Maj Jones begged her to intervene for the sake of an Englishman's reputation. Lord Wellingdon himself left no stone unturned at Whitehall, seeking assurances in favour of both the captain and the manager.

Unaware of these developments in England, Amarnath was preparing to take the first available flight to England from Bombay. His wardrobe trunk had already been sent to Bombay from Bhopal through a special messenger with instructions to send it overland to London from Marseilles as he was only carrying two bats, cricket boots and some flannels. On a Saturday morning, much to his discomfort, the Nawab of Bhopal received a cable from Whitehall. It clearly instructed him not to send Amarnath back to England and that if he was sent despite instructions, the consequences could be quite detrimental for him. It was a veiled threat to the Nawab's position as the ruler of Bhopal. The Nawab knew the English mentality well enough.

At 1.30 p.m., a message was delivered to Amarnath that the Board president had decided not to send him back to England. "I was devastated by this change of heart and the news. Since there was nothing I could do at that moment, I called the shipping office asking them to with-hold my baggage but it was too late. It had already left by the mail boat. Not only did I lose the opportunity to play in England, I lost my entire baggage, too."

Later in the day, the Nawab of Bhopal called him and explained the reasons for his decision. He even promised to compensate him for the financial losses incurred but Amarnath politely declined the offer. Amarnath now realised the futility of seeking help from any quarter. Thereafter, he decided to fight his battle with or without anyone's assistance. At this stage, he also knew he had nothing more to lose but everything to gain.

Taking leave from Bhopal, he proceeded to Chail, Patiala's summer capital, to join duty and keep Maharaja Bhupinder Singh posted on the developments. In Delhi, he met the press and threw a challenge to the Board. Though forbidden to give any interview and having been asked to proceed to either Allahabad or Jodhpur and to lie low, Amarnath rebelled and decided to make everything public. He stated, "Now that I have been disgraced publicly, I do not make any apology because I know that I have no reason to apologise. It was only with the object of doing my best for the team that I was anxious to go back by signing any form of apology that would assist me to that end. This apology letter was signed on Friday evening (July 17) as a guarantee demanded by both the captain and the manager."

Amarnath's interview with *Associate Press* was lucid. "It will serve no useful purpose to appear before the Board again in the role of a sinner. I have suffered enough humiliation by apologising from door to door. I am not indispensable to any team and nobody is; but if I am to play for India again, the Board must institute an independent enquiry into my case and obtain a public apology from the guilty party, whether it is myself or the captain or the manager. If they have done wrong, there is no reason why they should be ashamed to confess their error and express publicly their unreserved apology. I was asked to admit my guilt before any enquiry was made," he said.

To clear his name, Amarnath demanded an impartial and independent inquiry committee and even suggested the name of Duleep Sinhji as one of the members. Then, referring to Vizzy's last statement on discipline, Amarnath said, "Is it strict discipline or a joke that the captain of an international touring side should withdraw his own words twice?" In conclusion, he once again challenged the Board to publish Maj Jones' report and his statement and leave it to the public to judge. "I was shown a copy of the allegations against me made by the manager and while I do not wish to comment on it, I have no hesitation in saying that it contained no specific report on my behaviour."

But the Board decided to wait for the tour to end so that the committee could have full access to all the players' version of this incident.

On September 19, the Board met in Bhopal and had a stormy four-hour session relating to this episode but no decision could be reached. The meeting concluded the following day with the passing of a resolution on the proposal moved by Anthony de Mello on behalf of Southern Punjab Cricket Association (the Maharaja of Patiala was the president of this association) and seconded by Jasdanwalla of Bombay Cricket Association, that an enquiry be held into the Amarnath episode.

Just before the end of this infamous tour, the Nawab of Bhopal constituted a strong three-member committee consisting of Dr P Subbaroyan, president of Madras Cricket Association as well as a prominent lawyer and politician, and Sir Sikandar Hayat Khan, the former president of the Board and now acting governor of Punjab under the presidency of Sir John Beaumont, chief justice of Bombay High Court, to go through the allegations made by the captain and the manager as well as Amarnath's counter charges against the two. Sir Sikandar Hayat Khan attended a couple of meetings but his duties as governor of Punjab made it difficult for him to devote more time and he resigned.

When the Indian team reached Bombay on October 1, Dr Subbaroyan was away in Simla on work. Nonetheless, realising the urgency of the matter, Sir John Beaumont ordered all members of the team to appear before him, before dispersing to their individual destinations. Every player was asked to give his views of the tour and reply to a series of questions. Vizzy could not be questioned, as he preferred not to travel with the team. He came back later alone, unsung and quietly aboard the *Strathmore* along with the Indian hockey team which had won a gold medal at the Berlin Olympics.

With no decision made at the meeting regarding Amarnath's cricketing career, he was free to play till the verdict was pronounced. To keep public memory fresh, he arrived in Bombay to play a series of friendly matches at Kennedy Seaface (now Marine Drive area across the Gymkhanas) for the Hindu Gymkhana in early October. This opportunity allowed him to be in town when the other members of the team were to appear before the Commission. On October 6, many people arrived at Parsi ground to watch him play and he scored 40-odd runs. On October 13 , a larger crowd assembled at the ground and Amarnath did not disappoint as he scored a fine century, the local papers carrying every detail of his batting.

After the conclusion of the England tour, E D H Sewell wrote in *The Times of India*, "After Mohammed Nissar, Amar Singh and Amarnath, C S Nayudu was the best bowler on the tour but the captain never recognised his abilities. It was an absolute disaster for the team when Amarnath was sent back. The kind of form he was in, his bowling would have been useful in the first Test, his batting in the second and perhaps both batting and bowling in the last Test. As a batsman, Amarnath was opposite to Merchant. For him, attack was the best form of defence."

On January 8, 1937, the Board met in Delhi to discuss the findings of the Beaumont Committee. The report was brought to Delhi in a sealed envelope by the Board Secretary de Mello. The proceedings of the Board meeting were conducted privately. The press was barred access to its discussions. The report was obviously a very personal document and it was argued that it would be far better from the viewpoint of Indian cricket and the people concerned to keep its contents confidential.

Since the ugly affairs of the 1936 tour caused much furore in the public eye as well as embarrassment to the team and the Board, it was inevitable that certain portions of the report would be released to satisfy the agitated cricket fraternity. On a motion moved by Fyzee and seconded by Rashid, the Indian Board decided by ten votes to seven that the report should be made public.

On January 11, 1937, the Beaumont Committee report of the Indian tour of England with special reference to the Amarnath incident was issued to the press.

> The report criticised the Board of Control for inadequate organisa-
> tion in that too many players were sent and that there were no
> rules of conduct drawn up for them. C K Nayudu was criticised
> for his non co-operation with the captain. The Board appointed
> M K Vizianagram as captain, who had no experience of first-class
> cricket in England or captaining the side. The committee described
> his off the field success as brilliant but his handling of the team
> on the field as disastrous. There was a strong feeling in the team
> that he was not successful as a player–captain. He did not under-
> stand field placings or bowling changes and never maintained any
> regular batting order. At the Board meeting 17 players were selected
> to proceed to England and reported that L Amar Singh, Jehangir
> Khan, Dilawar Hussain and Nawab of Pataudi Iftekhar Ali Khan
> would also be available. Subsequently C S Nayudu joined, making
> it a 21-member squad but Amarnath was sent back.

> From the time they had joined the team in July, Jehangir Khan
> and Dilawar Hussain Khan played regular matches. After the third
> Test when Mohammed Nissar returned to India, S M Hadi also
> played in most of the matches. The result was, during most part
> of the season there were eight to 10 members of the regular team
> sitting idle. The traditional policy was to endeavour to play the best
> available team in all matches, yet the good players remained idle
> for weeks together. The case of Palia was illustrative, who played
> and played well in the first Test match but did not get to play a
> game for next two months despite being fit.

> The captain was reprimanded for allowing Dilawar Hussain Khan
> to replace Hindlekar as a wicket-keeper in the Test despite the
> former not even being part of the team.

> The committee felt that the selection of the team should not have

been left to the sole discretion of the captain. At the time of the selection of the team, there was already dissension among certain members and the team tended, from the earliest days on board the ship, to split into cliques. The manager of the team did not sail with the team. There was a general feeling amongst the members of the team that the captain had his favourites and that at any rate in later stages of the tour, one way to keep the captain happy and be in his good books was to avoid showing any friendliness and to show hostility towards C K Nayudu. In the view of the committee, from the evidence available, when the captain suspected there was a party against him which desired to have Nayudu as captain he endeavoured to meet the situation by creating a party of his own and showed favours to some members of the team and did not treat all members impartially.

With reference to Amarnath, the committee found him not guilty of the charges pressed by the captain or the manager and he was honourably exonerated. The committee also recommended that in future the manager and captain would have to consult the Board and the tour committee before any action of such consequence were taken. Vindicated by the report, an elated Amarnath got ready to concentrate on his career.

Later in his life, when Amarnath sat with his sons, he would often introspect about the whole episode. He suspected that the main cause lay elsewhere and he merely became the proverbial whipping boy. His thoughts would go back to a 1934 match between the MCC and the Delhi Cricket Association in which Maharaja Bhupinder Singh was included in the MCC team by Jardine. Lord Wellingdon was quite sore with the Maharaja due to an earlier showdown between the two and did not wish to see the Maharaja in the MCC team. He could do nothing about it except show his displeasure. The earlier incident had seen heated exchanges in which the Maharaja had snubbed Lord Wellingdon openly with the remark that he may be the viceroy of India but was also the servant of the crown whereas he was Maharajadhiraj .... Farzandey khas ..... etc. (a distinguished son of royalty equivalent, for example, to the Prince of Wales). Lord Wellingdon never forgot this humiliation. Was this an opportunity to show Maharaja Bhupinder Singh in bad light through him, the Patiala lad Amarnath, often wondered.

FOUR

PATIALA & THE PRINCELY CONNECTION

THE MAHARAJA of Patiala Bhupinder Singh's contribution to cricket speaks volumes about his love for the game. In 1932, the Board was discussing a trophy for the National Championship. Anthony de Mello, along with Vizzy, took a sketch of a proposed Wellingdon Trophy to Simla for approval by Lady Wellingdon. When Maharaja Bhupinder Singh heard about this, he checkmated everyone by proposing that the championship commemorate the name of Ranjitsinhji, who had passed away prematurely. Lord Wellingdon, himself an admirer of Ranji, agreed. Not only did Maharaja Bhupinder Singh donate a large sum of money for the Ranji Trophy, he was also the main force behind setting up a strong infrastructure for Indian cricket. It was his farsightedness that got the Board to run Indian cricket effectively in a manner similar to England's Test and County Cricket Board.

The Maharaja had always been impressed by the Lord's cricket ground in England. It inspired him so much that he dreamt of establishing something similar in India. The Brabourne Stadium in Mumbai and its pavilion owe their existence to the never-ending endeavour of Maharaja Bhupinder Singh. He influenced and convinced Governor of Bombay Lord Brabourne to part with some area reclaimed from the sea for creating a cricket stadium. To set the ball rolling, the Maharaja himself donated a large sum of money for the construction of the pavilion. Unfortunately, he didn't live long enough to see this glorious stadium host an international match.

For the Ranji Trophy, the teams were divided into four zones and before the top four teams played the semi-finals and their winners the final, the matches within each zone were played on a knockout basis. The reason for playing a knockout format was two-fold: First, it reduced travelling and second, the Board's finances were none too healthy. Sadly, the knockout format proved harmful to many aspiring cricketers. If their team lost their very first game, they had to wait until the following season for the next match. Ironically, the strong Southern Punjab team fell victim to this faulty system when it was caught on a wet wicket and skittled out for just 22 runs. Subsequently, the format was changed to league within the zones, allowing players minimum guaranteed matches.

That the Maharaja of Patiala loved to possess everything beautiful was no secret. If he could pick up the most expensive items in Europe without even a glance at the price tag, he also ensured that he had the best sportsmen under his patronage. The world wrestling champions, Gama and Imam Bux, won laurels under his patronage. The Maharaja is also remembered for creating the famous Patiala Peg — the large measure of whisky. His love for music was so intense, that a German bandmaster was stationed at Baradari gardens to conduct the Patiala band. With a glass of wine in his hand, he enjoyed classical Indian music in the evenings and the Patiala gharana was born and nurtured during his regime. It was probably the golden period for both sports and music.

If the Maharaja pampered people, he was also very strict with the dress code in the palace. It was unthinkable for a subject to enter the Moti Bagh Palace without a turban. "Though I had no work in the palace, I was summoned by the Maharaja on numerous occasions. I got two turbans especially tied and kept ready in a box just in case the Maharaja summoned me. One couldn't take chances," Amarnath said.

Mohammed Nissar, the burly fast bowler who lived in Lahore and visited Patiala only to play matches for the Maharaja, did not know much about the strict rules. Once, he went in to Moti Bagh Palace without a turban. As soon as the Maharaja saw the 250-pound Pathan, he thundered, "Nissar, go back at once and wear the turban." Quietly, Nissar withdrew from the palace and returned with a colourful *turrlaydar* turban, much to the satisfaction of the Maharaja.

On another occasion, when playing in Patiala, the buckle of Nissar's trousers snapped, causing the loose pair of flannels to slip down his waist. Understandably, he could not complete his over. Sensing his problem and the delay that it caused, the Maharaja ordered a belt so Nissar could keep his trousers in place, but none would fit his huge waist. Unable to let his main bowler go away from the field, the Maharaja came up with an idea. Laughing at the sight of his baby-faced fast bowler holding his trousers, he ordered the boundary rope to be cut to fit Nissar's waist. The match resumed but the boundary was shrunk by a couple of feet.

Off the field, Nissar the ferocious bowler, was a picture of childlike simplicity and credulity. How else could one explain his request to the mighty Secretary of State Sir Sammuel Hoare (later Lord Templeton) who, while congratulating him on his brilliant performance and on asking if he could do anything, was told, "Sir, my Principal (Government College, Lahore) has detained me, can you ask him to promote me?"

During the early twentieth century, all teams touring India played a fixture in Patiala, similar to Duke of Arundel's XI in England these days. These matches in Patiala were prestigious for the Maharaja and it was unthinkable for him to be on the losing side. Amarnath often described the pitch at Baradari ground as the best in India. It was rolled constantly after sprinkling water to bind the surface and at times rolled with the help of an elephant pulling a heavy two-ton roller. "The hardness of the pitch could be gauged from the fact that no elephant footmarks were left on the pitch. It was hard as rock and shone like a mirror in the afternoon and was ideal for stroke-play and fast bowling. Any batsman who played back-foot to a slightly short of a length ball had his stumps shattered due to the pace of the pitch. In the winters, the morning dew helped the seamers and invariably caused the downfall of many batsmen in the pre-lunch session."

Much later in life, Amarnath would often become nostalgic when he described the atmosphere at Rajindra Gymkhana during the matches against touring sides. The picturesque ground situated in the middle of the large but exclusive Baradari gardens were adorned like an Indian bride. Flowers of various colours and kinds decorated the pavilion. A cool breeze carried the fragrance of the exotic flowers across the ground. The entire place was covered with beautifully designed *shamianas* to offer shade to the visitors and guests. The outfield was always lush green and well manicured. The tall trees surrounding the ground added to its pristine beauty. Opposite the pavilion, stood a tall clock tower and a large scoreboard. It was a dream ground where a carnival like atmosphere prevailed for all to enjoy, whether playing or watching.

The facilities at the Baradari ground were the best in India and easily comparable with the best grounds overseas. But no one could match the hospitality of the Maharaja who could go to boundless lengths to satisfy his guests. The fantastic tales of hospitality and entertainment at the palace were carried to different parts of the world by anyone who had ever been privileged to experience them. The pomp and splendour dazzled the players attending the evening function, where the best of Scotch and rare wines flowed. With each passing minute, the evening livened up with music and dancing girls offering entertainment. After all this, the variety of dishes made it very difficult for a guest to make his choice. No wonder, such evenings left a lasting impression on the visitors. At the end of the game, and if the visitors had any strength left, the following day a *shikaar* (hunt), would be arranged to keep them busy. It was no surprise that every team touring India requested a game in Patiala.

Amarnath was perhaps one of the few who had experienced both Maharaja Bhupinder Singh's magnanimity and ire. The Quadrangular tournament in Bombay was not only prestigious but also very popular. When Yuvraj Yadvindra Singh replaced Prof D B Deodhar, a popular figure in this part of the world, as captain of the Hindus, members of the Hindu Gymkhana did not take kindly to this move. A large crowd at the ground heckled and hooted the young prince for taking the mantle from their beloved cricketer. Yadvindra Singh had a tough time during the match and this unruly behaviour disturbed his concentration.

After this incident, he decided not to play in this tournament. The Maharaja of Patiala was also annoyed and he ordered all his players to avoid playing for the Hindus in the Quadrangular.

Before the young prince returned to Patiala, he told Amarnath that he desired to watch the shooting of a film. Since Amarnath was himself quite a star in Bombay, he called up the famous producer, director and actor Chandra Mohan and requested him to let Yadvindra Singh watch a shooting schedule in his studio. Happy at the prospect of meeting both the young Yuvraj and Amarnath, Chandra Mohan made arrangements to entertain the duo. They spent some time watching the shooting of a movie and meeting other stars including Ashok Kumar and K L Saigal, who had come to meet Amarnath. The young prince was satisfied and they returned to their hotel.

The following evening, Chandra Mohan went to meet Amarnath. He congratulated him for passing the screen and voice test and offered Rs 5,000 as advance payment to him. A surprised Amarnath asked him what it was all about and when the tests had taken place. "When you came to watch the shooting," replied Chandra Mohan. "I have no clue about acting," Amarnath responded. "Don't worry, it is our headache to make you act," said Chandra Mohan. "Look Chandra, I am a cricketer with a reasonably good job. If the Maharaja comes to know of this, he will throw me out of Patiala. In case the movie flops, I'll be on the pavement. I better stick to cricket," replied Amarnath. Later, Amarnath laughed at the thought of watching himself on screen, running around trees with a heroine. "Thank God, I didn't accept the offer. I didn't want to make a fool of myself," he chuckled.

The following year, Amarnath was approached by the Hindu Mahasabha to play in a crucial match against the Muslims but he declined as per the wishes of the Maharaja. After a lot of discussion and persuasion, the officials impressed upon Amarnath that no harm would come to him and that they would convince the Maharaja and resolve any misunderstanding if it did occur. It was a peculiar situation. On one hand, was the honour of playing for the Hindus and on the other, his unflinching loyalty to the Maharaja. Having been convinced by the officials, Amarnath decided to play for the Hindus. He knew, however, that it meant annoying the Maharaja and being in his bad books as also the prospect of losing his job. "But being young and brash, one hardly gave a second thought to the consequences," he remembered.

He reached Bombay for this important fixture. The moment he walked into the pavilion with his kit bag, Amarnath was taken aback at the sight of Maharaja of Patiala sitting in the lounge. He tried to avoid eye contact but it was too late. Spotting him, the Maharaja gestured with his hand, beckoning Amarnath to him. Reluctantly, Amarnath walked towards the Maharaja and greeted him. Without acknowledging his greetings, Maharaja Bhupinder Singh said, "I think I made myself clear that no Patiala player would play for the Hindus without my permission."

"But Maharaj ... "

Before Amarnath could complete his sentence, the Maharaja said, "So it seems that you are quitting my service. I have heard that Nawanagar has offered you better perks. I'll see to it that you don't get that either."

Amarnath stood silently and listened. Luckily at that moment, one of the players came looking for him and told him that the skipper wanted to see him immediately. Thanking his stars, he took leave of the Maharaja.

At this time, India was going through a turbulent period with the Muslim League spreading the message of a separate identity even in sport. Mohammed Ali Jinnah delivered a lecture to Muslim students about this. Such speeches had some effect on the masses, but cricketers continued to have good relations with each other. Supporters of both communities came in large numbers to cheer their teams, adding fervour to the contest. Both sides played the game hard. The match started amidst loud cheering. The Hindus lost an early wicket to herald the arrival of Amarnath and he walked in to face Nissar, bowling at his fastest. The first delivery was a bouncer, which sailed over his head. The next whistled past his nose at lightning speed. Watching Amarnath in discomfort, Nissar grinned. "There is something wrong with him, he never grins at me," Amarnath told himself. "Shaking my head, I got ready to face the last ball of the over. This bouncer was bowled even faster than the last, aimed at my head. It flew over me and the wicket-keeper. Before I could react, it bounced twice before hitting the sightscreen."

After the over was completed, Amarnath walked up to Nissar and said, *"Tera dimag to kharab nahi hai? Gaind uchaal raha hai?* (Are you mad? Why are you bowling only bouncers at me)?"

Nissar smiled, *"Abe Amar, tere sar ke sau rupye rakhe hai. Maharaja Patiala ne kaha ke jitni bar maroonga, utne sau milenge. Kam se kam, ek baar to khaa ley, aadha aadha kar lenge.* (Amar, the price of hitting your head is a hundred rupees. The Maharaja of Patiala has said I would get as many hundreds as the number of times I hit you. Get hit at least once and I shall split the hundred with you)."

Amarnath had his wits about him. *"Tere ball khane ke baad, zinda kaun bachega* (Who will remain alive after getting hit by your bouncer)?" he asked.

Nissar tried desperately to earn the reward but he never managed to hit the target. Witnessing this keen tussle, Maharaja Bhupinder Singh realised the importance of the match and asked Amarnath to report in Patiala.

Presuming that the Maharaja had forgiven him, Amarnath reached Patiala and reported for duty. He was summoned to the Moti Bagh Palace immediately. The Maharaja said, "Now you are in Patiala, let's see who will save you for disobeying my orders." Amarnath felt as if he was struck by lightning but kept quiet. The Maharaja then stated that there were various complaints against him for not being serious while playing for Patiala. "It has been brought to my notice that you score runs in abundance away from Patiala. Tomorrow is an important game and if you don't score, then you will face my black rule." Not knowing what the rule was, Amarnath innocently asked, "What is it?" Looking sternly at him, the Maharaja replied, "You will get to know tomorrow if you don't get runs." Confused by these remarks, Amarnath returned home and asked a friend what the black rule was. The friend told him, "It means either the dungeon or a death warrant." The very thought of spending time in the dungeon as a prisoner, not to mention death, petrified Amarnath. By evening, he was down with fever due to fear. Fortunately for him, he managed to score enough runs to satisfy the Maharaja and thus save his skin. It was a close shave, he remembered.

LALA IS BORN

If Amarnath had his admirers in Patiala, he had adversaries too who were envious of him because of the special favours he received from the Maharaja. These people looked out for any opportunity to disgrace him in the eyes of Maharaja Bhupinder Singh. The opportunity came their way in the thick of the cricket season when Amarnath requested the Maharaja for leave to go to Lahore to see his ailing grandparents. The request was granted without any delay.

During the cricket season, Lahore hosted many tournaments. Another local lad by the same name — Amar Nath scored a century in one of the matches. The local paper reported the game in some detail. When this news reached the opportunists, they rubbed their hands with glee. They told the Maharaja that his favourite *chokra* (kid) was, in fact, fooling him. Unaware of these developments, Amarnath reached Patiala after a few weeks with his grandparents. He was summoned to the palace as soon as he reached Patiala. Amarnath realised something was drastically wrong and before entering the palace, one of his friends informed him of the conspiracy. The Maharaja flew into a rage when he sighted Amarnath and was in no mood to listen to any explanations. The angry Maharaja blew his top each time Amarnath started to say something. Aware of the repercussions if he did not clarify the situation, Amarnath played the emotional card. He cited various instances to convince the Maharaja of his unflinching loyalty and sincerity. It worked, though with great difficulty. The smile returned to the Maharaja's face and he pardoned him but not without a warning. To avoid repetition of such a situation, Amarnath had to do something. He then remembered that everyone in Kapurthala called him *Lalaji* owing to his father's background of being a businessman. He decided to prefix Lala to his name. Over the years, this prefix became as popular as that of another Lala — Lala Lajpat Rai of Punjab. As coincidence would have it, they were both referred to as the 'Lion of Punjab' in their own fields.

Having sampled the Maharaja's fury, Amarnath was now to receive his generosity in 1938. Maharaja Bhupinder Singh had sponsored a strong English team to tour India under Lord Tennyson. As usual, the Baradari ground and the beautiful Rajindra

Gymkhana were decorated tastefully for the match on January 11, 12 and 13. The Maharaja himself led the Patiala XI, with the Yuvraj as his deputy. After winning the toss, the home side batted first but found the English attack too hot to handle. With the exception of Engineer and to a lesser degree the Yuvraj, none of the batsmen managed to score anything substantial and the side was bowled out for 142. Maharaja Bhupinder Singh hardly uttered a word but his expression conveyed disappointment at the poor show of his so-called strong team.

During the break, the Maharaja looked at Amarnath in the dressing room and said, "*Chokre* (boy), can you get them out for less than 142 runs?"

"I'll try my best, Maharaj."

"What try! If you get them out within Patiala's score, I will donate a village to you as *bakshish* (gift), it's a promise!"

Feeling thrilled at the prospect of becoming a zamindar in one day, knowing fully well that the task was uphill one, Amarnath decided it was worth giving it his best shot. Since the moisture had evaporated from the track, it had started playing easier. The English relished the home attack to an extent that they batted the remaining part of the day without difficulty. At lunch the next day, they were 251 for five. By now, all chances of possessing a village had vanished into thin air. When the match resumed at 2.30 p.m., the Maharaja had retired to the palace since he had not been keeping well and had been advised rest. Cricket was his first love and he continued to defy the doctors. Amarnath tried very hard to dismiss the tourists. He was successful too but not to his satisfaction. He captured three wickets, Amir Elahi, two and Frank Warne, one, to be among the lucky bowlers. Lord Tennyson XI batted through the second day and put up 445 for nine on the board.

On January 13, the final day of the match, Lord Tennyson declared the innings closed at their overnight score to try and force a victory. The Maharaja did not turn up for the match as he was still recuperating from the fatigue and the late night dinner he had hosted for the teams at the palace. The Patiala second innings did not begin well as the first batsman returned to the pavilion rather early. This brought Amarnath to face the English pace battery of Arthur Wellard and Bill Edrich. After the late night, he felt sluggish and uneasy in the morning. To top it, he had managed very little sleep courtesy the Maharaja's late departure for rest. His body and eyes ached as he walked like a zombie to the middle to face the English attack.

"The first ball cut back and hit me on the left thigh. It was a painful blow as there was no thigh pad those days. After rubbing the area, I got ready to face the next delivery. The next ball also cut back to hit me in the groin, leaving a stinging pain and a nice red mark. I was desperately trying to focus on the ball but my eyelids were heavy and I could not sight the ball too well. The bowler must have noticed my plight and realised his chances of capturing another wicket as he repeated the last delivery. It hit me on the inner thigh. The pain was so excruciating that I collapsed on the crease, writhing in agony. The 12th man rushed to the ground with a jug full of water. I washed my face and splashed my eyes with the cold water and even wet my head to get some relief. After a few minute's rest, I felt better and my vision cleared. Fortunately till lunch, I managed to stay unbeaten with a half-century along with Havewala, the Bombay player, on 34. We had taken Patiala to 141 for four," remembered Amarnath.

"While I was busy removing my pads, the musical tunes of the military band indicated Maharaja's arrival at the ground. Before entering the dressing room, he had a fleeting glance at the scoreboard, which gave him the picture of his team's performance. Dressed in his white flannels and Patiala blazer, a scarf with blue and golden stripes around his neck, the Maharaja exchanged greetings with the English team and the other guests before entering our dressing room. With his back resting against the long table in the middle of the room, the Maharaja looked around with his piercing eyes till his focus stopped at me.

'Chokrey, are you also out?'

'No, Maharaj, I am batting.'

'Who have lost their wickets?'

'Your Highness, Joginder, Warne, Saeed and Yuvraj saheb have been dismissed,' his ADC replied.

"By now, one could sense he was losing his composure. He looked at Warne and said, 'Frank, you better forget about playing,

I think you stick to your coaching the princes only. Joginder, you need to be sent to the stables to look after the horses.'

"Turning to his son, he said, 'Yuvi, I think cricket is not your cup of tea, though I had great hopes from you. You better stick to tennis.'

"Finally, he focussed on Saeed and said, 'Ah! Saeed my boy, you are prospering! You seem to have added extra pounds of flesh all over.'

"Turning to Liaqat (prime minister of Patiala), the Maharaja said, 'Get some carpenter to chisel the extra flesh from Saeed's buttocks. He has gone too fat to move in the field.'

"There was pin-drop silence in the room and everyone's eyes were glued to the floor. None dared lift his eyes till the bell rang, indicating that the umpires would be out in the next few minutes. The moment Maharaja left the room, all the players took a deep breath and heaved a sigh of relief."

After lunch, Amarnath and Havewala batted cautiously to retrieve the situation. Both scored centuries much to the Maharaja's joy and satisfaction. Just before the tea interval, Havewala lost his wicket but the long and fruitful partnership had pleased the captain as it had saved the team from a collapse. When Amarnath walked into the dressing room with an unbeaten 109, the buoyant Maharaja greeted him with a broad smile and a sense of satisfaction. He said, "Well done! You have saved my honour."

The men in the dressing room could understand his happiness as the words came straight from his heart. Amarnath knew that this was the best opportunity to seek the Maharaja's favour. Before he could think of anything, Havewala complained to the Maharaja that while playing the crucial match saving innings, he had broken his (Gunn & Moore) Autograph bat. The Maharaja waved to his personal staff and out of nowhere came two Gunn & Moore bats. He autographed them and handed one each to Havewala and Amarnath. This insipid request made Amarnath livid, for his chances of receiving a better reward for saving Patiala's honour had been spoilt.

With the main batsmen already back in the pavilion and with the home side only a few runs ahead of the tourists, Amarnath knew that the match was still not saved. Just before the end of the tea break, he walked up to the Maharaja, who was getting ready for his batting. A *nafar* (servant) was busy tying the Maharaja's pads while another his shoe-laces and a third, adjusting his abdominal guard. "Maharaj, we are supposed to have a group photograph of both the teams after the match, but with light likely to fade at that stage, the clarity of the picture may not be to Your Highness' satisfaction. If Maharaj gave orders, then the photo session could take place now and the match could commence later," Amarnath requested.

Impressed by his favourite *chokra's* suggestion, the Maharaja conveyed to Lord Tennyson his desire to get the group photograph taken. The English captain had no choice but to accept it gracefully. Getting the teams together at the last moment and making proper seating arrangements took forty-five minutes. When the game resumed, Amarnath was dropped in the first over by Hardstaff in the slips. In the next, the Maharaja swung his willow merrily and scored three runs. After the over, Amarnath walked up to his captain and told him that the light had faded and he was finding it hard to sight the ball against the lush green background. The Maharaja agreed with him and called the English captain for consultation. He told Lord Tennyson, "Since the chances of a result are remote and the light is poor, we should call off the match as a draw." There was nothing that the visiting captain could do but agree. The match was called off almost an hour before the scheduled closing time. Each English player then moved forward to shake hands with the Maharaja and thank him profusely for his fine hospitality and a wonderful game of cricket.

Happy with the outcome, the beaming Maharaja then walked briskly ahead of Amarnath towards the pavilion in a jolly good mood, acknowledging the thunderous applause and a rousing welcome from the royal ladies sitting in the special enclosures and the nobility and friends at the doorsteps of the pavilion. The Maharaja had kept Patiala's honour and dignity intact till the next battle.

After packing his kit bag and changing into a fresh pair of whites, Amarnath looked for an opportune moment to speak to the Maharaja. He knew saving the honour of Patiala from the jaws of defeat had its effect on the Maharaja. Finding a vacant space next to him, Amarnath approached him and said, "Maharaj,

I am going to England to play in the Lancashire League this summer."

"Yes, I know. I have read that in the newspaper. Your leave for that period has been sanctioned but you will receive the full amount of your salary on your return. Happy?"

"Yes, Maharaj," Amarnath paused, "if I could ... get my salary in advance, it would help me in purchasing my passage to England."

"I have read your contract and it says that your club Nelson is paying you the first-class passage money separately."

"Yes Maharaj, but I will get the money on reaching England."

"Why don't you cable them to send you the amount in advance?"

"What will the club say? That Maharaja of Patiala's officer does not have enough money to buy his passage, that he is begging them for an advance."

"What! What did you say? Repeat that again."

Everyone around was aghast with Amarnath's frank replies and they feared punishment, but Amarnath knew that the Maharaja was very happy with his effort and he repeated the sentence. After hearing it, the Maharaja turned his head and looked over his shoulder and called his prime minister. To everyone's surprise, he said, "Book this bloke a first-class return passage on my account. Get five best four-piece woollen suits stitched for him and also give him 5,000 rupees to enjoy life during the voyage. But, do not entertain his request for advance salary as he will blow that up, too."

It will be pertinent to point out that the salary of an officer was not more than Rs 200 per month those days. Then he smiled at Amarnath and asked, "Happy now?" Amarnath could not have asked for a better reward after losing an opportunity to get a village as a gift.

Taking leave and permission from the Maharaja to play some matches in Bombay, he travelled along with Havewala first class in the train. During the journey, Havewala said that he was not impressed by the Maharaja.

"I was told that he is very generous but look what I got?

A bat and a few hundred rupees for my efforts! What did you get?"

When Amarnath told him about his reward, Havewala refused to believe him. "Why didn't you tell me all this at that moment?" he said. "Never," replied Amarnath. "This is a princely state. If I had told you there, the Maharaja might have divided 5,000 between us!"

Poor Havewala cursed his luck throughout the journey and was left praying for another opportunity.

In 1938, when Yadvindra Singh ascended the throne of Patiala, he carried on the family tradition of encouraging sports in general and cricket in particular. During his rule, Amarnath was initially given the charge of the entire sports department and later, had the added responsibility of being Southern Punjab Cricket Association's honorary secretary. The young Maharaja had very closely observed the court intrigues and knew from experience who he could rely on. Amarnath was not only his friend but also a counsellor for cricket.

Some people could not digest this proximity. Frivolous complaints were often lodged against him but none led to any action. "My relationship with Maharaja Yadvindra Singh was on a different platform. He always came to the ground early for the matches and on the pretext of inspecting the wicket took me to the centre. It was here that we discussed everything, including the complaints filed against me. Those exclusive ten to fifteen minutes clarified everything and our friendship continued for a long time."

By 1938, the Ranji Trophy was considered an emerging threat to the Pentangular because it had a larger representation both by the states and the players. Maharaja Yadvindra Singh raised a formidable Southern Punjab team for the 1938 season which defeated Northern India and then later North West Frontier Province (NWFP) to reach the semi-finals against Sind. Amarnath produced an all round performance against NWFP (87 runs and capturing six for 36 and four for 17). Sind too had a successful run to the semi-finals, defeating Bombay and Nawanagar.

On January 10, 1939, Sind made a good start and scored 339 with the last pair adding 80 runs against the strong Southern Punjab attack led by Nissar, Amarnath and Amir Elahi. To rub salt into their wounds, the Sind bowlers proved more devastating as well. The Southern Punjab batting crumbled against an accurate attack and just about managed to save the follow-on. With a 142-run deficit, the favourites were facing imminent defeat. The young Maharaja had laboured hard to pick the best talent in north India but was disappointed with his team's performance. The large crowd at Baradari ground was not amused either and the much-touted players now became objects of ridicule. "I spoke to the Maharaj and requested for an all-out attack to redeem our prestige."

With nothing to lose, the Southern Punjab team entered the field like wounded tigers and what followed in the next fourteen overs, neither Yadvindra Singh nor the large crowd could have imagined or foreseen. Amarnath and Mohammed Nissar in their seven overs each, demolished the strong Sind batting for 23. Amarnath returned with a remarkable spell of 7-5-2-4 wickets and Nissar five for 16. At the prospect of chasing a modest total of 166 and playing the final for the first time, some impatient players started celebrating the victory well before it was actually achieved. Unexpectedly, within a few overs the Sind bowlers claimed both the Southern Punjab openers. Like a true hero, fresh from his bowling exploits, Amarnath played a swashbuckling innings of 95 not out to give the home team a seven-wicket victory. His record of most economical bowling analysis remained intact for twenty years, till he himself bettered it in 1959 against Southern Punjab while representing Railways, his bowling analysis reading 7-7-0-4. Apart from being a remarkable bowling feat, it proved his physical fitness and stamina.

Amarnath had fond memories of the times off the field too, especially his promotion to the rank of captain in the Patiala Army. "When the news of my selection for the 1946 England tour reached Maharaja Yadvindra Singh, he was very happy. He invited me to the palace and congratulated me. During the course of our conversation I brought to his attention my low rank of lieutenant in the Patiala army. He immediately agreed and called his ADC and ordered him to get 'three crowns' signifying the rank of a captain. Handing me the rank, he said, 'Henceforth, you will be addressed as Captain Amarnath.' It was probably the quickest promotion ceremony. I was thus promoted to the rank of a captain with all the perks."

CHAIL & TRAINING

"Maharaja Rajendar Singh of Patiala (father of Maharaja Bhupinder Singh) was the first Maharaja to engage English cricket professionals to coach in Patiala. He had the top of a 8,000-foot high mountain in the Simla hills (Himalayan ranges) chopped off to create the highest cricket ground in the world which is still in use. He, on the occasion of his cousin, the Maharana of Dholpur's birthday, presented him with the hill station of Chail, with all the buildings recently erected and furnished at a cost of several lakh rupees. It was like King Edward VII, gifting Sandringham to one of his European cousins. Fortunately, the Viceroy intervened and asked Dholpur not to accept Chail as a birthday present.
The Magnificent Maharaja by K Natwar Singh

The extravagance was deep rooted in the psyche of the House of Patiala, though in Maharaja Bhupinder Singh's reign it surpassed all limits.

The British in India found the summer heat of the plains unbearable. To continue the Imperial work in summers while enjoying the cool climate, was like a dream to them. They found in the high Himalayan ranges a perfect answer to their needs. The sleepy town of Simla, with its pine and oak trees, combined with the cool climate reminded everyone of England. The sleepy town came alive during the summers with the arrival of viceroys/governors-general, and the Imperial staff. The area of the Mall was exclusively reserved for the Europeans or the royalty.

In the early part of the British conquest of India, it was the English who imitated the Maharajas or the Nawabs, but by the late nineteenth and early twentieth century, this attitude had changed. Now the new generation royalty emulated the overseas rulers practically in everything. Patiala kept pace, even choosing European nicknames to allow their overseas nannies to call them easily without having to try the tongue-twisters that they found the Indian names to be. Trousers and other European dresses replaced pyjamas, salwars or other traditional dresses. If the British had a summer capital, so did the royalty, moving to their respective summer capitals at the earliest possible time.

In the night, the streetlights of Simla could be seen well below Chail. Early April, Amarnath and his family would also move to the cool climate of Chail where the Maharaja stayed till September. He spent quite a few years in this summer capital and had fond memories of the place. If he was not in England playing league cricket, he was playing limited cricket in Chail. He understood the advantage of remaining fit and knew that there was no better place during the off-season than Chail to provide him with an ideal climate to work on his fitness. It was a boon, which allowed him to play cricket till the age of fifty-two, (though he retired from Tests in 1952, he continued to play Ranji Trophy till 1960-61 and first class cricket till 1963–64). This routine started in 1936 and continued till 1956, when Patiala merged into Pepsu and later, Punjab.

Apart from having the highest cricket ground in the world, Chail offered the players a magnificent view of the snow-clad Himalayan ranges. To reach the ground, the cricketers had to climb twenty-odd steps. In the middle, was a concrete strip on which coir matting was rolled out for the matches. On one side stood a large oak tree with a *machaan* provided with a wooden ladder. From this vantage point, one could get a panoramic view of the great mountain ranges of the Himalyas including Simla. The nets were in a corner near the oak tree.

Before Amarnath arrived with the entourage at Chail, the entire paraphernalia along with servants would move in two trucks from Patiala. Amarnath was a fitness freak, his programme and strict diet were jotted down to the minutest details months in advance. Since a majority of Patiala cricketers stayed back in the plains, training would be a lonely affair. Special trainer shoes, sweat shirts, woollen socks, cardigans, etc., were purchased at Lillywhites, London, for this purpose.

The training routine would commence at 5.30 a.m. each day. Amarnath described this as highly satisfying and enjoyable but very exhausting because of the altitude. The ground was just a few minute's walk from his Oak Cottage, built in typical English design. The temperature would be below ten degrees Celsius and the ground was invariably covered with dew and mist. "I always waited for the sun rays to hit the ground, the drops of dew would sparkle like a million tiny diamonds, always such a pleasing sight," Amarnath said. To keep the chill winds at bay, heavy woollens were used. No doubt, it kept the body warm but it also added extra weight at an altitude of 7,500 feet.

The exercises started with twenty minutes of jogging around the boundary, followed by plenty of long strides and fast sprints. The first half-hour warmed up his body completely and he would then proceed with his favourite exercise — skipping the rope. The waterproof cotton rope with ball-bearing wooden handles enabled him to continue his skipping uninterrupted till he completed the target of 4,000. In case he tripped halfway, he would commence skipping all over again. He always advocated skipping very strongly because it helped the batsman's footwork (it became an integral part of his sons' training, too). After a few minute's rest, stretching and other exercises would be performed rigorously. Next, came the exercises in which special attention was paid to the back and stomach muscles. The entire session would last an hour and a half. By now, he would be perspiring profusely with his clothes drenched. Without wasting any time, he would briskly walk back home.

At home two servants, Bir Singh and Somi, would be ready in attendance. Quickly, his shoes would be removed and he would then be tucked into the bed with his woollens on and covered with a quilt and a blanket. With Amarnath covered from head to toe, a five-minute alarm would be set. The effect was astonishingly similar to a sauna bath. "When the quilt was removed after five minutes, sweat dripped from my clothes and the sheet was always drenched. Immediately, I would get into a tub of hot water provided by the *hamam* (a traditional Persian method of warming water in the medieval times) and relax for ten to fifteen minutes," Amarnath recalled. Seldom during his career did Amarnath allow his waist to increase beyond thirty-two inches, whereas his chest was forty-four inches. At 8.30 a.m, breakfast would be served. The usual menu consisted of fruits, cornflakes, two half boiled eggs, toast with butter and coffee.

After a little rest, he would attend office at 10 a.m to see if there were any instructions from the Maharaja. Since Amarnath was the Southern Punjab–Patiala Cricket Association honorary secretary, he would be constantly busy. There was plenty of paper work as the telephone was available only at the palace and the Maharaja's office. Normally, official work did not consume much time. Nevertheless, he had to be in office just in case the Maharaja decided to pay a surprise visit. At 1 p.m. he would have lunch, comprising chicken soup, boiled vegetables, chicken or mutton stew with a loaf of bread. At no stage did he indulge in oily or fried food.

Net practice would commence at 2 p.m., and Amarnath batted regularly for half an hour with six bowlers operating, one after another to complete a round. The day a bowler managed to trouble him at the nets, he would go back to the basics in front of the large six-foot high mirror in the verandah to check and correct his mistake. He would shadow practice continuously in front of the mirror till the mistake was ironed out. To keep his bowling effective, he bowled for an hour with the new ball and another half an hour with the old ball, mostly leg cutters. At no time would he relax or bowl with a reduced speed. "I was so accurate that I could hit a coin placed at good length spot nine times out of ten," he remembered. "The practice session was always serious and lengthy, concluding with the discussions, observations and remedies around 5 p.m. or so."

Since Chail had very few officers, interaction with them was normally only at the club. It was here that news of the outside world would be available, though slightly late as everything was first communicated at Patiala or Chail, depending upon where the Maharaja was. Dressed in his black dinner suit, Amarnath would often reach the club at 8 p.m., not because he had a desire for drinks but more as a social obligation. Being a teetotaller, it was difficult for him to keep pace with the other officers, who loved their Patiala pegs and which they drank merrily till late in the night but Amarnath returned home early. A few Sundays were booked for friendly matches and in case Maharaja Yadvindra Singh was keen on a game, instructions were conveyed to the ground staff. Special arrangements were made for lunch, tea and other facilities for the Maharaja to enjoy the cool sunny day and cricket. The ground wore a festive look and many waited for the Rajmata's (Maharaja Bhupinder Singh's wife) attention. The occasion allowed officers and other officials to pay their respects and present their families to her. Some families deliberately came in pathetic attire. A concerned Rajmata would enquire about the cause of their conditions. Sad stories would be told and they would go back richer, some with money and others with promotions.

In case there was no match on a Sunday, which happened often, Amarnath went for his countryside training. "It was a great experience to be in the woods and near nature all by myself," Amarnath recalled. "I would leave Chail early in the morning after breakfast for Kandaghat railway station, a distance of about 18 miles by motorcar through the winding roads of the mountains. It took two and a half hours to reach. But I preferred to take the narrow path barely three-feet wide. I trekked across many mountains and then through the woods to reach my destination. Since it was part of my fitness programme, I enjoyed every bit of it. The jungle and the mountains were infested with leopards, bears, snakes and other wild animals but it never bothered me, as I was obsessed with my training. All the same to protect myself, I carried a *ballum*, a long stick with a sharp spear at one end. It was hardly a protection but it was considered handy by the hill people."

The narrow path was dangerous and steep because of its slippery surface and a sudden drop of thousands of feet on one side. "I crossed many hills, rivulets and thick jungles to reach Kandaghat railway station," Amarnath said. "Once there, I would relax at the platform consuming a couple of cans of sardine and then topping it with hot tea, exchanging pleasantries with the railway staff till the train arrived at 1 p.m. If I found any friends on the way to Kalka, I would have a chat with them and get any possible news. If not, I would get ready for my journey back home. With no streetlights or signboards, the homeward journey would be tiring and treacherous because of the steep climb and the setting sun. One hardly came across anyone to ask for directions, in case one was lost. Only the footmarks formed the path and there would be so many such marks made by the local people leading to their cottages. Any wrong path through the jungle was likely to lead to an unknown area. With dusk falling, one could in all probability become a nice sumptuous meal for either a leopard or a bear.

"The other major hurdle was crossing the rapidly flowing water of the rivers. Since I couldn't swim, I had to look for the shallow part of the river to cross. To keep my clothes dry, I would undress completely, fold my clothes and keep them high above the water while crossing the river. On one occasion, while I was crossing the river with my trousers, shirt and sweater on my head and shoes tied to the *bullum*, a leopard stood on the other side drinking water and staring at me. Having crossed the river more than halfway, there was no way I could outrun the animal. I held my breath and told myself, 'Beta, abhi toh paani pait may ja raha hai, thori daer may tu jaiga (It's water that the leopard is drinking now. Soon, he will be feasting on you, son).' Fortunately, the big cat was not hungry or perhaps did not like my appearance. It turned and walked back towards the bush and vanished, leaving me stunned and petrified. I don't know how long I was in the water, but yes, that was scary!"

Amarnath narrated the story of his close encounter with the leopard to his friends at the club the following day. In turn, they conveyed this to Maharaja Yadvindra Singh. Being an old friend and a well-wisher, the Maharaja spoke to Amarnath and asked him not to take such risks. "You do not swim or carry any firearms, you must only be an eccentric," he told Amarnath. But Amarnath could not be convinced and passed it off as a freak incident. Instead, he started telling the Maharaja the advantages of these journeys. "While going down the narrow path, the knees and ankles get strengthened and while climbing, the back and the thigh muscles become stronger. Now you tell me, Maharaj, whether it is a good exercise or not?" Realising the futility of dissuading him from undertaking the dangerous drill, Yadvindra Singh tried to convince him to carry a weapon for his safety but Amarnath never carried the extra load as it meant an added burden while trekking. The routine continued much to his satisfaction and thrill without coming across any leopards, though the slow moving python crossed his path in the jungle many a time.

MOIN-UD-DOWLA
& THE GUARDIAN OF PRINCES

One evening, Lala Amarnath's sons asked him which match in his long career was the most memorable. Apart from his debut Test, he said, the final of the Moin-ud-Dowla Gold Cup in 1934 gave him great satisfaction.

The Bombay Freelooters had won the tournament in 1932 and 1933. As per the rules of the tournament, any team courting success over three successive years would win the gold cup outright. Vizzy, realising the importance and sensing a chance, raised a strong team with his finances. At the prospect of losing his Gold Cup forever, the worried Nawab Moin-ud-Dowla sent an SOS to Maharaja Bhupinder Singh. Since Vizzy had crossed swords with Patiala on a number of occasions, this opportunity seemed godsend to settle scores with the petty zamindar. Promptly, the Maharaja despatched a note to the Nawab promising to shoulder the responsibility of protecting his cup and then went about the task of raising a formidable team. To send the team as Patiala XI to face the Freelooters seemed below the Maharaja's dignity. In order to counter Vizianagram's Freelooters, it was proposed to name the team appropriately as the Patiala Retrievers under the captaincy of the Yuvraj. The preparations for this encounter and the long journey to the Deccan kingdom was nothing short of war. But there was a slight difference. It was a battle royal to be fought on a cricket field.

As captain of his side, Vizianagram had secured the services of Learie Constantine (later knighted by the king) from the West Indies. Constantine was then considered one of the fastest bowlers in the world. Along with him, Ramji and Amar Singh were also drafted to man the pace on the matting wicket. Vijay Merchant, Colah, Marshall and Jai formed the strong batting line-up. To assist himself, Vizianagram had the services of Rajkumar of Alirajpur to form a formidable side good enough to defeat any team.

There was nothing that Vizianagram did which the Maharaja of Patiala could not match. With his immense influence among the princes, he gathered a galaxy of stars to face his enemy. C K Nayudu, Navle, C S Nayudu, Nazir Ali, Wazir Ali, Mushtaq Ali, Mohammed Nissar, Amarnath and the Australian player employed as a coach at Patiala, Frank Warne.

Just four days before the big fight, four main players from Nawanagar who were in Vizianagram's team were asked to withdraw by the Jamsaheb. It was a clever ploy orchestrated by the Maharaja to weaken the Freelooters. Vizianagram chickened out on receiving this news and withdrew from the team at the prospect of facing a definite defeat at the hands of Patiala Retreivers. Instead, he named Rajkumar of Alirajpur as captain.

With the battle lines drawn, a huge crowd of around fifteen thousand turned up for the finale. All vantage points in and around the race course ground at Secunderabad Gymkhana were occupied by the excited and boisterous spectators.

Batting first, the Freelooters found the pace of Nissar too difficult to negotiate. Since Amarnath kept wickets and had faced Nissar on numerous occasions, he found him probably the fastest bowler in the world in his first four to five overs. Here, Nissar was really enjoying bowling on the coir matting much to the discomfort of all batsmen. Amarnath found Nissar's physique similar to that of a great African rhino. He was about 6ft 3in tall with a huge frame. Like a rhino, he would pick up speed with each step, sending dust flying around his boots, with the ground protesting under his weight, before unleashing the ball at lightning speed. Being good friends, Amarnath often pulled Nissar's leg saying, "If someone put his ear to the ground while you were bowling, he would run in panic thinking an earthquake has struck!"

With each step of his long bowling run up, the crowd clapped, cheered, whistled, egging Nissar to bowl even faster. Nissar did not disappoint and made the ball rise awkwardly from a good length to cause problems for the Freelooters batsmen, dismissing them for just 125. Though the target didn't seem too difficult to achieve for the strong Patiala team, they too found the lethal deliveries of Constantine difficult to handle on the matting. Except Wazir Ali, who single-handedly withstood the West Indian's thunderbolts with a fighting knock of 91, none of the Patiala batsmen could do much. Wazir received blows on his body a number of times but never flinched. This courageous innings enabled the Retreivers to gain a slender lead of 56 runs, which seemed quite substantial.

During lunch on the second day, Amarnath was discussing various aspects of the game with Constantine, when two telegrams reached the ground. One was addressed to the skipper of the Freelooters, Rajkumar of Alirajpur, wishing him all success in this prestigious contest and the other to the West Indian. The message from Vizzy promised Learie Constantine plenty of money in pounds sterling for every run he scored and more benefits for each scalp captured.

The Freelooters' second innings responded better largely due to the fighting 134 by Palia. He faced Nissar with more authority and confidence. With Merchant playing a sheet-anchor role,

Palia did the bulk of scoring and the Freelooters piled up a good score. The match was now entering an interesting stage with almost two days' play still left and an outright result quite possible. When the Freelooters' second innings terminated at 233, a target of 179 runs did not seem difficult for the Retrievers.

With prospects of monetary benefits on his mind, Constantine devised his own plan and new tactics to dismiss the Patiala batsmen. He bowled with fire and precision. His deliveries either jumped awkwardly from good length, hitting all batsmen on their body or the gloves or sailed menacingly past their heads. Soon, the uncomfortable Retrievers were forced into submission. With the scoreboard reading 30 for five wickets, Constantine's plan was working successfully. Between total annihilation and victory stood only one batsman, Amarnath. He too was subjected to fierce short-pitched balls but the theory backfired. Being primarily a back foot player, he cut Constantine square of the wicket or pulled him through midwicket or hooked in the fine leg area with ease. Amarnath utilised the crease so well that the short deliveries looked harmless to him.

Vijay Merchant witnessed this innings and lauded it in an article meant for Amarnath's testimonial brochure as the finest ever he watched, as his team was at the receiving end. He added, "On coir matting, Constantine made the ball lift from the good length and his short-pitched balls passed Amarnath's head and ears. While Wazir Ali at the other end kept moving away from the line of the ball, Amarnath moved into them and hooked them with rare accuracy and power. Never in my career have I seen such hooking of short fast balls rising from good length and the manner in which he was able to keep the ball out of the reach of the fielder's hands at deep fine-leg and square-leg spoke volumes of his greatness as a batsman. To others, he scored on the off side but to Constantine he pulled or hooked anything that was short. In two cases, he even late cut them through the slips to the third man region, which was untenanted. That innings was an object lesson in batsmanship — particularly in the matter of effectively dealing with fast and short-pitched balls bowled straight at the body or in the line of the stumps."

This fierce contest continued much to the delight of the large crowd, who enjoyed every bit of the keen tussle. Finally, when the game ended in favour of the Patiala Retrievers, Amarnath had scored an unbeaten 104 out of his team's 179 runs. The Nawab profusely thanked him for saving his favourite gold cup. The rules were changed and the winners were from then on given a replica of the gold cup. When the news of the splendid victory reached Moti Bagh Palace, Maharaja Bhupinder Singh was on top of the world. He had achieved a victory against Vizianagram. To commemorate this occasion, a special caricature of each team member was made to remind him of the victory and the players involved.

Cricket brought Amarnath close to many royal houses. He was friendly with the Maharajas of Cooch-Behar, Nawanagar, Nalagarh, Junagarh and many others from Rajasthan and often stayed with them. "It was always a fabulous vacation and the topic of discussion — cricket. Once, while enjoying the hospitality of the Jamsaheb of Nawanagar, I was asked if it would be fine for me to go for a hunt. Presuming it to be similar to a tiger hunt of North India, I did not relish the idea of chasing the tiger with a gun. Yet, declining the invitation would have seemed rude, so I accepted.

"Next day early in the morning, the Jamsaheb along with his servants arrived in a jeep at the guest-house and I cursed myself for being brave. After half-an-hour's drive, we reached a vast stretch of land with no tiger in sight. I was very happy. Looking at me, Jamsaheb waved at the servants and they brought two young cheetahs, chained and blindfolded. Finding me confused, the Maharaja stated that it was a unique hunt, with no shots fired. Then pointing his finger in the direction of the blackbucks, he removed the blinds of the cheetahs and released them. The agile cheetahs galloped at high speed closely followed by us in the Jeep in the direction of the blackbuck herd. Within a few minutes, the hunt was over. The cheetahs had managed to kill one blackbuck (deer) by the time we reached. By now, I was mentally and physically relaxed as my fear of chasing the tiger had vanished. The cheetahs were chained amidst growling protests and moved a little distance away from the dead blackbuck. I watched the entire show with relief and amazement, till another request of my friend sent shockwaves. Holding both these ferocious animals with chains, he asked me to step down from the Jeep and come for a photo session. My heartbeat was fast and legs a little weak at the prospect of holding the killer beasts who had just tasted fresh blood. What if they attacked me I thought." But nothing of the sort happened and Amarnath proudly pasted this photo in his personal album to show his bravery!

With the hunting expedition accomplished successfully, he met the Jamsaheb in the evening to celebrate the occasion with a few other people. After dinner, he was presented with two blackbucks mounted on wooden shields as mementoes. Once the others departed, the Maharaja asked him if he would be interested in joining his service permanently. "I will pay any salary you deem fit to coach the princes and represent my State. Along with it you will be provided a car, house, a fleet of servants," the Jamsaheb announced. Presuming it to be just a joke, Amarnath casually asked Jamsaheb, "What will be my status?"

"You will be the guardian of the princes," came the reply.

"Your Highness, please give me some time to think and consult my family."

The Maharaja understood the reason for Amarnath's hesitation and did not pursue the topic further. But whenever they met, he would always jokingly say, "I am still waiting for your reply."

FIVE

PENTANGULAR, MARRIAGE & PROFESSIONAL

THE HISTORY of Indian cricket dates back to the early nineteenth century when English settlers from the East India Company wielded the willow now and then in Calcutta. But the real influence of this game took roots in Bombay when the Parsis, whose ancestors migrated to India centuries ago from Persia (now Iran) took a liking for cricket. The interest in the game led to the founding of the Oriental Cricket Club in 1848 for the Parsis. Soon, cricket started becoming more competitive and matches were held between the Europeans and the Parsis in Bombay and Poona. The growth and popularity of cricket led the Hindus to form their own club called the Bombay Union Hindu Cricket Club in 1866. The Muslims lost no time in joining the fray as well. Though initially this tournament was played once in three years, its growing popularity saw it turning into an annual affair.

The Presidency matches that were friendly contests between the Parsis and the Europeans from 1895 to 1906, later took the shape of a triangular contest among the Europeans, Parsis and the Hindus. From 1907 to 1911, the results were normally in favour of the better organised and experienced Europeans who won the tournament thrice and the Parsis twice. The popularity of the tournament became more intense with the arrival of the Muslims and thus came into existence the Quadrangular tournament from 1912 to 1936. Since the competition was tough and stakes high, only the best got the opportunity to play. Later on, the Rest XI was included to give a chance to other aspiring cricketers who failed to find place in these teams. The Christians greatly benefited from it as they could not get into any of the other religious team. This inclusion also helped cricketers from all communities who otherwise wouldn't have got any chance to participate. Now more matches were played, allowing the cricket crazy people of Bombay to enjoy the game for a longer duration. The death of the Quadrangular gave birth to the Pentangular in 1937 till it was terminated in 1944 for good due to various reasons including political ones. By then, however, it had done yeoman service to Indian cricket for almost half a century.

As this was a first-class tournament, it provided ample opportunity to all cricketers to demonstrate their skills amidst a charged atmosphere. An outstanding performance ensured them a good chance to make it to the Indian team. With this motive, a galaxy of stars played serious cricket and set many records. The clashes in the name of religion were intense and each community came in large numbers to support and cheer their respective teams. Thanks to the Quadrangular and later the Pentangular, many great names surfaced and enabled India raise a formidable team in the early stages of her international cricket.

The tournament was based strictly on religion, with every team collecting the best possible talent to win this coveted trophy. If the Hindus consisted of distinguished players like C K Nayudu, Prof D B Deodhar, Lala Amarnath, Amar Singh, Vijay Merchant, etc., the Muslims too possessed great personalities like Mohammed Nissar, Wazir Ali, Nazir Ali, Dilawar Hussain and Mushtaq Ali to name a few. The Parsis, the oldest club in the tournament along with the Europeans, had Dr Kanga, Jamshedji, Vajifdar, Palia, Havewala among others to form a formidable side. The Europeans were best placed as their players could come and participate from England, Australia or any other part of Europe. Frank Tarrant, Frank Warne (Australia) A L Hosie, Wilfred Rhodes, Harold Larwood, Joe Hardstaff and Denis Compton (England) assisted the Europeans on a number of occasions.

Amarnath's association with the Quadrangular came much after he became a celebrity in Indian cricket. He could not play much in the Pentangular earlier due to various factors. In 1937, he missed the tournament due to a protest by the Hindu Gymkhana against the seating arrangements at Brabourne Stadium. With not much international cricket available, Amarnath was keen to establish his batting prowess in the Pentangular. The 1938 season provided him an opportunity to break the long-standing record of highest individual score set in 1924 by A L Hosie (200) and he did it in style by scoring 241. It was a marvellous achievement as no Indian, and that too a Hindu, had ever come close to breaking this record. For the large crowd at the ground, it was another treat, reminiscent of his Test hundred against England not very long ago. All bowlers including Vijay Hazare came in for severe punishment. It was batting at its best. Every stroke was placed with precision and power so tremendous, that fielders had little chance to intercept them. Such was his dominance that day that the eleven players seemed inadequate to stop his flow of runs. Brabourne Stadium was on fire.

When Amarnath broke Hosie's record, a large number of his fans rushed in to garland him. In a few moments, his face disappeared beneath dozens of garlands draped around his shoulders and arms. "While trying to get rid of these flowers, I noticed a young man rushing towards me with a bottle in his hand. I was scared and prayed for my safety, but soon found my fears unwarranted as he turned out to be an ardent fan who had got drunk while enjoying my batting and now, he was in the middle to offer me his drink. I politely refused the champagne as I was a teetotaller, but nevertheless, thanked him for the gesture. After putting my name in the record books, I was floating on cloud nine," Amarnath said.

Describing this innings, Hazare wrote in his book *Cricket Replayed*: "I watched with mixed feelings his 241 in the Bombay Pentangular in 1938. I said mixed feeling because I was at the receiving end. In between toiling for long hours I could admire his stroke-play. It was difficult to place a field for him as he just did what he liked with the attack. My solace was that I got him in the end but at what cost! Tired as I was, I walked away happy at having seen this knock."

In the evening, Amarnath was honoured by the Hindu

Gymkhana members for setting a new record. It was a great honour for the entire community and the celebrations continued till late in the evening. If there were long speeches describing this innings, there were many expensive gifts awaiting him. He was presented with many silver cups and other valuable gifts. A Raja present at the ground, was so overwhelmed that he presented him with a tea set worthy of a Maharaja, consisting of twenty-odd pieces of gold and silver arranged on a musical table with lights shaped like grapes. The Hindus were confident of winning the tournament that year but they missed Amarnath in the final as his marriage had been fixed for that time. The Hindus had to wait for a year to avenge their defeat in a keenly-contested final at Brabourne Stadium on November 25, 26, and 27 against their arch rivals, the Muslims.

In 1940, the Congress was fighting a battle on two fronts, one against the British Raj and the other against the Muslim League. Mahatma Gandhi called for the Pentangular tournament to be banished in December 1940. The remarks were extensively reported by the *Bombay Chronicle*. "I should like, therefore, those who have anything to do with this movement to stop the matches to broaden the issue and take the opportunity of considering it from the highest standpoint and decide once for all upon banishing the communal taints from our life whilst the blood bath is going on," said Gandhi. This call touched Amarnath's heart and soul — and indeed, of the other Hindu cricketers — and they boycotted the tournament.

The All India Muslim League leader M A Jinnah preached something quite different. In late January, while presiding over a function at Cooperage, he enjoined the Muslim students assembled there to consider themselves Muslims first. It was a speech totally in contrast with Gandhi's call for integration of all communities in sports but Jinnah was out to burn the very fabric which bonded the sportsmen. The tournament continued despite several protests and the dharnas by students and Congress members. The following year, Amarnath received an invitation to play in the Pentangular for the Hindus but he declined. "It was unthinkable to play in the tournament anymore after the communal clashes and Gandhiji's call," he told us. But many prominent Bombay players including Vijay Merchant, C S Nayudu and Vijay Hazare continued to play in the tournament.

In 1943 Anthony de Mello said there was nothing communal about the tournament. According to him, "The tournament had given India very thrilling and top class cricket, played in a very healthy competition." This seemed like a desperate attempt by the captain of a sinking ship. Perhaps the loss of revenue from gate money was the reason. The Pentangular was passing through a very critical stage and it finally wound up in 1944. But for Amarnath, it was the end of the road in 1940 itself. "Country comes first, then religion or cricket," he said with pride.

MARRIAGE IN 1938

Despite having conquered the cricket arena and the hearts of many a damsel in India and abroad, Lala Amarnath was unable to find a suitable match. Since he could not make up his mind, he left the choice of his bride to his grandparents and concentrated on his cricket. Those days, marriages in Punjab and United Provinces (now Uttar Pradesh) were arranged either through close relatives or barbers who knew details of all eligible bachelors in the area. In his case, it was an aunt who played a key role in finding the match. He was slightly sceptical of the proposal since not even a photograph of the prospective bride was sent to him for approval. Vesting his faith in his grandparents, Amarnath hoped they would find the best girl for him. Whom he saw at the engagement was a beautiful girl of sixteen. Wrapped in a peach silk saree, Kailash Kumari was the daughter of Charan Das, a leading sugar agent and president of the Kanpur Chamber of Commerce. He also dealt in silver and gold bullion in his daughter's name since he felt she had brought him prosperity as soon as she was born.

After the engagement, when Kailash Kumari was told by her mother Panna Devi that she would be travelling to Lahore and staying in *Paree Mahal* (Palace of the Fairy), she was very excited as she had read many stories of the palaces of kings and nawabs. The prospect of staying in *Paree Mahal* was like a dream come true for the young girl who had hardly stepped out of her house and had spent much of her time reading fairytales.

On December 8, 1938, Amarnath's marriage with Kailash Kumari was solemnised in Amritsar in a large house near *Haathi darwaza* (Elephant gate). It was a very cold night and as was the practice, the main ceremonies were slated for 1 a.m. in the open. To show off her fabulous jewellery and Tanchoi silk saree especially woven for the ceremony, Kailash Kumari did not wear any woollen protection. She remembered the event and how cold she felt. After the *bidaai* (farewell), the couple travelled to Lahore by car, barely twenty-five miles away. The journey was pleasant for the new bride as she sat snuggled in her fur coat bought by her husband in London only a few months earlier.

After an hour or so, the car stopped in front of a huge iron gate leading to a massive building. What she saw was both beyond her dreams and brought her down to earth. It must have been the most beautiful palace in terms of architecture and design of a bygone era but it was not in a condition she had expected. It had belonged to a nawab who loved his wine and women. It was said that he dressed his concubines as fairies and spent his evenings enjoying their music and dance under the influence of wine. After his death, the massive structure was neglected. Various stories around the *Paree Mahal* made it worse. One such was that the soul of the Nawab returned each night to haunt the place. But one look at the palace told a different story. It was probably lack of funds and the disinterest of the Nawab's descendants, which led to the dilapidated condition of the palace except for one section, where Amarnath and his wife lived for some time.

The couple stayed in Lahore for a few months before travelling to England in April and on returning to India settled down in Patiala.

LANCASHIRE LEAGUE

Lala Amarnath's desire to play as a professional cricketer materialised when Nelson Cricket Club signed him for the 1938–39 seasons. It was a big achievement for him as Nelson Club recognised his abilities as a leading player, despite his infamous exit from the 1936 tour of England. He was an instant hit with his team-mates and the people of this small town. The wet conditions in the league made him the most dangerous bowler. It was here that he developed and mastered his lethal delivery

— the leg-cutter. The league also taught him the art of reading wickets, which came handy in his long career.

Since counties did not encourage hiring the services of overseas players, the Lancashire League offered an opportunity to many cricketers from around the world. The most sought-after was George Headley, popularly known as 'Black Bradman' due to his batting prowess. In the league, every rival club feared him, large crowds made a beeline to watch him and he hardly disappointed. Other batsmen envied his scoring skills in conditions which were considered difficult. Despite being jealous of his talent, each player admired his skills and he proved it with his averages.

About his own experience in the league, Amarnath said, "I was a free-flowing batsman in India, where the ball would come nicely on to the bat but found my technique coming to naught on slow, damp wickets. Even harmless half-volleys caused me problems. I played too early to these deliveries and the ball came slow off the pitch resulting in a catch. Amar Singh was a grand success with the bat. He was a strong man who loved to hit the ball in the air and most of his shots landed on the rooftop of the houses across the street. I often imagined the plight of the bowlers if C K Nayudu had played in the League. Surely, many people would have sued him for breaking their windowpanes. Though Amar Singh was a better bowler than me, I beat him in bowling because I hit the target more often due to my in-swinging deliveries as compared to his outswingers, which missed the wickets."

Gradually, Amarnath settled down in both departments of the game. The Lancashire League had a tradition of collecting hat money, once a batsman reached a half-century or captured five wickets (this tradition still continues in Lancashire and Yorkshire leagues). Amarnath was earning extra money in each match. "I always used half my hat money to treat my teammates to beer after the game." Thursday evenings were spent in the club devising strategies for the coming game. As things were moving in his favour, he hardly contributed anything to the discussions.

The game against Headley was a big event for any club, as maximum beer was consumed that afternoon and the gate collection was also high. Amarnath was amazed that many theories came up on the eve of this much-awaited match. His silence prompted the captain to ask him for his plan to get Headley out. "Don't worry, George won't last too long in the middle," he said. The excited captain and the rest of the team tried hard to know the plan but Amarnath was not keen to divulge it and kept laughing. Before leaving the club for his cottage, he called his team-mates and said, "Consider our opponent already one down." Before the baffled team-mates could realise what hit them, he was gone.

Amarnath opened the attack with the new ball and in his first over, he had the opening batsman plumb in front. The close-in fielders appealed but he shook his head and said, "missing the leg stump". The umpire, who was about to declare the batsman out, was impressed with Amarnath's sporting spirit and knowledge of the rules and changed his mind. There were a few more close shaves. While others appealed loudly Amarnath shook his head. On one occasion, his captain walked up and asked, "Pro, are you playing for my team or theirs?" By now, the umpire was fully convinced that the batsman would be out leg before only if Amarnath appealed.

Soon, the struggling batsman found his wickets shattered and Headley walked in, bubbling with confidence. The Nelson skipper asked Amarnath if the field needed any re-adjustment. "Yes," Amarnath replied. Looking at Headley and smiling, he said, "Place all the fielders around his bat in a semi-circle." Thinking that Amarnath had said that in jest, the captain repeated the question but got the same response. Shrugging his shoulders, the captain gave in. Headley smiled in disbelief. He had never been given such a vast opening in the field to score freely. Finding his would-be victim relaxed, Amarnath grinned and got ready for the kill.

He pitched an in-swinger outside the off-stump, getting the ball to hit Headley's front pad. Amarnath jumped, appealing loudly while the wicket-keeper and slips were not so sure. The umpire was confused. He was thinking that the ball would have missed the stumps but seeing Amarnath appeal so confidently, he raised the dreaded finger, much to Nelson's joy and Headley's disbelief. He stood there shaking his head and looking aghast at the decision, before walking back. Headley was furious and kept cursing the umpire all the way to the pavilion. Amarnath had kept his word and the dreaded Headley had not lasted long. After the match, Headley walked up to Amarnath and asked if he was out leg before.

"The umpire felt you were out," Amarnath said.

"Ah! That umpire, he must be bloody blind or ignorant of the rules or maybe both," said Headley. The two parted after a long discussion, wishing each other luck for the rest of the season.

The rules in the League were drafted in such a manner that each club would play the other twice, once at home and the other away. In the second half of the season, Nelson got ready to face the infallible Headley on his turf. Amarnath had won the first round against the West Indian and knew the same tactic would not work again. Out of habit, he always reached the ground early and did so on this occasion, too. He checked the wicket and found it ideal for batting. "I knew we were in for some rough treatment from the West Indian that day," he said.

Lost in thought, Amarnath walked back towards his dressing room when he saw the same umpire who had given Headley out, walking towards the middle. Amarnath was delighted to see him. He waved to him and on meeting him exchanged a few notes about the League and his health, especially his eyesight. The last query made the umpire raise his eyebrows. "My eyes are fine. Why do you ask?" he said. Sensing he had hit bull's eye, Amarnath narrated his short conversation with George Headley and his poor opinion of this umpire. Hearing these comments, the umpire burst out in anger and requested Amarnath to hit this fellow's pads and leave the rest to him. Having received an assurance from the umpire, he walked happily to the dressing in great spirits. The Nelson players could not believe their pro was smiling while they were tense. Unable to hold their curiosity any longer, a player asked him if he was okay. "Yes, I am fine, I just got him out," he said, pointing his finger at Headley, who was taking a knock outside the dressing room.

When the game commenced, Amarnath got rid of the opening batsman and Headley came in to the middle. This time the Nelson skipper didn't ask Amarnath but arranged the fielders as in the earlier contest. Amarnath smiled at his opponent but

Headley was in a pensive mood and ignored it. "He was serious and did not acknowledge my greetings making me a little uncomfortable," Amarnath recalled. Headley negotiated every delivery with his bat with ease but without scoring. In the next over, Amarnath bowled one ball, which hastened off the track to hit him on the left pad while playing on the back-foot. Amarnath leapt in the air, appealing for leg before along with the close-in fielders. Everyone knew it was a futile appeal, as the ball would have missed the leg-stump. The appeal was upheld much to the team's joy and disbelief. But Headley couldn't believe his eyes, given out again by the same umpire! He walked back but not before giving vent to his feelings.

After the game, Amarnath tried to speak to Headley but he was quite sour. Later, Sir Learie Constantine, the famous West Indian player, tried to patch up the differences between them but Headley wouldn't speak to him for the rest of the season for his role in his cheap dismissals. "I didn't do anything wrong, I was paid by my club to get rid of all the batsmen and I did it in a perfectly legitimate manner, bowling and appealing," Amarnath remembered.

The season was very fruitful in terms of runs and wickets, which came in abundance. Amarnath was enjoying life on and off the field. His cottage was always open to his English friends who came regularly to taste Indian curry. He was a good chef himself, cooking Mughlai dishes. His wife Kailash was an excellent hostess despite being able to speak only a few words of English. The couple was much in demand. With matches being played on weekends, they had plenty of time at their disposal. To take his newly-wed for sight-seeing, he bought an Austin Morris but could not use the car since he neither had a licence or boasted of much driving experience. To wriggle out of this situation, he approached the club President Hopkinson to help him get a licence. His fame and Hopkinson's connections expedited the request.

Within a day, an officer came to his place to conduct a driving test. It was an embarrassing situation as he knew what lay ahead — denial of the driving licence since he had no experience of handling a vehicle. But Amarnath had a pleasant surprise when the officer turned out to be an admirer of his. He invited the officer inside the house for tea and he felt confident thereafter. As soon as the officer saw the new Austin Morris, he expressed a desire to drive it himself. Happily, Amarnath allowed him to take the wheel and occupied the passenger's seat. The two drove to the countryside when the officer asked him to take over. "We were on a road which had no intersections or traffic. I simply drove straight and passed my driving test," Amarnath said.

In 1939, war clouds were looming large over the horizon due to the critical political situation in Europe. England was sensing war with Germany. Under these circumstances, Amarnath requested Nelson to release him early so that his departure to India was not jeopardised in case hostilities between Britain and Germany broke out. The club accepted his request but his early departure deprived him a good chance of capturing 100 wickets in the League, needing only a few wickets in the last two matches to reach the landmark.

The journey to Southampton in the night was long and slow. As a precautionary measure, the authorities had banned the use of car headlights. Under these circumstances, his inadequate experience of driving combined with the darkness and journeying in moonlight seem like an eternity. At one turn, he almost drove over a cliff. By the time they had reached Southampton, the ship had already set sail for India.

The late arrival turned out to be a blessing in disguise, as the ship which they were to board was hit by a torpedo from a German U-boat and sank. News of this sinking and the loss of lives reached Kanpur, sending family members into the despair. Their tears dried when a cable, intimating the change in the Amarnaths' travel plans, arrived. The atmosphere transformed from mourning to celebration. Sweets were distributed to Brahmins and the poor in thanksgiving to the Almighty. But the journey back home was scary, as news of the Allies' ships sunk by German U-boats reached the ship regularly. The couple survived the nerve-wracking journey but their new car could not survive the Nazi bombing of England.

Amarnath had to wait for nearly a decade before he played as a professional in England, this time for the Radcliffe Cricket Club in the Central Lancashire League. He replaced Frank Worrell for a season and was shaping well, before a foot infection forced him to miss a few matches. He was operated upon but the corn kept cropping up. Despite that, he proved successful. Many offers came his way to play as a professional but his commitment to Patiala forced him to decline all offers and he never went to England after 1950.

AUSTRALIAN SERVICES TOUR 1945

The Board of Control for Cricket in India's plan for a regular series with England or Australia was washed away with the advent of Second World War. Between 1936 and 1945, Indian cricketers were deprived of international competition, though Tennyson and Ryder's team did fill the vacuum a bit. These matches were played without the sanction of ICC and the performance in such matches did not receive its approval.

When the War ended in 1945, the BCCI hurriedly arranged a short tour of the Australian Services players stationed in Asia or returning from Europe. Though again unofficial in nature, it came handy for the Indian cricketers and gave the selectors an opportunity to choose the best team for the tour of England in 1946. During their two-and-a-half-month tour, the Australians entertained everyone with their cavalier attitude and delightful approach towards the game. If the tiny Lindsay Hassett displayed superb batting skills, then Keith Miller won the hearts of all with his lusty hitting and fierce bowling. The team covered the length and breadth of the country, leaving most of the players familiar with every custom of the land.

The match between the Princes XI and the Australians brought almost the entire city of Delhi to the Ferozshah Kotla ground. With the uncertainty of the War over, it was once again carnival time. To keep this atmosphere alive, Hassett did not disappoint the large gathering and scored a century in each innings. Amarnath also came up with a scintillating knock of 163 at an almost a run-a-minute pace to remind the Australians of his batting prowess. The feast of runs sent a positive signal to the cricket-loving spectators, who turned up in large numbers at the venues.

"I reached Bombay for the first 'Test' match. In the evening, I was relaxing with a cup of tea when the receptionist informed me that a Bhutto wished to meet me," Amarnath recalled. "I immediately recognised the name, as I had known his father Shah Nawaz Khan for quite sometime and had met young Zulfikar at every match I played in Bombay. This youngster was very vibrant by nature and always boasted of his cricketing abilities, may be good enough for local matches. His other interest was movies and he was head over heels in love with his favourite heroine, Nargis. Despite his boastful nature, he was quite a likeable person. I told the receptionist to send him up to my room. The moment he walked into my room, I said 'So Zulfi, have you come for some complimentary passes?' He replied in the affirmative without any embarrassment. 'Why can't you buy tickets like the other guys, surely you can afford that?' I asked him. 'Sure, I can but I won't,' he said, making me give him two passes. Before leaving my room, he said 'When I become the prime minister of Pakistan, I'll return all your favours.' I laughed and told him to first be in a position to buy tickets. Of course, Zulfi did become the president of Pakistan on December 20, 1971."

The first 'Test' at the Brabourne Stadium produced some of the most breathtaking cricket witnessed on this ground. It was such a fine display of both batting and bowling that nobody left their seats till the last ball was delivered for fear of India losing the match. Winning the toss and batting first on a true strip, the Australians posted a huge score of 531. John Pettiford collared the Indian attack as he scored a magnificent century. Cec Pepper (95), Lindsay Hassett (53), James Workman (76) also played attractive cricket. The large crowd had never witnessed such awesome batting before and enjoyed every bit of it, wishing it had come from the home side. When the tourists bowled, they stuck to a line and length, frustrating the free stroking Indians. Unable to penetrate the field, the Indians committed one mistake after another to be in a hopeless situation. Amarnath (64) and Hazare (75) tried to retrieve the situation with some resolute batting but it was not enough. The Indians were followed on. The second innings also did not bring any smile to the faces of the crowd and everyone sat with their fingers crossed, praying for a draw. Luckily for the home side, Amarnath and Merchant consumed invaluable time, scoring half-centuries. The tourists were set a 113-run target in half-an-hour's batting. The match ended in a draw, but in fact it was a moral victory for the Australians.

The teams then travelled to Calcutta for the second Test match at Eden Gardens. This ground had always left happy memories with every cricketer who played here. Back in 1945, Eden Gardens looked very different from today's imposing concrete structure that overlooks the ground. The pavilion was made of wood at the ground level with a sloping tile roof. Lush tropical green plants and colourful flowers decorated the seating area. When the match commenced, the ground was overflowing with a knowledgeable crowd and each day produced absorbing cricket. It was also a high-scoring game where the bat dominated the ball. For the tourists, Pettiford continued from where he left off in Bombay. In the company of Richard Whitington, he tore the Indian bowling to shreds and the Australians scored 472. The memory of the Bombay Test and the value of occupying the crease kept coming back to them, as well as the result it produced. Merchant, Hazare, Mankad and Amarnath ensured a respectable total for the home side. This match ended in a draw as well.

The series reached its climax in Madras and Indian supporters went to watch the finale in large numbers. When the Australians batted first, they found the early morning moisture helping the bowlers. Much to the home team's delight, some wickets fell but Hassett (143) and Pepper (87) rescued their side with a respectable score of 339. The Indians also found the bowling not easy and wickets tumbled at a regular interval. Before the total could reach 100, the top four Indian batsmen were back in the pavilion. The prospect of another collapse loomed at this stage. Luckily for India, Amarnath was scoring freely with his usual gusto. With young Rusi Modi growing in confidence, he destroyed the menacing pace attack with a fine innings of 113 in just two hours and twenty minutes. After his departure, Modi cut loose to score a fabulous 203 to swing the game in India's favour. Having gained a substantial lead, the tourists couldn't take the pressure and folded up in the second innings rather cheaply to let India score a six-wicket victory.

The series demonstrated Amarnath's class as the country's leading all-rounder. He had exhibited his batting skills in all 'Tests' and bowled well in Calcutta. With not much cricket to be played after this series, he had booked his berth for the tour of England.

"At the end of the tour," wrote R S Whitington in *Sporting Life*, "having watched Merchant, Amarnath, Modi, Hazare and Mushtaq Ali, we (Hassett, Miller, Carmody and I) classed Amarnath as India's finest batsman. His hundred in Madras after India, chasing 339 had lost Merchant, Mushtaq Ali, Kardar and Hazare cheaply, was an innings of which Australia's MacCartney or McCabe would have been proud."

The series produced many good individual performances but Hassett and Merchant's captaincy left many wondering which of the two was more defensive. Both skippers carried a negative approach towards the game. Once the match commenced, the fielding side adopted every conceivable method to ensure safety first and waited for the opponents to take chances, which none took. This attitude became so prominent when the going was a bit tough for the Australians in Bombay and Calcutta. Despite being in a good position to win, Hassett never applied any pressure. The Indians won the last Test, not because of good captaincy but due to fine batting by Modi and Amarnath — and the fatigue of the Australians.

SIX

COMEBACK ONE – ENGLAND TOUR, 1946; LALA TURNS BOWLER

I T WAS a foregone conclusion that Vijay Merchant would be the obvious choice to lead India on the tour of England after he led the side to victory against the Australian Services. But the Board of Control for Cricket in India was always most unpredictable when it came to filling the important posts for tours. Many names would spring up like mushrooms and the still atmosphere in the Board's corridors would come alive. It was no different for this tour, coming India's way after a gap of ten years. The first major bout on the cards was for the the post of manager. The contest between Homi Contractor and Pankaj Gupta showed a major shift in the re-alignment of several groups. The atmosphere in the Madras office of the Board resembled a war council meeting. Pankaj Gupta understood the power of the north and, with its help, won the contest by a handsome margin to secure the post.

The officials then began to concentrate on the other position, captaincy. The Nawab of Pataudi, Iftikhar Ali, who had not played for England after the Bodyline series and had missed India's tour of England in 1936 owing to personal reasons, expressed his keenness to lead India. This caught Merchant's supporters off-guard but they were not convinced about Pataudi's seriousness. The Nawab was known to change his mind. This time they were wrong. With India on the threshold of independence, the Nawab desired to make a career in foreign affairs. He saw cricket as a great avenue and the tour as godsend. To materialise his plan, he sought the Maharaja of Patiala's help. In return, the Nawab of Pataudi played for Southern Punjab against Delhi to demonstrate his fitness and intentions.

Though the royalty tag had been useful in the past, the scenario was changing. If commoners like Mohandas Karamchand Gandhi and Jawaharlal Nehru could lead India in the political arena, any commoner could lead India on the tour of England in 1946. The Bombay Cricket Association proposed Merchant's name for captaincy and laboured hard to convince the other members to support its candidate. Though the results of the matches against Australian Services did not reflect any loss, Duleep Sinhji's report on Merchant's captaincy cast a shadow on his chances.

The pro-Merchant lobby, realising the strength of Patiala & Co, raised several questions about Pataudi's nomination and his past record. This was the only way they felt they could win the sympathy of the people who mattered. The lobby told other members that it did not doubt Pataudi's calibre or skills as he had proved for the English during the Bodyline series, but his health remained a big concern. Moreover, he had not played much cricket in England or India for a pretty long time. These allegations failed to make any impact on most of the Board members.

Despite the Board being a divided house, all realised the importance of the tour and wished to take no chances with India's image. The memory of the 1936 tour was fresh and continued to haunt the members. A repetition of such an episode was likely to jeopardise their future. It was a well-known fact that the majority of the players had formed a strong bonding with a certain group while playing for their state or religious team in the Pentangular or other tournaments over the years. To avoid any conflict of interest, a neutral person was the best choice and the Nawab of Pataudi, with his exceptional record, fit this perfectly. He belonged to no particular group and he carried the royalty tag but treated everyone as an equal due to his long stay in England. Yet, he was not acceptable to Bombay. With neither group ready to accept the other nominee, the Board put the captain's post to vote. In a close contest, the Nawab of Pataudi won with ten votes to eight. As Southern Punjab Cricket Association honorary secretary, Amarnath played a prominent role in securing crucial votes for the Nawab of Pataudi.

To ensure a smooth tour and to avoid repeating the 1936 mistake, the Board appointed Merchant vice-captain. To help these two, a tour Selection Committee consisting of senior players including Amarnath was formed. It was truly an Indian team that left the Indian shores with patriotic feelings. All members moved as one unit, thereby allying fears of disunity. This tour was of special significance for Amarnath, as it was exactly ten years earlier that he had been sent back in disgrace. He had fought that battle hard and had emerged victorious. Now, he was back with the Indian team as one of its main players. "There were mixed feelings when I landed in England as part of the Indian squad. It was nice to be back but I felt cheated when I looked back," he said. Being optimistic by nature, he looked forward to prove his class as a complete cricketer.

Before reaching England, Amarnath was considered the team's leading all-rounder and was feared by rival bowlers. Many of them had suffered from his flashing blade. With the experience of having played on English wickets, he looked forward to an enjoyable summer. It was definitely a marvellous tour for Amarnath not so much as a batsman but as a bowler. The Indians didn't have the services of either Mohammed Nissar or Amar Singh, hence the onus fell on his shoulders. Never one to shy away from challenge, Amarnath took on this responsibility and did his best for the team.

FIRST TEST, LORD'S

The Indians played attractive cricket on the tour, even though conditions were not suitable. This attitude made them popular with the crowd which came in large numbers. Before the first Test match, *The Times* wrote: "Although it is not an Australian team who are to be the guests on this refreshing occasion, no more worthy substitute could be asked for than the All India team, who, in extremely unfamiliar conditions, have been giving pleasure wherever they have played." Nothing better or appropriate could have summarised the image of the team. The first post-Second World War Test began at Lord's on June 22 under bright sunshine after a spell of heavy rain. A whopping crowd of 30,000 entered the ground after standing in queues for more than an hour. For the people of London, it was a historic cricket contest after a long, disastrous war. What was amazing was that 26,513 people paid for the tickets and the rest were MCC members or guests, according to *The Cricketer* magazine. They came to enjoy the game and applauded at every possible opportunity to encourage the players.

For Amarnath, it was a nostalgic moment, as he had survived many unpleasant moments in his career to play his fourth Test after a gap of 12 years and 160 days. (He still holds the world record for the longest time span between two Test appearances and the Indian record for the longest career spanning nineteen years). Physical fitness, total obsession and commitment kept him going. Considering the long interval, it is doubtful if the present generation of cricketers would have remembered the make of the bat, the endorsement on their flannels or even hoped to represent their country. His prime years were behind him and he was now thirty-five and yet very fit. "Look at those 12 years, no official Test matches were played. Whatever were played were unofficial Tests as they did not have the ICC sanction. I scored runs, including centuries, and took wickets but they didn't count. Then came the War to deny me the use of my best years and talent," he lamented many a time.

India won the toss and elected to bat on what seemed a good batting track despite there being a little moisture in the wicket. With the outfield being slow due to the recent rain, boundaries were hard to come by. To make matters worse, Alec Bedser exploited the conditions and ripped through the strong Indian batting with a seven-wicket haul. The Indian batsmen never looked confident throughout the innings, with the exception of Rusi Modi, who remained undefeated with 57 out of a total of 200. India's plight would have been worse had Modi been caught by Hammond in the slip off the first ball off Wright. It was a grand beginning for the home team.

The euphoria had hardly settled down in the gallery when England's prominent openers Cyril Washbrook and Len Hutton walked towards the middle amid thunderous applause to face the seemingly none-too-potent new ball attack. What was presumed as an innocuous Indian attack by the indomitably strong English batting soon became extremely hot to handle. Amarnath, with his couple of paces run up and double-arm action, sent shock waves one after another, not only in the hearts of the home supporters but also in the dressing room. He had Hutton caught at short-leg attempting a cover drive. The next ball was a leg-cutter pitching on the leg-stump and knocking over Denis Compton's off-stump. The batsman couldn't believe his eyes, nor could anyone else. The Indians were jubilant with the early success.

Hammond managed to deny him a hat-trick and added precious runs but not without hiccups. In his pursuit to dominate the bowling, he found Amarnath's in-swing tempting to drive. The ball curved between his bat and pad to shatter his wicket. At the other end, Washbrook tried his best but the close-in ring of five fielders finally consumed him off Amarnath. England was stunned at 70 for four and Amarnath was making all the batsmen dance to his tune. If only chances had not been floored at the critical moment, the complexion of the game could have been different. Hardstaff played the innings of his life and with able support from Gibb rescued England.

Terrence Prettie of the *Manchester Guardian* wrote: "Amarnath is transformed. He develops shrewish venoms, a niggling, nagging character. He takes an easy but alert four paces run up and double hop as he delivers the ball. As the ball leaves his hand, his eyes glued on the batsman, his teeth glittering in a superior, snarling grin. He is bitterly hostile, volted with energy and desperately keen to go on with the game and hardly waits for the ball to be returned to him before heading back for his run-up. Paul Gibb, the number six batsman of England, died a dozen deaths against Amarnath in the late afternoon."

The close-in fielders not only missed half chances but also floored many simple catches. Hardstaff (205) and Gibb (60) took the home side to 428. On the second day, the King Emperor honoured the players with his presence and the teams were introduced to him. Amarnath bowled his heart out in a marathon spell to finish with figures of 37-18-118-5. Vinoo Mankad and Vijay Hazare, capturing two wickets each, supported him from the other end.

The Indian second innings was more solid and runs came at a fast pace. Mankad and Amarnath scored a fine half-century each but the rest failed to consolidate after a good start. Wickets fell when the bowling looked least penetrating. Amarnath and Hindlekar fought hard and added 59 runs to save India from an innings defeat. India lost the Test by 10 wickets but it was a personal triumph for Amarnath, excelling both in batting and bowling.

The result of the Test did not dishearten the Indians who continued to play attractive cricket to win most of their games against county sides with ease. Merchant, Mankad and Amarnath produced stunning performances to become the backbone of the team. It was so different from the team of 1936 when everyone watched his back. Now they laughed, cracked jokes and pulled each other's legs and enjoyed the cricket.

SECOND TEST, OLD TRAFFORD

After the sensational collapse of the much-touted English middle-order barring Hardstaff and Bedser's outstanding bowling, the rest of the home side looked jaded at Lord's. The Indians also gave glimpses of their batting prowess and bowling abilities but unfortunately, it was as individual efforts, though Amarnath excelled in both departments. Tickets were booked in advance for Old Trafford, Manchester at ten shillings and about 20,000 went to the ground. A couple of days before the Test, Amarnath was nursing a swollen knee and it became a grave concern for the skipper. He wanted his best bowler to be fit. He enquired from him how he felt about his injury.

Amarnath was himself keen to play the Test match and convinced Pataudi that he would be fit by that time. He ordered a big but unripe grape fruit, salt, mustard oil and turmeric. After heating the oil, he cut the grape fruit in two halves, applied turmeric on them and warmed them on the frying pan. He then tied the warm fruit on his knee, changing the two pieces constantly. This was an ayurvedic remedy to treat such injuries. "I was myself a bit sceptical of the remedy which had been passed on to us many generations ago but the result was unbelievable," Amarnath recalled.

The match was delayed due to rain and Pataudi put England in to bat after winning the toss. The decision, however, back-fired. Washbrook and Hutton gave England a good start and by the end of the opening day, they had piled up 236 for four. The contest between Amarnath and Hammond was interesting. If Hammond hit him to the fence, there was loud cheering from the crowd but when Amarnath hit Hammond on the pads and appealed, Pataudi apologised to Hammond after the over. "It was strange that the Indian skipper would regret the appeal. After a while I walked up to Iftikhar Ali and said jokingly, 'Nawab saheb ab aap Hindustan ke liye khel rahe hai, thori appeal may madad kijiye (You are now playing for India, help me with the appeal).' The Nawab of Pataudi smiled and thus ended the friendly gestures."

The following day, the crowd swelled to 22,000 but the game was delayed by overnight rain. Mankad and Amarnath exploited the conditions and England was bowled out for 294. Amarnath sliced through the middle-order. Compton going on the backfoot, was caught plumb in front, Hammond was again bowled while attempting a cover drive and Hardstaff found the leg-cutter taking an edge to Merchant at slip. He bowled un-changed from one end in another marathon spell of 51-17-96-5, which seemed unlikely only a few days earlier with a swollen knee. The long spell helped India but it had an adverse effect on his batting. He was not a youngster anymore but any advice to him always proved futile as he did what he felt was right. Amarnath went to England as a stock bowler but conditions made him the shock bowler.

With Mushtaq Ali back in the side, his opening partnership with Merchant looked balanced and strong. The contrast in style, though both were equally effective, was there for all to see. If Merchant placed the balls in the gaps with a quality of a master craftsman for easy singles or boundaries, Mushtaq threw cau-tion to the winds and came down the wicket to Pollard, Bedser and Voce to play unconventional shots to the bowlers' horror and the delight of the dressing room. Being nimble-footed and sharp-eyed, he often walked towards the bowlers, forcing them to stop midway in their run-up. Runs came in abundance from their blades and it looked as if it was a repetition of the 1936 opening partnership but Mushtaq (46) missed an in-swinger from Pollard and his entertaining innings terminated at the score of 124.

"From this point, a remarkable change came over the game," *The Cricketer* magazine noted. "The Indian captain decided to alter his batting order, but what did he gain by it?" Promoted to No. 3, Kardar fell to a magnificent caught and bowled effort by Pollard and soon it was a regular procession of Indian batsmen. India lost seven wickets in an hour for only 36 runs and all the hard work of the opening pair proved useless. Sensing another victory in the offing, a larger crowd turned up to cheer the home side. India did not last long and was all out at 170. At 11.45, the English second innings commenced and their intentions became clear. Hammond wanted quick runs but it was not easily possible. Amarnath had studied each batsman and exploited his weakness. Attempting to play on the on-side Hutton was caught off a ball, which moved from leg to give wicket-keeper Hindlekar an easy catch on the off side. Soon, Washbrook fell leg before to a quicker delivery from Mankad. Hardstaff, ever since his double century, found Amarnath difficult to negotiate and once again the leg-cutter did the trick, clean bowling him for zero. The English batsmen tried desperately to score rapidly but found Amarnath, Mankad and Hazare hard to score off, Compton, however, played a gem of an innings (71) and England declared their innings at 153 for five. Amarnath had bowled 30 tight overs and captured three wickets. He was now India's leading wicket-taker.

Hammond's declaration gave India three hours to achieve a target of 278 runs, but the start was dreadful. India lost Merchant, Mushtaq and the Nawab of Pataudi with just five runs on the board. Modi and Hazare fought hard till tea to take India to 70 without further loss but the final session saw Bedser strike back again, reducing India to 87 for six. Soon, the last pair was in the middle negotiating the deadly pace attack. With little luck and attitude, Hindlekar and Sohoni survived the tense but exciting moments of the match. India saved the match by a whisker.

Having kept the series alive, the Indians maintained their popularity with the crowd. The outcome of the last Test remained the hot topic with everyone in London. The Nawab of Pataudi had done an exceptionally good job by keeping his flock together and used his resources judiciously. It was undoubtedly the most popular and respected team ever to touch English shores. Pataudi, like his team-mates, looked forward to the last contest as an opportunity to level the series and return home as equals.

The team reached the centre of politics and social hub, London, and anxiously waited for its last major battle. Unlike Vizzy, who carried thirty-six boxes, personal servants and an ADC on the tour, the Nawab of Pataudi had none to match but he strongly felt the need and a desire to have an ADC in London. The reason to acquire an ADC at the fag end of the tour was probably linked to the invitation he had extended to some influential friends for a social evening at his hotel. He did not want them to go directly to his room and usher them in personally. After all, he was a Nawab and wanted to maintain his image in a place like London. Unable to find any solution, he thought of Amarnath as the ideal person to rescue him from this predicament.

He sent Amarnath an urgent message, asking him to see him. On reaching the captain's room, Amarnath enquired if everything was in order. "Amu, I need your help very badly," the Nawab of Pataudi said. Being good friends, they spoke both in English and Urdu.

"*Kya hai?*" (what is it?)

"I have invited some important people over drinks this evening and I want you to be my ADC for one evening."

"*Kuch paisa waisa bhi milega* (Will I get paid for it)?"

"Yes, I'll pay you 30 pounds."

"No! I'll charge you 50 pounds."

"Agreed. You have brought your army uniform, haven't you? Please wear that."

"*Na bhai, mujhe naukari se nikalwana hai kya* (No brother, do you want me to lose my job?)"

"Okay then, what would you wear?"

"A black dinner suit."

"That's perfect. Done!"

"Please tell the receptionist not to send anyone to your room without my permission. All those who wish to see you must report to my room."

"Thanks for all the help."

"It's okay, after all, friends are supposed to help one another."

Unfortunately, the plan went haywire, when Begum Pataudi landed in London apparently without any intimation and showed up at the hotel. When she told the reception that she wished to go to Pataudi's room, she was denied permission. Instead, she was asked to meet his ADC. Infuriated and surprised by these instructions, the Begum marched to the ADC's room. Since Amarnath had never met her before, he politely requested her to wait and entered the Nawab of Pataudi's room. By this time, the Nawab had received information about a lady wanting to meet him. Not sure who she was, he presumed she was a fan. But when he heard the description of this lady, he stood up in disbelief and understood who she was. Realising the faux pas they had committed, the Nawab of Pataudi requested Amarnath to escort her to his room without any loss of time. Amarnath apologised to the Begum for keeping her waiting and escorted her to Pataudi's room and left them to sort out what might have been unpleasant moments for the skipper.

Later, in the evening the guests arrived and left but the fifty pounds never showed up. Amarnath never let the Nawab forget that. The Nawab of Pataudi always said, *"Amu, marva diya tha* (Amarnath, you almost got me in trouble)."

Rain followed the Indians and on the first day, play was not possible till five in the afternoon. India scored 79 runs without loss in an hour and a half. England secured the first break the following day when Mushtaq Ali was run out by a direct throw from Fishlock. Wickets fell around Merchant, who kept one end blocked and scored a century. "Merchant, if ever a man did, held his side together, and well as he batted, we doubt whether he would consider it one of his best innings," *The Cricketer* wrote. "Merchant had batted well, if almost entirely on the defensive and it is seldom indeed that so fine a batsman found the ball so often hitting the edge of his bat. He was eventually run out, Compton running from forward short leg making a perfect centre and kicking the ball with his left foot into the wicket."

At one stage, it seemed that India would not put up a decent score but Mankad and Sohoni helped the team to 331. India, for a change, was in the driver's seat. When England batted, Amarnath and Mankad bowled immaculately to keep Hutton and Washbrook on the defensive. The match was interrupted by rain and finally it had to be abandoned when England was three down for 95. It was an anti-climax to the series, which had been played in great spirit.

With the series complete and Pataudi's health taking a beating from the arduous itinerary, Merchant replaced him as a captain for the match against South England. Unfortunately, he pulled his groin muscle and had to retire from the match, leaving Amarnath in charge for the rest of the period. By nature, Amarnath was aggressive and impulsive. He loved taking chances, whether bowling or batting and now he was in a position to try the same in a new capacity — as captain. He declared the Indian innings closed at 253 for three wickets, giving the home side three hours and a fair chance to achieve the target. This act left many in the Indian dressing room wondering if it was not audacious! There was panic at the prospect of losing the game. Merchant was also upset but could do little as it was the captain's decision and Amarnath was now the leader. At one stage when South England was cruising comfortably at 204 for four, it looked as if he had committed an error but a change of bowling end did the trick. India won the game by 11 runs. The victory showed him as an aggressive and innovative leader, always ready to exploit his opponents' weaknesses to his team's benefit.

Writing about Amarnath and the Indian summer of 1946 John Arlott wrote: "Merely by seeing him walk you knew he (Amarnath) was an athlete: he might have been a footballer or a boxer, moving with the rhythmic jaunty certainty that spring from the close, mental and muscular sympathy of the born games player. It was difficult to see that he ever bowled a bad ball. There was thought behind every ball …. faultless length above all. He would redden a patch the size of a soup-plate on the wicket with his immaculate pitching of the new ball on the length. His bowling so subtly varied, that few batsmen dared to take liberty with him; he forced most of them completely on defensive. … He morally bowled batsmen two or three times in an over, and little catches flew from the edge of half-hypnotised dead bat to scurry past his fieldsmen: it was then that one appreciated his superlative excellence. A man of exceptional strength of character, it was impossible to remain indifferent to him; all who met him reacted violently. As a raconteur, explosive with gesture, laughter implicit in every part of his body, he was magnificent. Under all lay a cold thought and the strength."

Paying tributes to Amarnath, *The Wisden* almanac wrote in 1947: "Amarnath revealed the unlimited strokes at his command, his driving and square-cutting being of delight. In bowling, he kept an almost impeccable length, moved his inswing probably more than any bowler in England, mixed these with a cut leg-break of some venom. His quickness off the pitch also troubled his opponents but much of his good work was wasted by the gathering of the slips and the short-legs, who were not quick enough to hold on to the snicked catches."

Though the tour ended on a positive note, the manager was, nevertheless, asked to submit a full report with details, an indication that certain heads were to roll. Since Pankaj Gupta had the best of relations with most of the players and those who mattered in the Board, he did not annoy anyone. He wrote back to the Board that he was unable to provide the details of the tour because the report he had prepared had been lost on the way back home. When the officials pressurised him to reveal the truth, he wrote back, "When I was compiling the report of the tour on the deck of the ship, a strong gale blew all the relevant papers in the sea. I have none of those left nor do I remember the details." It was some excuse but it worked.

Iftikhar Ali, Nawab of Pataudi died on January 25, 1952 of a massive heart attack while playing polo in Delhi.

SEVEN

CAPTAINCY ON TOUR
OF AUSTRALIA

It is not the men, it is the man that matters.

NAPOLEON BONAPARTE

ONLY A couple of months before the tour of Australia, India achieved Independence. Unfortunately, the hope and vision with which the battle for Independence was fought under Gandhi's non-violence movement turned ugly. Massive celebrations were overshadowed by displacement of hundreds of thousands of people on either side of the border. The sufferings of the displaced were enormous, physically and mentally, as frenzied mobs looted their properties and slaughtered them. Lala Amarnath also suffered, though not physically but mentally and financially. His ancestral home in Lahore was lost forever along with a majority of his silver and gold trophies, which were in a huge Burma teak showcase. All those cups and trophies that could not be displayed were in an open basket in a corner of the room. Among the trophies stood the Gunn & Moore non-jar bat with which he had scored his century on his Test debut in Bombay and he literally worshipped the bat. The new, unpacked Persian carpets, specially purchased for a new house, along with the most expensive Belgian crystalware presented to him by the royalty were also lost forever. Fortunately, at the time of Partition, he was in Patiala but his dream home was lost forever. What remained in his heart were sweet memories of Lahore, which he cherished till his end more than half a century later.

Amarnath never liked to talk about the unpleasant journey from Patiala to Delhi which he undertook just after Partition. However, sometimes he did speak about it. "I was named captain of the India team for the Australian tour, the Board asked me to reach Delhi to finalise the team," Amarnath recalled. "Normally, the journey from Patiala to Delhi via Ambala would take four hours or so. But the short journey between Patiala and Ambala seemed to take an eternity with the train halting every mile for no apparent reason. Then to my horror, I witnessed a blood bath in my compartment by a frenzied mob. It was a nightmare. I had a narrow escape. I noticed a few well-built men looking and whispering to one another and then pointing fingers at me.

"When I got down at the platform of Ambala station to await my connection to Delhi, a superintendent of police recognised me and asked what I was doing in Ambala in such terrible circumstances. When I told him the reason and the incident in my compartment, he called his junior to get a *karra* (steel bangle worn by the Sikhs) and asked me to wear it for safety. While talking to the superintendent of police, I saw the same group approaching us. They greeted the police officer with folded hands and then looking at me and the *karra*, they said, 'Thank God, you have it. We were planning to kill you before Karnal, thinking you belonged to another community'. The very thought still sends chills down my spine," Amarnath recalled.

"Watching my expression, the officer directed a constable to ensure safe passage for me till Delhi. Though led by an escort, the journey after Ambala to Delhi was hardly comfortable, as it seemed to take forever. The train was overcrowded but with a little luck I managed to travel in the guards' coaches for some distance before the train was stopped. Chaos prevailed every-where. Every delay made me angry, frustrated and a little scared, too! With no information coming about the train's departure, I was forced to change trains to try and reach Delhi. To continue with my journey, I even got into a goods train heading towards Delhi. In the confusion, I was separated from my escort and I had to bank on prayers again. These journeys were cut short by chain-pulling incidents or massive demonstrations on the tracks and I had to fall back on another mode of transport.

"Finding the Railways so badly affected, I decided to travel by road in local buses, trucks and even a bullock-cart. There was no water or food available during the journey. To make conditions worse, the mercury was touching its peak. Being hungry, thirsty and perspiring, I stood in a queue at one of the gurudwaras, which was serving free roasted gram and jaggery to the refugees. Eating grams and drinking water under a tree, I closed my eyes and hoped that this was a bad dream. But it wasn't. My kit bag and suitcase were next to me, the former dearer to me than life itself. At no stage, did I allow the kitbag to be separated from me. By the time I reached Delhi, I was in a terrible condition but, thankfully, in one piece. After checking into the Swiss Hotel (which existed at a junction on the road from Kashmere Gate to the Oberoi Maiden's Hotel), I managed to clean myself but the experience of that nerve-wracking journey was etched in my mind forever," Amarnath said.

The journey from Delhi to Calcutta was much better and Amarnath checked in to the Great Eastern Hotel where the team had assembled before departure. The strength of the team was drastically reduced when three important members opted out. Mushtaq Ali was mourning the death of his brother and conveyed his inability to make the tour. Rusi Modi cried off due to an injury which required immediate attention while Fazal Mahmood declined to accompany the team as Lahore was now part of Pakistan and he was not an Indian citizen. Despite the absence of these great players, the spirit of the team was high and Amarnath was about to make history by becoming the first captain of independent India. "When I looked back at the 1936 incident, which almost ruined my career and this great honour, I was convinced that destiny had been kind to me and maybe, something more was in store for me!"

The Governor-General Viscount Mountbatten was among many who cabled their good wishes to the team. It was a tour on which everyone was focussed and hoped for the best results. This tour heralded a new mode of travel to Australia by a visiting team. Normally, all teams travelled to Australia by sea but the Indians were to become the first team to alight from a specially chartered MacRobertson-Miller Dakota aircraft at the Guildford airport. Till then, no visiting team had ever travelled by air. The series was also the first between the two sovereign nations.

Lala Amarnath flanked by Gul Mohammad (left) and P Sen at Melbourne Railway Station, 1947/48.

Lala Amarnath and Vinoo Mankad at Melbourne Cricket Ground 1947/48.

Lala Amarnath (in black bow tie) standing next to the Indian Prime Minister Pandit Nehru at Governor General House in New Delhi at a function with other team members in 1948.

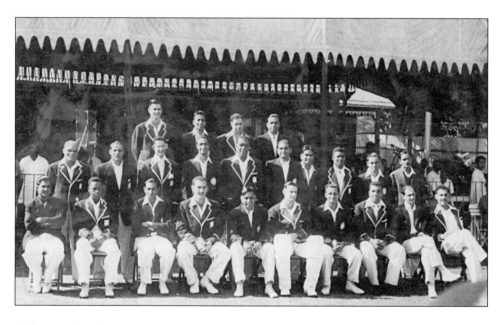

The Combined India and West Indies teams in 1948. Lala Amarnath is seated on the right of John Goddard (padded).

Lala Amarnath and John Goddard, the West Indies captain, after the toss at the Brabourne Stadium, Bombay, 1948.

Lala Amarnath and Abdul Kardar, the captains of India and Pakistan, meet
Abdul Kalam Azad (seated) in 1952.

Another victim of Lala Amarnath; caught and bowled.

Lala Amarnath (tossing coin) with Pakistan captain Kardar in the inaugural Test match between India and Pakistan at Keorzhah Kotla, Delhi, 1952.

Top: Lala Amarnath being introduced to General Ayub Khan, the president of Pakistan, at Sialkot in 1954. Vinoo Mankad is in the background.

Right: Lala Amarnath with Vizianagram (Vizzy).

Opposite: Lala Amarnath with his trade mark pipe.

Lala Amarnath, aged 50, in the nets at Bangalore in 1961, preparing to lead the Board President's team against Pakistan.

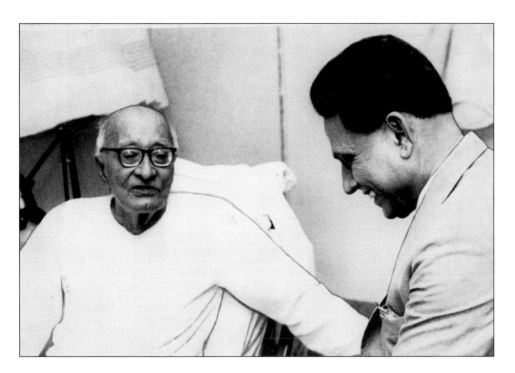

Lala Amarnath with C Rajagopalalchari, the last governor general of India at Madras in 1970.

With the Primer Minister of India, Indira Gandhi in 1983.

The President of Pakistan, General Zia-ul-Haq with Lala Amarnath to this left and others.

Lala Amarnath (left, second row) with other former world cricket captains at a reception in Adelaide.

Lala Amarnath, cricketer turned journalist.

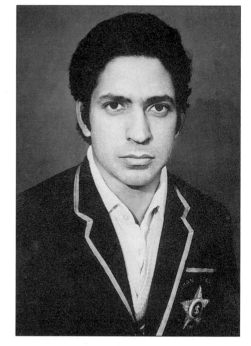

Lala Amarnath's sons. Top: Rajender, the author, with his father and Sunil Gavaskar. Bottom left: Lala with Mohinder. Right: Surender.

The newly married Lala Amarnath and Kailash Kumari on their arrival at Nelson Cricket Club in 1939.

Lala Amarnath at home with his wife on his last birthday September 11 1999.

Lala Amarnath, aged 88, relaxing in his garden.

The Indians were no threat to the mighty Australian side led by Don Bradman. By the Don's own admission, he was in the best of health and form after a long lay-off. Amarnath described his opponents as being so good that if a World XI team were to be picked, at least nine of the eleven players would have been Australian.

The Indian team flew to Australia in two batches, due to an acute shortage of seating space. In the first group, only thirteen players and the manager Pankaj Gupta could be accommodated. The other four players, C Rangachari, Chandu Sarwate, Rai Singh and Ranvirsinhji joined the party later. It was probably for the first time that such arrangements were made. The neatly dressed Indians, led by Amarnath, charmed the crew with their perfect etiquette on the flight from Darwin to Perth. Chief air hostess Hillary Johnson was so impressed by him that she became his secretary on the tour. "She was a great source of inspiration in making the tour so memorable and successful," he remembered.

The tour opener against Western Australia was spoilt by the rain depriving the tourists of any real feel of the hard and bouncy wickets of Australia. If this was a damp squib, then P Sen brought smiles to Amarnath's face when he handed him a cable from his wife in India, announcing the arrival of his fourth child but his first son, Surender on October 14. Nothing else could have been more pleasing than this news. Like a devout Hindu, he had laboured hard for many months, washing wells and feeding cows at dawn each day as part of the rituals ordered by a saint. With his prayers answered, the jubilant Amarnath threw a party in honour of his son. In his short speech, he announced the arrival of another 'immortal', who would not only make him proud but also his country. Surender did emulate Amarnath, scoring a century on debut against Sri Lanka in an unofficial Test and then in the Test against New Zealand team at Auckland in 1975. It is the only instance when father and son have scored a century each on Test debut.

From Perth, the team flew to Adelaide to face Bradman and company, South Australia. The conditions at Adelaide Oval were ideal for batting. The hard and bald strip offered no assistance to either spin or pace, enabling the home side to put up a big score. Neihuus, Craig and Bradman made mincemeat of the

Indian attack, scoring fine centuries. The first day alone produced 379 runs for the loss of only three wickets. It was not cricket but fireworks by the batsmen. Bradman was ruthless and by lunch on the second day, South Australia had made 518 for eight declared. The Indians had heard about this run-machine but were experiencing his might for the first time. Bradman batted for just 152 minutes and scored 156 with the help of 22 fours.

The Indian reply was equally impressive, despite the loss of two early wickets. But unlike the South Australians, the Indians threw away the advantage playing casual shots and were soon 164 for five wickets. Batting lower down the order, Amarnath walked in amidst the ruins. He launched a blistering counter-attack, which caught the bowlers and Bradman by surprise. Neither the pace nor the spin attack could stop the power-packed strokes of Amarnath. The huge crowd enjoyed every bit of it. Bradman was so over-awed by his scintillating display that to keep Amarnath away from the strike, he kept the off-side fielders deep on the boundary line, allowing easy singles. Instead, Amarnath waited for the right delivery and dispatched it to the fence with power and precision. Finally, when he fell after 187 minutes, he had made 144 and the Indians were well placed.

To infuse life into the match, which would otherwise have ended in a draw, South Australia went for quick runs but not without paying a price. The Indians, by now, had gained some experience and kept picking wickets. Bradman declared at 219 for eight, leaving the Indians a target of 286 in 180 minutes. The Indian second innings got off disastrously, losing five wickets for only 60 runs. Playing for a draw seemed the only option for the Indians, when Amarnath walked in to join Mankad to repair the damage.

The unbroken partnership of 175 runs took only 112 minutes. Mankad scored a fine century but Amarnath remained not out six runs short of the milestone. In the last five minutes, he tried desperately to reach the three-figure mark, scoring 21 runs in the last over. This dazzling display of footwork and brutal power generated tremendous interest in the public. Since the captains had agreed before the toss to closing the game half an hour early on the final day, India fell short by 51 runs but had ample time to board the train to Melbourne.

"The partnership, which today produced 175 runs, was worth

coming a long way to see. It was a grand exhibition of batting, which one would expect to see only after earlier batsmen had plastered the bowlers and the board with runs. A dull partnership would have been permissible, or forgiven, but Amarnath stuck to his pledge made in Perth, that his team would try and play bright cricket, even at the risk of being defeated," wrote Arthur Mailey.

Mesmerised by his batting skills, the newspapers took a lot of interest in Amarnath. One headline screamed 'India's star cricketer reads palms' and the report was accompanied by a photograph of the Indian skipper. The crew of the aircraft gave evidence that Amarnath had read the past and foretold the future of the co-pilot, engineer and hostesses. The pilot Capt Klenig said when the plane arrived at Perth, "Amarnath was so accurate that I wouldn't let him read my palm." But when Amarnath was asked, he simply smiled. Anything connected with the country of the maharajas and nawabs fascinated the Australians. They enquired about snake-charmers and the great Indian rope trick. The Indian players' names also tested the Australians. To help the locals pronounce them properly, the newspapers changed their spellings. Lala Amarnath was spelt as Larlar Arrmarr-naart; Amir Elahi as Ameer eelah-eee; Nayudu as Nigh-doooo; Phadkar as Fud-ker. The Indian cricketers were entertaining the Australians both on and off the field.

Despite the weather remaining unpredictable, the touring party was enjoying the constant attention of the media and the people by what they did away from the ground. On the off days, the team was like a small family spending time together, playing with a deck of cards or cooking in the wild. Their skipper was a master chef in Continental and Mughlai dishes. Though Amarnath had been among the runs, he was very concerned about his bowling attack, which had been at the receiving end in the state matches on the covered pitches. He wondered about his team's plight against the full Australian batting under conditions in which it found the task of bowling out state sides extremely difficult. It was this factor, which forced him to opt for uncovered pitches in the Tests. It was his ill luck that the Indians were caught on the sticky dog pitches more often than the Aussies. Only once were the mighty Australians caught on such a surface and they failed to score.

The team had an interesting character in the manager Pankaj Gupta. His short stature and Hitler-style moustache attracted attention and he could converse on any topic including sports or politics for hours. He had the distinction of holding a world record for being nominated manager of the Indian teams in various sports the most number of times. He was so efficient in his duties that the tour progressed without any hurdle.

Apart from exhibiting his skills on the field, Amarnath also won hearts off the field. The tour was packed with various dinners and other important functions, and as the leader of the team, he had to make speeches. Despite not being experienced at this, he sent the audiences into rapturous laughter with his wit and presence of mind. He was a born entertainer and knew how to be the cynosure of all eyes and these functions gave him plenty of opportunity to excel in this field too.

On one occasion in a packed house with Lord Mayor Connelly, Deputy Premier Field and President of Victoria Cricket Association J A Seitz and many other luminaries, he said, "Ladies and gentlemen, I can exhibit batting for long hours and bowl for an hour at a stretch but I am afraid I cannot give long speeches." There was sustained applause. He had caught their attention and continued to enthrall them with his anecdotes.

When the team assembled for another function at Melbourne, Amarnath stole the show again. Sharing his experience with his audience after receiving a drubbing from Bradman in the last encounter, he said, "We Indians had the good fortune of watching Bradman but he made us run for cover." Then looking at Hassett, he said, "I hope my good friend Hassett would be kind enough to give us a break and get out early to allow us time to relax." The tiny Australian batsman just sat there and smiled at the touring captain's request.

If Amarnath and his team were showered with praise, former Governor-General Lord Wavell was at the receiving end. His remarks that a cricket match was a waste of time was severely rebuked by the Australians. At Launceston, A T Marshall said, "Lord Wavell may be a great soldier but he is a poor psychologist. If during the past twenty-five years, Germany, Japan and Russia had been engaged in Test matches with England or Australia, things might have been different. In ten days, Amarnath, the captain of the Indian team, by his glorious batting had done more to bring the people of Australia and India together than a sackful of haggling politicians could do in ten years."

India could not have asked for a better ambassador than Amarnath at this juncture. R S Whitington, writing for *The Times of India* said: "Following his stroke-studded 144 today, India's captain would have been the last person to agree with Lord Wavell's statement that 'cricket' is a waste of time. Amarnath certainly did not waste any time. He many a time danced five to six feet down the wicket to drive Dooland and Oswald and leave the fieldsmen flat-footed."

Although Bradman was a big name in South Australia, Lindsay Hassett, Neil Harvey and Bill Johnston, to name a few, received no less recognition and respect in Victoria. The result of the last match had created immense interest for this fixture. People came in large numbers to watch them but the innings started on a pathetic note. At this juncture 'Percy Taylor' described Amarnath's popularity in a local daily: "Twenty-one thousand spectators had come to see the wonder batsman. When his name appeared on the Board, the crowd applauded vigorously and continued till the batsman was halfway to the wicket."

Arthur Mailey, the former Australian Test leg-spinner reporting for *The Sun*, wrote: "The dramatic prelude to India's batting performance was sufficient to demoralise a team of hard boiled veterans. Three wickets (Mankad, Rangnekar and Hazare) down for no score on the board was not a particularly pretty sight, especially when many of the following batsmen were short of practice and unaccustomed to a pitch which unlike Adelaide graveyard showed some sign of life. Then came Amarnath looking somewhat bored, but with his lips well set and dangerous gleam in his eyes, the same gleam in Adelaide he faced a position as helpless. Many of his beautiful, well-timed drives were wasted on judiciously-placed fields and he was compelled to play lofted shots over the head of the cover fieldsman. Many connoisseurs were beginning to fear that this adventurous stroke had departed with the golden age of Australian cricket, but Amarnath showed that it was not completely out of fashion. Speaking as a slow bowler, the more I see of Amarnath, the more I shudder."

After lunch, the floodgates opened and the feared Victorian attack ran for cover. "Amarnath cut, glanced, glided and steered the ball with artistry and audacity," wrote *The Age*. The worst treatment was reserved for the slow bowlers, who found him almost at hand-shaking distance, hitting them all over the field. When the Indian innings closed at 403, he had contributed more than half of the score, remaining undefeated at 228 in 372 minutes with the help of only 10 boundaries. If the outfield had not been damp and slow, he may have crossed the 300 mark that day, wrote a local daily. Another critic described his innings as the best played on the ground after Victor Trumper. Describing his innings, Hassett said, "There are not many batsmen playing today who hit their off and cover drives as hard as Amarnath."

With each outing, Amarnath was capturing the hearts of cricket crazy Australians, who turned out to watch him in thousands and went back satisfied. It was a great comeback by the Indian captain, after he had failed to score in the opening match on a treacherous wicket at Perth. The Indians were capturing the imagination of many newspaper writers as probably one of the best stroke-playing teams to visit Australia for many years. "With them (Indians) has come a cricket spirit almost entirely new to first-class cricket in Australia," wrote *The Age*. "By their sporting attitude on the field and their unaffected natural manner off it, they have quickly established themselves in the heart of all Australian lovers, even though pronunciation of their names is often distorted beyond recognition. The Indians subscribe to the belief that a cricket bat should be used to hit a cricket ball as hard and as often as possible and they follow this principle whenever it is humanly possible. In Amarnath, India possesses the finest batsman in the world today. The tourists' captain revives a period of batsmanship long since dead among either Australians or English. Combining wonderful footwork with uncanny timing, Amarnath is not afraid to move yards down the wicket to give himself a chance of using his unlimited range of strokes. As a captain of Patiala forces, Amarnath maintains stern discipline over his team but is extremely popular. Overflowing with energy, he takes great care of his physical condition."

Unlike previous captains, Amarnath was a team-man to the core and loved to be with the players all the time to make everyone feel part of the group. Arthur Mailey experienced this and wrote in one of his columns during the Victoria match: "Amarnath played a magnificent innings but he takes no credit for it. He is grateful for his team-mates' assistance. When he was invited to a glamorous supper last night, he replied 'No, thank you sir. I am having coffee around the corner with my team.' This explains the Indians' loyalty to their captain."

Another correspondent wrote: "Amarnath joked with his team members on and off the field but there is no mistaking the fact that he is their leader. When the team is fielding, he raises a finger or claps his hands and the player he wants dashes to the position he indicates. Amarnath knows the rules but plays the game the sportsman's way. During the game at Adelaide, Gul Mohammad left the field to change the studs in his boots and Rangnekar the 12th man ran on to fill the vacancy in the field but Amarnath waved him back. During the luncheon interval, I asked Amarnath why he did this and he said 'Gul Mohammad was not sick or injured. He had just left to change his shoes. I could not allow a man to replace him.' Such was Amarnath's commitment to the game and its laws. He always believed in playing straight and within the framework laid down by the Laws of Cricket."

When the Victorian batsmen faced the Indian attack, they found Mankad and Amarnath's bowling difficult and were bowled out for 273. Sensing another victory, Amarnath asked his batsmen to get quick runs and set Victoria a target of 334 but Hassett decided to play for a draw much to the displeasure of the crowd. The game was finally called off midway on the final day when Hassett appealed against the bad light. The crowd was disappointed by this action at a time when Amarnath was making all efforts to continue the game but the contest was over without any result.

Enjoying their success and popularity, Amarnath along with some of his team-mates went for the Melbourne Cup to try their luck in the famous horserace but the weather froze them. Mobbed by the press for his comments, he expressed satisfaction at the atmosphere and admired the crowd, especially the beautiful ladies and their hats, but in the same breath bemoaned the cold weather.

Undefeated and popular, the Indians arrived at Sydney. Speaking at the press conference, Amarnath said, "We will play as we have in the other states and hope to have an enjoyable match. To date, we have only one complaint about Australia — the weather!" In the evening, manager Gupta and he made bright speeches at the New South Wales Cricket Association reception held in honour of the tourists. "It was one of the happiest functions of its kind for many years", wrote E E Christensen in *The Sun*. Both manager and captain stressed the fact that the Indians play cricket for fun and enjoy the spirit in every fixture. "I have told my boys that it does not matter who wins or loses so long as we have a good game," declared Amarnath.

The game against New South Wales was tipped as a battle between the sharp blade of Amarnath and thunderbolts of Keith Miller and Ray Lindwall. Unfortunately, he fell sick due to gastroenteritis and a swollen liver. The doctors advised him complete rest but he put aside their decision. He told them, "I cannot let down my fans, who have stood for a long time in a queue to watch me play." Amarnath did take the field to keep faith with the public but he was too weak. He wore two sweaters on the field but the strain was too overbearing and he retired to his hotel room. The Indians were like a herd of sheep without their shepherd. What could have gone wrong with his health? A doctor diagnosed the problem: Amarnath's enormous love and appetite for good food had caused him to overeat. He was ordered two days rest. When the press visited him, he complained of starvation. "I have had only water for the last fifty-six hours and no food. If only I could be allowed to eat, I would regain my energy."

Feeling a little better, he requested Gupta to allow him to play but the request was turned down on the doctor's advice. Confined to his bed and frustrated, he listened to the proceedings and also the bad news of his team's first defeat on the tour on the radio. Later, he missed the much awaited visit to the Sydney Harbour. The press covered the match extensively, also reporting special bulletins on Amarnath's health. Since his reputation as a good cook was splashed all over the country, one correspondent found this a golden opportunity to learn how to prepare Indian curries. Without bothering about his health, he invited the reporter to his room and offered to demonstrate his skills in the hotel kitchen. When this news reached the manager, he was furious and reprimanded him for his childish behaviour. Unable to demonstrate the preparation of a curry, Amarnath dictated the recipe to the journalist to publish it in the newspaper for the benefit of all those who relished Indian food.

After a few days rest, a recharged Amarnath got ready to face the most formidable opponent, the Australian XI led by Bradman at Sydney Cricket Ground. It was almost the full strength Australian team with the exception of Lindwall, who was nursing a muscle injury. This game was especially important to Don Bradman, who had scored 99 first class centuries and was about to join the elite group of ten English greats led by Jack Hobbs (197), Patsy Hendren (170), Wally Hammond (156), Phil Mead (153), Bert Sutcliffe (149), Frank Woolley (145), W G Grace (126), Andy Sandham (107), Tom Hayward (104) and Ernest Tyldesley (102). Thousands poured into the ground to see Bradman become the first Australian to reach the milestone of a hundred first class hundreds.

The Indians batted first on a good track but their innings was a roller coaster ride, on top at one stage, only to drop down to a nightmare. They managed 326 runs. The fall of each wicket was loudly cheered, as the large crowd had come to see their hero perform a historical feat. Bradman did not disappoint the large gathering with his appetite for accumulating runs. There was pin-drop silence when Bradman got ready to face Kishenchand at 99. Bradman had faced every Indian bowler in his previous encounter but this move of Amarnath's perplexed him. He was not sure what kind of deliveries Kishenchand bowled. He played the first ball carefully, but the next, he pushed for a single to reach his century. Bradman, always a cool batsman, showed his emotions for a change when he jumped up and pumped his fist in excitement. Much later, Bradman acknowledged this shrewd move of his counterpart that made him a bit suspicious and extra cautious at that moment.

Bradman and Miller enthralled the large gathering with wonderful shots. Once these two departed, the innings folded up at 380. The Indian second innings was cruising smoothly when Amarnath decided to throw a challenge to Bradman to score 251 runs in 150 minutes. According to Bill O'Reilly, "It was a coura- geous and sporting declaration. Amarnath could have utilised the remaining time for batting practice for his men and delayed the closure of the innings thereby eliminating all chances of defeat." But the Indian captain loved challenges and thrived on chances. Bradman picked up the gauntlet and it meant entertain- ing cricket till the very end. The fierce battle ensued for the next two and a half hours. Not only was each stroke of the home side applauded, any fielding attempt or bowling performance of the Indians too received equal appreciation. When Amarnath intercepted a powerful stroke, a section of crowd from the hill clapped and whistled and remarked, "Ooh! La! La!" In the end, the gallant Indians won the match by 47 runs thanks to Amarnath's astute captaincy and Mankad's fine bowling.

Inspite of India's victory, the game is best remembered for Bradman's hundred and Brown's run out by Mankad at the non-striker's end in his bowling stride. Though this action created a big controversy, relations between the two teams continued to be cordial till the tour was over. With this success, the image and popularity of Amarnath reached its zenith. To show their appreciation and honour the Indians, a sailing competition named 'Welcome India' was staged by the Australians. They invited Amarnath to give away the Indian colours as a prize to the winning team of a 18-foot league sailing race.

Having achieved the most unexpected at Sydney, the Indians reached Brisbane to encounter Queensland with their confidence high. Only one thought was worrisome — the opening pair. The absence of good opening batsmen continued to haunt Amarnath since he understood the importance of this position if the Indians had to excel. He had tried different combinations but found them wanting. On top of it all, he had players like Rai Singh and Ranvirsihnji, who made this trip not for their abilities but because of their connections in the Board.

The home side batted first and posted 341 mainly due to the fine efforts by Arthur Morris, who scored an attractive century and Mick Raymer (82), before Mankad cut through their innings with a quality spell. The Indians, like in all previous matches, faltered against the pace attack and spin early in the innings, with only Mankad holding fort. Amarnath joined Mankad with the scoreboard at 77 for three to face Colin McCool, who with his teasing leg-spin had earlier troubled the English batsmen and presented the tourists with their biggest challenge. "Amarnath, on this tour, had been successful against all other Test slow bowlers and it was interesting to see whether he would add McCool's scalp to his belt," wrote Arthur Mailey in the *Sunday Telegraph*. Amarnath produced another sterling performance, scoring 172 not out in 278 minutes with 10 fours and a six before running out of partners. The Indian innings terminated at 369. McCool came in for special treatment from his flashing blade. Each tossed up delivery was met down the track and converted into a full toss or half volley and driven firmly. When McCool dropped the ball short, he employed his favourite late cut.

Summarising the innings, Mailey wrote: "Amarnath stood well over the high rising balls from Carrigan and executed two of the most delightful back cuts I have ever seen in years — shots so glorious and artistic that they should have been reserved for the connoisseurs of a southern capital." He was in a belligerent mood and no bowler, whether slow or fast could disturb his concentration. "Once to the fast bowler Smith, he walked straight down the pitch and with a beautiful full backswing, coolly lifted him straight over mid-on for a lovely six," Percy Beames reported. Amarnath was now the leading batsman in Australia and seemed to have hit the purple patch!

With the match evenly poised, Queensland played brisk cricket and scored 269 for five in even time before declaring its second innings to instil interest in the match. It was cricket played to the gallery. McCool, fighting for his place in the Australian team, retrieved a bit of his reputation by scoring a quick century. The target of 242 in two hours and 35 minutes was always a difficult proposition but the Indians decided to pursue another victory. The chase began well, the first 50 coming in only 20 minutes but a defensive field setting made runs hard to get. Unmindful of these tactics, the Indians continued their hot chase, losing wickets often. In the last over, India needed 24 to win with a wicket in hand, with Kishenchand facing McCool. He played the first three deliveries easily but read the fourth one wrong, when he offered no stroke to a ball pitching in the bowler's rough outside the leg stump. The ball turned viciously and shattered Kishenchand's stumps from behind his back. Though the Indians lost the encounter, they won the hearts of all with their positive attitude. "It was cricket par excellence where the result was secondary. It was the spirit with which it was played, that was truly the champion," remarked one critic.

FIRST TEST MATCH

The big day arrived for both nations to start their official Test engagements at Brisbane. Before the commencement of the historic Test, Amarnath disagreed with Bradman to let the pitches be covered during the Test. Bradman tried to reason out the drawbacks of rain-affected pitches but Amarnath refused to accept the bait as the Indian attack had been hammered by state sides under good conditions. It would be suicidal, he felt, taking chances against the strength of the Australians. He knew the best chance would be to catch the home side on wet wickets. He stuck to the tradition of leaving the pitches at the mercy of nature.

If Amarnath evaded this trap, another rule applicable in Australia put the Indians in a disadvantageous position. The rule allowed the fielding team the option of taking the second new ball either at the score of 200 or on completing 40 overs, whichever came earlier. Amarnath said this unfair rule was loaded heavily in favour of the home side but could do little. The Australians, with a battery of fast bowlers and only one spinner in the team had a hard ball all the time. On the contrary, the strength of the Indian bowling was spin and they came in to bowl only after 15 to 20 overs. By the time the spinners (Mankad, Nayudu or Amir Elahi) found their line and length, the new ball would become due. In true sense, spinners got to bowl only ten overs each at a stretch.

As if all this confusion was not enough, India found the eight balls over too long to complete. Being so accustomed to six-ball overs, the Indian bowlers at times walked away from the umpires after the sixth ball or the fielders moved to other position presuming the over to be complete. Despite the dice being loaded so heavily in favour of the home side, the Indians did not protest.

On the historic occasion in Brisbane, Don Bradman used a Cartwheel five-shilling silver coin, which turned to be out lucky for him when Amarnath called his favourite 'heads'. Without any hesitation, the home side batted first on what looked like a perfect track. Disappointed with his luck, Amarnath drew first blood when he had Brown caught behind early in the innings. The Indians had to wait for a long time for their next success, as Bradman gradually mastered the limited Indian attack on a placid wicket. "No batsman had ever made me feel that I could not dismiss him but Bradman was something else. His body language demonstrated as if he was possessed by some extra terrestrial power. Early in the innings, Bradman hardly played any flashy strokes, placing the ball for singles or twos, or maybe, hit the odd boundary. By the time one looked at the scoreboard, the Don was already in his thirties or forties, thereafter there was no restricting him," Amarnath recollected.

"My form was immensely superior to anything I had shown against the Englishmen the previous year, simply because of further improvement in my health during the winter months," Bradman wrote in *Farewell to Cricket*. Runs flowed with ease and in abundance from his bat. Apart from Bradman's stupendous 189 and Miller's half-century, no batsmen made any impression. Amarnath was forced to share the responsibility of long spells with Mankad since his other bowlers failed to make an impact. He bowled 39 overs, equal to 52 six-ball overs and captured four for 89. Despite being fit at the age of thirty-six, the long spell did make him a little tired and stiff.

Australia was sitting pretty at 309 for three when there was rain on the second morning. Play was delayed as both captains disagreed regarding the resumption and the umpires had to take curator Farquhar's advice before play started. The wicket was sprinkled with cut grass and rolled with a light roller. As expected, the freshly-rolled pitch played easy but with each passing minute, it started playing tricks. Australia lost five wickets for 73 runs when Bradman closed the innings at 382. Once the sun came out, the drying surface was like a glue pot, playing tricks on the batsmen. The ball rose awkwardly from a good length or skidded at ankle height to play havoc with the Indian batsmen and they were shot for a paltry 58. Only Amarnath held firm for a while before one delivery from Ernie Toshack stood up to have him caught by Bradman for 22.

Following-on on a treacherous wicket, India started the second innings also disastrously and by the end of play, India was 41 for four. The entire third day was washed out. With the sun coming out and a southwest breeze drying the wicket, batting was difficult. Miller, Lindwall and Johnston made the ball fly all over the place. With no protective gear like helmets, padded gloves, arm guards, thigh pads or chest pads available then, the best method was to use the bat. But under these conditions, even this became useless. After initial damage by the pacemen, left-armer Toshack captured six for 29 and his mind-boggling match figures read 11 for 31. India lost the match by an innings but there was still a ray of hope. What stood between India's success and defeat were undoubtedly Bradman and the weather.

SECOND TEST IN SYDNEY

The second Test was like a homecoming for the Indians. They had fond memories of their encounter against the Australian XI whom they had defeated not so long ago. The toss had played a crucial part in the outcome of the last Test match and the Indians prayed Amarnath would win it this time. India included its two best leg-spinners Amir Elahi and C S Nayudu, apart from Mankad to strengthen its spin department and Amarnath hoped that they would enjoy bowling on the spin-friendly surface. Unlike modern day cricket, the toss was done in the presence of two umpires, in the ground close to the pavilion. Luck favoured Amarnath as he changed his mind from customary 'heads' and called 'tails' to win the toss.

Winning the toss was like winning half the battle, particularly on uncovered wickets. The team batting first had a distinct advantage of using the fresh surface as was evident in the first Test. Without any hesitation, Amarnath opted to bat first but Lindwall, Miller and Johnston's pace got the top order cheap. Once the shine was gone, spinners Ian Johnson and McCool caused ripples in the Indian line-up. The advantage was lost when wickets fell at regular intervals. Desperate to put up a decent score, Kishenchand (44) and Phadkar (51) played a good innings but luck seemed to have deserted the Indian skipper. When on 25, he stepped outside his off-stump to fend away an off-break from Johnson. The ball turned more than expected and glanced from his left calf on to his stumps. The spinners had the lion's share and India was all out for 188.

A lot was expected from Australia on the good wicket. Its innings was progressing smoothly, when Mankad caused a stir in the dying moments of the opening day by running out Brown for leaving his crease too soon. It was a peculiar situation but Umpire Barlow had no hesitation in giving the batsman out. Fearing a reprisal from the gallery, the Indians were amazed when a crowd of 20,000 applauded as if commending the bowler for his vigilance. Brown's lapse was surprising after similar incidents had happened in two earlier matches against Indians. With the clock now showing 6 p.m. and with only three deliveries remaining for the close, Bradman fulfilled a captain's responsibility by coming himself to the crease.

Overnight rain washed away the second day's play. Despite inspections of the pitch by the two captains and their disagreement, Amarnath was keen but Bradman wasn't. The conditions at Sydney Cricket Ground left both Amarnath and Mankad smiling when they noticed small puddles at good length areas. They knew that the wet surface was going to be difficult for batting. When play resumed on the third day under a bright sun, the mighty Australian batsmen, including Bradman, looked vulnerable. To make their lives miserable, the Indian captain shuffled his bowlers in quick succession. Hazare eventually consumed Bradman, who was struggling on a treacherous track. Once he departed, the rest of the batting folded at 107.

With more rain forecast, Amarnath was keen to see his team score as many runs as possible before he could declare and put pressure on the home side. To allow the wicket to play easy for sometime, he asked for the heavy roller to smoothen various spots. The batting order was shuffled to achieve this task, but the wicket continued to torment the batsmen and India was soon reduced to 61 for seven by the end of play. India had an overall lead of 142 and prayed for a sunny day. For Australia, a defeat loomed for the first time since 1938. Fortunately for them, rain had the final say. The last day was washed out much to the joy of the home team. India had missed the golden opportunity to beat the Australians. All his critics admired and agreed with Amarnath's argument in favour of an uncovered wicket if the Kangaroos were to be beaten, or even contained.

THIRD TEST IN MELBOURNE

With the series still open and the infallible Kangaroos now slipping on the wet surface, Amarnath saw a ray of hope catching the home side again under similar conditions. The third Test generated tremendous interest after India had cornered favourites

Australia in Sydney. The toss in the previous Tests had proved vital and both captains knew its importance in the unpredictable weather. When Bradman flipped the coin for the third time, Amarnath called 'heads' and immediately cursed himself for making the mistake he had committed in Brisbane, but it was too late. Australia won the toss and batted first before a packed stadium of 50,000 people. Though Amarnath and Mankad got rid of Morris and Sid Barnes early, Bradman (132) was in an irrepressible mood. He collared the Indian attack and dominated the proceedings in the company of Hassett (80). Australia was in a commanding position at 268 for two but once Bradman fell to Phadkar, the home side found Amarnath (four for 78) and Mankad (four for 135) unplayable and was bowled out for 394. This collapse proved that Australia was not too superior to the Indians but for one man making all the difference.

For a change, the Indian openers gave the team a solid opening stand of 124, with Mankad (116) in his best form. But his fall led to a mini collapse after tea. Barnes produced two magical deliveries to get rid of Hazare and Amarnath. The second wicket brought deafening cheers from the gallery as Amarnath's double century was still fresh in everyone's mind. Remembering his dismissal much later in life, he said, "After bowling another long spell, my body was sore and stiff. A simple straight delivery hastened off the track and hit me on the pad and I couldn't move a muscle." India finished the day at 262 for six, which gave more satisfaction to the home side than the Indians.

Rain once again played its part at night and the crucial seventeen-yard area was found soaked in the morning to assist the bowlers. Sunshine and a stiff breeze enabled the wicket to dry up and allowed the proceedings to be resumed a little later. But the conditions made the ball play tricks. One delivery from Miller flew and stung Phadkar on the glove. The impact was so enormous that his bat fell. Miller picked up the bat and walked across the pitch to tap the area from where it rose. It was indeed a great show of sporting spirit. Sensing the devil in the pitch, Amarnath declared the innings closed, 103 runs behind Australia.

It was a shrewd move designed to catch Australia on the sticky dog pitch and it proved correct. "In a dramatic 40 minutes before lunch India captured one Australian wicket for 11 runs.

India was only to blame itself that Australia then was not in a much worse position, for in this period four easy catches were dropped. If the chances had been accepted, or even two of them, India's chances of its first win would have been bright. It didn't matter that two of the tail-enders went immediately after lunch, for then Bradman produced his first-class batsmen," wrote a special correspondent in a Melbourne daily. After lunch, Australia were four down for 32 but Bradman's decision to shield himself, and other main batsmen at a crucial times by changing the batting order worked. The tail-enders did a commendable job by occupying the crease and consuming valuable time in the middle. With the sun shining brightly and a strong breeze, the effect of rain evaporated, making batting easy for Bradman (127 not out) and Morris (100 not out) to put pressure on India.

Once again, overnight rain delayed the start. Both Bradman and Amarnath inspected the pitch at 11.35 a.m. For once, Amarnath agreed with the home captain to start the game at noon, hoping that the Australians would bat for some time but Bradman declared the innings closed on the overnight score. India was again caught on the drying surface.

Writing in *The Herald*, P J Millard said: "The Indians may have magnified the difficulties of the wicket, but it is questionable whether the Australians would have done better." The task of achieving 359 on a tricky wicket was always difficult. Once the effect of the heavy roller was gone, the two-paced wicket and the craters at good length became the batsmen's nightmare. Deliveries of Lindwall, Miller and Johnston either skidded or rose sharply causing grave concern. If this was not enough, Johnson spun his off-spin at right angles. Australia bundled out India for 125 in 118 minutes on a rain-soaked wicket to win the third Test.

Percy Beames wrote: "Rain had been the Indians' toughest opponents in the Tests so far, but the visitors could take some consolation from their performance on yesterday's Melbourne gluepot." Bill O'Reilly wrote in his column: "Amarnath was unlucky. He did everything, and more perhaps than 'a good captain' can do in such circumstances, but the Fates were unkind."

Leaving this defeat behind, the team travelled by air to beautiful Tasmania with its morale still high, and popularity intact. If hundreds welcomed the smiling Indians, then thousands came to the ground to watch them. At this time of the season, both Amarnath and Bradman were running neck to neck for the thousand-run mark in first-class matches in Australia. Despite his failures in the Tests, Amarnath continued to surge ahead of Bradman in the aggregate with good performances in the games against the state sides.

Amarnath did not deprive the large crowd of another fine innings. With his usual gusto, he thrashed every bowler during his stay of 141 minutes. Runs flowed fast and in style to enable the spectators to enjoy every stroke from his blade till he was dismissed for 171. These sparkling innings in the state matches and poor score in the Test matches baffled his supporters. While discussing the Australian tour, one day I asked my father to analyse the reasons behind these adverse performances. "I had been bowling far too many overs in each innings in the Test matches, which made me a little tired and stiff. I should have bowled less and batted lower down the order to recuperate my energies. But this situation never came nor did I give it any thought, may be due to over-confidence. In the State matches, I hardly bowled long spells, which kept me fresh and I scored plenty of runs," he said.

From times immemorial, a majority of cricketers have always been superstitious about the kit or their number in the batting order. Some batsmen prefer odd, while others prefer even numbers as lucky for their success. Amarnath mostly preferred odd numbers in his career. To give them confidence, cricketers have been known to wear their old caps, trousers or shirts. Even the use of a particular bat or tying of shoe laces or putting on the left or right pad first plays an important role in their mind during the matches. Amarnath was not different. For the Australia tour, he carried as many as eleven Gunn & Moore Autograph bats but found only one to his liking. It weighed 2.2 pounds and swung easily like a fly swat. He once told us he scored 972 runs with this bat alone and when it broke against Tasmania, he was convinced that his luck had bid him good-bye.

Amarnath was a complete cricketer and loved explaining the finer points of the game to his team-mates. If anyone brought his problems to him, he would not only explain the intricacies theoretically but also practically. Before the fourth Test, he was not happy with the young wicket-keeper Sen's gathering. Since

Irani had not kept wickets well, the only choice was to continue with Sen in the team. To show this youngster the art of keeping, he decided to don the gloves. It was indeed, a fine gesture but uncalled for before the Test. He had not had any regular practice for a long time. The last time he had kept wickets was in 1935. The squatting and bending gave him sore muscles the next day. "I was so stiff that I could barely bend down to tie my shoe laces or pick up anything," he remembered.

After a few days' rest, the team drove down to Launceston to face Tasmania. Once again, he was in top form and scored another century to become the first to complete 1,000 runs in the season ahead of Don Bradman. He was thoroughly enjoying batting on good wickets but in the Tests it was the glue pots that troubled the team.

FOURTH TEST IN ADELAIDE

Happy with their performance in the last two games, the Indians reached Adelaide in a good frame of mind. The strip was bald and easy-paced. Amarnath was desperate to win the toss but the coin seemed to invariably fall for the opposite side. "We were massacred on a slow pitch by Bradman (201), Barnes (112) and Hassett (198 not out) as I watched the show from the slips," he said. "It was frustrating, as I could not bowl due to a severe chill behind my shoulder and a blow on my knee." The plight of the Indians knew no bounds when Gul Mohammad messed up an easy run out of Hassett at 59, when the batsman was stranded in the middle of the pitch. Australia posted a mammoth 674 and Amarnath could bowl only nine overs with great difficulty. In the dying moments of the second day, India faced the daunting Australian attack. In the last over, Keith Miller got two wickets off successive balls to put India in a precarious position.

Sensing more trouble, Amarnath promoted himself to face Miller and Lindwall. For a change, there was no rain following the Indians and he relished batting on this good surface. Within half an hour, he galloped to 46 before a harmless full toss from Johnson forced him to play a lofted shot to deep mid-on where Bradman took an easy catch. He rued this stroke for a very long time as Hazare and Phadkar scored centuries without any hiccups. India scored 381 but it was not enough to save the follow-on. The second innings commenced horrifically when Lindwall sent Mankad and Amarnath packing with his express pace. Suddenly, the ball was swinging and gaining the pace off the wicket and India folded under pressure. The only saving grace was Hazare's fantastic batting as he became the first Indian to score a century in each innings of a Test.

FIFTH TEST IN MELBOURNE

The last Test in Melbourne was almost jeopardised by the assassination of Mahatma Gandhi on January 30, 1948. There was a frantic exchange of cables between manager Pankaj Gupta and the Board of Control for Cricket in India, which acted on instructions from the Government of India. India did stay on to play the last Test match. On the eve of the match, all members decided to pay homage to the Father of the Nation and later salute the tricolour. "I was shocked when Amir Elahi and Gul Mohammad refused to salute the tricolour because they had decided to migrate to Pakistan at the end of the tour. Later, I spoke to them alone and expressed my annoyance at their attitude. Gul Mohammad apologised for getting swayed by Amir Elahi's illogical arguments," Amarnath said. If there was this unpleasant incident, then there were many lighter moments on the tour. Bradman's phenomenal form was a headache for the Indians and they dreaded dropping any chance he offered. In one game, Amir Elahi dropped an easy catch of Bradman. Feeling guilty and annoyed, he slapped his forehead with his palm and looking at the sky said "Allah!" Amarnath, fielding in the slips, was more candid in his remarks when he said, "Now Allah alone can get him out!"

The Test commenced after the teams and the spectators observed a two minutes' silence as a mark of respect to Mahatma Gandhi. The Australians wore black arm-bands during the Test to share their guests' grief. This Test was in no way different than the earlier results. The Australians continued to dominate and controlled the game. It was undoubtedly a one-man show with Bradman scoring 1,124 runs in the matches he played against the tourists. In the Tests alone, he scored 715 runs at a staggering average of 178.75, which made all the difference in the series. Despite failing in the Tests, Amarnath aggregated 1,162 runs on the tour at an average of 58.10. To make up for his batting lapses, he proved to be an economical as well as India's most successful bowler.

Though India lost the series to a superior Australian side, it left a marvellous ever-lasting impression on everyone Down Under. Bradman, writing in his book *Farewell to Cricket* said, "Throughout the whole of the tour, I found Amarnath and Peter (Pankaj) Gupta absolutely charming in every aspect. They co-operated in all conceivable ways to try and make the games enjoyable and the most wonderful spirit of camaraderie existed between the Australian and the Indian players. Lala, as he was called, certainly believed in speaking his mind at all times and was not averse to expressing his opinion in regard to controlling authority or an individual but in Australia he did it with utmost courtesy and tact. Amarnath was a splendid ambassador. I look back on the season with him as my opposite number as one of my most pleasant cricket years."

"My feelings are to this chap (Amarnath) for his great-hearted leadership," Jack Fingleton wrote. "There are things he does which in our Australian conception of the game we do not agree, but that, when all is said and done, is purely only our opinion and, the fact remains that nobody could do more than what Amarnath has done at critical periods here and many could do less. He had endeared himself to the Australian people."

"The Indians and the West Indians, and to a lesser degree New Zealand and South Africa have not developed the necessary 'hard shell' for Test match play", wrote Walter Hammond in *Cricket My Way*. "What they have lacked so far have been two necessary factors — pitiless strategical leadership of the sort epitomised in Jardine and the spirit of aggression and domination. It was, therefore, with a particular interest that I watched the Indians in Australia in 1947–48 demonstrating the first beginnings of the two necessary acquirements. The chief reason for the change undoubtedly lay in the leadership of the Indian team by Amarnath. His experience in Lancashire League had taught him the hardest aspects of captaincy and shown the imperative need for a captain to analyse the play and the personality of each of his opponents just as a professional boxer has to do. His handling of the Indian team in Australia in 1947–48 was masterly, all the more because his material was patchy and weather against him with a cruelty that amounted almost to personal persecution."

Paying a tribute to Amarnath, Mailey wrote in the *Illustrated Weekly of India*, "Whatever shortcomings the Indians have, they are fortunate to possess an admirable captain in Amarnath. Being closely associated, I have had an opportunity to observe Amarnath's influence on the team. His knowledge of Australian pitches is superior to Bradman's. His choice of heavy-light rollers and the decisions regarding the staying powers of the pitches, and when to employ certain bowlers, etc., has been invariably correct."

EIGHT

STORMY PETREL

I N THE 1940s, the Board of Control for Cricket in India was under the influence of its president, Anthony de Mello. He was a powerful man and functioned in a typically imperial style and often told the Board members that he was the Board. He took all decisions without consulting anyone. This attitude did cause some heartburn but none dared question or oppose him due to his connections in high places, first with the British and later with some top Congress leaders.

On the eve of the Australian tour, when the press went to interview Lala Amarnath at the Great Eastern Hotel in Calcutta, de Mello was also present. Instead of allowing the captain to answer the questions, de Mello gave written replies to all their queries and asked the press to publish them. Amarnath was furious but controlled his temper. Once de Mello left the room, Amarnath tore the paper to pieces. He sat down with the journalists and answered all their questions. When Amarnath's replies were published the following day, de Mello was livid but could do little. He kept quiet and waited for the team to come back. He hoped to strike hard at Amarnath by having him replaced as India's captain as punishment for defying him.

The desire to punish could not materialise because of the popularity and the goodwill generated by the Indian team on the tour of Australia. Amarnath and Pankaj Gupta received special attention and were described as outstanding ambassadors of independent India by the Australian press and Donald Bradman. This praise startled Amarnath's adversaries, who were waiting for an opportunity to sack him as captain.

The Indian captain, contrary to the system prevailing now, was elected through a ballot involving all associate members of the Board. For the series against the West Indies, whispers of Vijay Merchant replacing Amarnath as India's captain started doing the rounds. But the divided West Zone helped Amarnath's cause. Baroda didn't agree with Merchant and instead proposed Hazare's name to lead, as he was found more suitable after his fine batting in the Tests in Australia. When the groups failed to reach a consensus, the lobbying became intense to push their individual candidates for the captaincy.

Amarnath had enemies but he was not short of friends and admirers, who saw in him an ideal person who could save Indian cricket from the influence of the bygone days of the Raj and the dictates of the Board president. The members, once again, put their faith in his captaincy and nominated him for the series against the West Indies. It was a special series for Amarnath, as he became independent India's first captain not only to lead the team overseas but at home, too. Amarnath was also making history, leading India in the inaugural Test against another team. Within a year, India was opening its frontiers to other national teams, whereas previously, the contest was confined only to England. With the advent of every new series, his status rose sharply and he was enjoying another fresh wave of popularity.

The first Test was played at Delhi's Ferozshah Kotla ground. It was a big occasion for everyone to watch the Indians play against two Ws (Everton Weekes and Clyde Walcott) from the Caribbean islands. All roads leading to the ground were crowded by ticket- seekers and there was a carnival-like atmosphere inside. India's first Prime Minister Jawaharlal Nehru, an ardent cricket fan, added to the ambience with his presence. He came along with his Cabinet colleagues and enjoyed cricket and bright sunshine at the ground. Such was his love for cricket that he continued the practice, not missing a single Test match till his death in 1964.

The perfect wicket and fast outfield helped the batsmen to dominate the proceedings in a high-scoring match, resulting in a draw. But the Test did produce a brief confrontation between Amarnath and Umpire Naik over an appeal, followed by what is now known as the 'hat incident'. The umpire reported the matter to the Board. Although, it was a frivolous incident, it gave Amarnath's enemies an opportunity to point fingers at him.

With each passing day, de Mello was collecting material to nail Amarnath. If the Board president thought he was smart, Amarnath was no lame duck. Shrewdly, he kept his eyes and ears open following de Mello's moves without confronting him. Apart from being India's captain, Amarnath was also Southern Punjab Cricket Association honorary secretary, which gave him a number of opportunities to attend the Board's meetings and he knew the functioning and politics in the BCCI all along. Though the situation was not so alarming, he sensed trouble ahead.

With his Test career at stake and unnecessary needling from de Mello and his cronies in the press, Amarnath kept his cool and concentrated on the game. He used all his resources and energy to attain perfection and success but unfortunately lost another series 0–1 despite a heroic effort at Bombay. It was probably for the first time in the history of cricket that a player captained the side, bowled, batted, fielded and even donned gloves behind the wickets. "When the regular wicket-keeper P Sen was injured and although the opposing skipper sportingly allowed the reserve stumper to keep wickets, Amarnath refused to avail himself of this generosity. As a matter of fact, he himself had refused the opponents this opportunity in an earlier Test. In the Tests, no quarter is asked for and none is given," stated Hazare in his book *Cricket Replayed*. Amarnath exhibited his wicket-keeping skills by taking five catches behind the stumps.

Amarnath and de Mello had been at loggerheads ever since the press conference in Calcutta but their personality clash erupted in the open during the second Test in Bombay, first on the eve of the Test and later, when de Mello walked into the dressing room at lunch and demanded the batting order from Amarnath. The captain declined to accede to the demand. This act of defiance infuriated de Mello and he just blew his top. "I am the Board president and have the right to see the batting order," he hollered. Amarnath replied, "You may be the president of the Board but I am the captain of the team. It is my prerogative to keep the batting order within the four walls of the dressing room and not put it up for public display." This argument during the Test made the other players nervous and tense but Amarnath remained cool and concentrated on the job on hand.

Such an incident hardly misses the media's attention and it was blown out of proportion. A distorted version started appearing in the newspapers pointing fingers at the Indian captain. "Since I was under a contract with the Board, I kept quiet but various articles started attacking and blaming me for this unpleasant incident, which was unfair," Amarnath remembered. Rumours started going around in the Board corridors that de Mello was contemplating serious action against him for his outburst and may perhaps even sack him midway through the series. Fortunately, nothing of this sort happened and the series continued uninterrupted but the undercurrents were felt by all in the BCCI.

The final Test at the Brabourne Stadium witnessed a fierce battle, with the fortunes swinging like a pendulum till the very end. On the fourth day, when the West Indies suddenly collapsed against the pace of Banerjee and Phadkar and the spin of Mankad, Amarnath saw a chance to square the series. Unfortunately, India lost both openers early. To keep up the tempo, Amarnath decided to lead from the front and promoted himself from No. 7 to bat one-drop and counterattack the West Indian pace bowlers and also redeem some of his lost reputation as an aggressive batsman. Though his was a short innings of 39, he added 72 runs with Modi to set the ball rolling. "India lost both Mushtaq Ali and Ibrahim very early in the second innings. Who could have expected at this stage that India would rise to the occasion and give a battle royal to their redoubtable opponents, as everything seemed lost at this stage," wrote J C Maitra in *Indian Sports Flashback*. "It was, however, to the everlasting credit of Lala Amarnath, India's skipper, that he infused courage and hope in the timid hearts of his mates. Like a Trojan, he stepped into the breach and not only turned the tide of India's misfortune but set a brilliant example to his followers to overcome their nervousness. Tired though he must have been by the unaccustomed duties of the wicket-keeper, he set aside his lethargy and discomfort and went all out to change the disheartening complexion of the game."

Sensing defeat, the West Indians resorted to some of the

worst time wasting tactics ever. So obvious were their actions that the crowd booed and hooted them but could do little to help the home side. In a desperate move to hold on to the solitary victory, wicket-keeper Walcott walked halfway down the boundary line to collect throws and then walked back to his position in leisure. Strangely, neither umpire reprimanded the tourists for their unsporting spirit. Time was of great value and both teams knew its importance. The drama reached its climax when Phadkar waited to face the last ball of the over from Jones with India requiring six runs to win. The task seemed achievable with another minute and a half to go after this over but inexplicably Umpire Joshi declared 'over' without the last ball having being delivered. At the same time, much to the horror of the batsmen and the crowd, he removed the bails signalling the end of the match with the clock showing a minute and a half still left. It was an anticlimax for the large crowd which had shouted itself hoarse, held its breath and kept its fingers crossed, expecting a grand victory. "Was it bad luck, miscalculation or something more sinister?" Amarnath wondered.

Once the West Indies departed, de Mello came out openly against Amarnath, targetting his method of handling the team. To settle this matter without any delay, de Mello convened a meeting of the Board in April 1949 and immediately afterwards, announced to the press that the Board had unanimously agreed to suspend Lala Amarnath from playing any cricket in India. When the media enquired the reasons leading to such a drastic decision, de Mello boldly said misbehaviour and misconduct were the prime reasons. Unable to convince people without giving reasons behind the suspension, de Mello called a press conference and handed out an official copy to twenty-odd newspaper representatives, mentioning various points of Amarnath's alleged misconduct.

The charges read as follows:

Your last minute decision not to captain and play for the States XI at Baroda against the West Indies, thus commencing the tour with an 'incident,' enabling the Press to assign motives to both you and Baroda Cricket Association.

Your late arrival in Delhi before the first Test match, contrary to the request made to the team by our Honorary Secretary, thus depriving India of an organised net practice by our players.

Your request for additional bonus to the team, which was threateningly made to me during the Test match in Delhi. stating your request was made at the request of all players.

Your request for additional payment to you as 'captain' for out-of-pocket expenses in entertaining friends in your Delhi hotel.

The umpire Naik incident during the first Test in New Delhi. I had to hang my head down in shame because of your behaviour. Umpire Naik has submitted a written complaint, which has not yet been dealt with by the Board.

Your last minute decision not to captain North Zone in the Zonal tournament in Bombay, which had been especially organised to select the team for the second Test in Bombay.

Your late arrival for watching the Zonal tournament, contrary to your promise to me in Delhi.

Your not informing me of the severe accident to your foot at Poona. You were definitely unfit to play in the second Test match.

Your demand for further increase in the bonus of Test players in view of the fact that they are required to be at the Test centre a full two days before the match.

Your deliberate carelessness in not collecting your team for:

The Progressive Group's reception presided by HE Governor of Bombay.

Party by HE Governor of Bombay at Government House, Bombay.

Your arrogant and rude behaviour to me in your room No. 21 at CCI, when the team had collected to meet me at my request on the eve of the second Test. Mr. Pankaj Gupta, Mr. Berry Sarbadikary and at least eight members of the team were present.

Your arrogant and rude language to me at lunch on the first day of the second Test match. Mr. Pankaj Gupta was present.

Your unintelligible 'indiscipline' speech at the reception of the Bombay Cricket Association at CCI, Bombay, remarking that "You will make an open exposure of many controversial matters in Indian cricket."

Your visit to Ahmedabad after the second Test match where (though severely injured and unfit to play in Bombay), you played in a match out of which, it is alleged, you derived monetary gain.

Your late arrival once again at Calcutta, depriving our team of organised net practice.

Your accepting a large purse in Calcutta without intimation to and permission of the Board. Mr. Gupta, in reply to my enquiry at the Board meeting, stated that a sum of Rs 5,000 was paid to you at Calcutta. I had informed Mr. P Sen (our wicket-keeper) during the first Test match that it was been universally stated that Calcutta had 'bought' his inclusion in all Test matches.

Your disregard of the Board by not replying to the under-noted letter from me, dated January 8, 1949 and delivered to you through the Military Secretary to His Highness, the Maharaja of Patiala.

Your not even seeing me in this matter (of both Calcutta and Ahmedabad) when you arrived in Bombay from Madras on February 2.

Your not sitting with your team for lunch during the fifth Test match in Bombay.

Your statement at a lunch in Bombay on February 9, charging the Board with power politics, which was reported by the UPI (and not API)

Your continued insulting and disregard of the Board by not replying to our first letter dated January 8, 1949 and yet another dated February 21, 1949, which was sent to you 'Registered Ack-due' and which was duly received by you on February 24, 1949.

Your interview to the *National Herald* dated April 2, 1949 charging me personally, the Selection Committee and the Board with intrigues against you.

Your speaking disparagingly to all and sundry about what transpired in the Selection Committee room, thus depriving India of the best efforts of selected players.

These charges were then dispatched to Lala Amarnath along with the letter from de Mello which said: "Having given you a full statement of your deeds on indiscipline, I shall make observations which are relevant in enabling you to have the whole picture of my submission to the Board meeting on April 10, 1949 and to realise how demeaning of discipline you have been and how great your guilt is in the face of years of ultra-kindness to you by the Board and me. Although at the Board meeting at Delhi on August 15, 1947, I had stated that I did not consider you to be a suitable captain for India in Australia, once you had been appointed, I did everything in my power to help in making your captaincy a success and, as a matter of fact, overlooked your misdeeds."

It was a desperate attempt by de Mello to project himself as a saint, who had been kind and magnanimous when dealing with Amarnath who paid him back through disobedience and disrespect. To demonstrate his largeheartedness and kindness, de Mello gave another list of complaints.

I did not charge you with neglect when you left the Poona camp after only a bare day or so.

I did not charge you with indiscipline when you gave a Press interview at Colombo on your return from Australia, although you were prohibited from doing so under your agreement and also similar to Bombay.

You promised the Board to send your report on the Australian tour, which as yet has not been received.

When in Delhi, I presented you with two (just imported) Autograph bats to welcome you as our captain again.

In Bombay, I gave you Lillywhite cricket kit, which had only just arrived from England.

I accompanied you to the VT Station on your way to Poona after the Zonal tournament and also made suitable arrangements for your stay and comfort there.

Even after your arrogance and rudeness to me in your room on the eve of the second Test match in Bombay — (I agreed to have the meeting in your room because of your sore foot) — I wrote the next morning (morning of the second Test) to wish you luck with the toss and in the match.

I also met you later in the dressing room before the match and shook hands with you and wished you luck.

My patience with you, however, had been exhausted after the second Test in Bombay, when your misbehaviour was so ungrateful and so glaring and I felt that your conduct generally was not befitting as India's captain. I wrote to Mr. Pankaj Gupta that if he had put your name down for a speech at Calcutta for the official dinner, during the third Test, he should kindly withdraw it. I also wrote to Rao Sahib Ranga Rao at Madras that no Indian player should be billeted in Government House, Madras. The reason for these two moves by me was not that I wish you to enjoy yourself with your speeches and your luxury in the Government House, Madras, but felt now that if you continued with your misbehaviour as at Bombay, I would have no alternative but to seek Board's sanction for you being removed from the captaincy during the tour. Therefore, I preferred to take precautions and avoid unpleasantness during the tour by the West Indies."

To make his case airtight against Amarnath, de Mello then directed his attention towards the interview given by Amarnath to the *National Herald*, Lucknow, and made a long list of allegations to pin him down. He stated:

It is a gross misstatement to say that I quarrelled with you on the eve of the second Test match in Bombay. I did charge you with disregard of the Board and Mr. Pankaj Gupta and the team are witnesses. Mr. Gupta has, in several letters to me, since then stated that he had advised you to see me immediately and apologise for your misbehaviour.

There has been no Press propaganda against you to which the Board has been a party.

There was never before, or till April 10, 1949, any talk of another captain except when after the second Test match at Bombay, I stated to Mr. Pankaj Gupta and other members of the Selection Committee that I would have to take action against you if you continued to misbehave as you did in Bombay. Even then the only captain mentioned was Mr. Mushtaq Ali who had been agreed to by the Selection Committee of which you were a member.

It is grossly malicious to state that I, or the Board, had some persons in view as a nominee for future captaincy.

No canvassing by anybody in the Board has been carried out for the appointment of another captain.

All that has appeared in your interviews are malicious concoctions of your own mind.

Concluding his letter, de Mello stated: "You have now before you in crystal clear manner the full position relating to your misbehaviour in which you have been wallowing during and after every tour since your selection as captain. I have not made any reference to your misbehaviour in 1944–45 after the Ceylon tour of which you are aware and of which I had then spoken to you and also the misbehaviour reported to me by Hon'ble Dr Subbaroyan in the train incident at Cawnpore (Kanpur) in the autumn of 1947 (before you left for Australia) when two hon'ble members of the Indian Constituent Assembly reported your misbehaviour and decided on legal action against you."

After reading his letter to Lala Amarnath and also the allegations, de Mello produced a letter addressed to him by Amarnath and read it to the journalists present: "I have just received your registered letter which has surprised me a lot to know that you did not receive my previous letter. I am herewith sending you a copy, which will answer your purpose. I regret that I could not write to you earlier being away from Patiala on a long leave."

Frustrated by this casual reply and cool attitude, de Mello produced a long list of favours the Board had supposedly bestowed on Lala Amarnath.

1. 1936 — From perdition, we gave you back to the Indian cricket.

2. 1937 — Recommended you to Lancashire League for a professional contract.

3. 1944–45 — Your appointment as vice-captain in Ceylon.

4. 1946 — Recommended you to HH the Maharaja of Patiala for special consideration. You were given a 'captaincy' in the Patiala Army and a handsome bonus of Rs 3,000 before you left for England.

5. 1947 — Your appointment as captain of the team to Australia. Recommended you for leave on full pay and another bonus by HH the Maharaja of Patiala before you left for Australia.

6. 1948 — Your appointment as captain versus West Indies in India.

The public at large was left with a sour taste when the Board president made vague allegations against the captain, who till recently was described as India's best ambassador by the Australian media. In his blind pursuit to punish Amarnath for standing up to him, de Mello forgot that he had been captain of India and any allegations directed at him involved the reputation of the country he was representing. Unmindful of the consequences, de Mello went about on his mission. Conflicting stories started appearing in various newspapers, which compelled Prof D B Deodhar (who had resigned as selector in disgust and despair from his post when de Mello insisted on sitting in the Selection Committee meeting in Poona for the Australian tour in his capacity as Board's president) to write to Prime Minister

Jawaharlal Nehru and Deputy Prime Minister Sardar Vallabhb-hai Patel to intervene. He also requested these leaders to probe the Board's functioning. To clear the atmosphere, Prof Deodhar recommended a panel of three to conduct an impartial inquiry into this whole affair. This insalubrious controversy made head-lines abroad, too. When the media interviewed Don Bradman in Australia asking for his comments about Amarnath, the legendary Australian described him "as a charming person. It is surprising that he is involved in such a controversy."

When the news of the suspension reached Amarnath, he reacted by issuing a statement to the press, asking the BCCI not to hoodwink people and to make all charges public. Once done, he would reply to each one of the charges. "Let the learned peo-ple of India then decide who is wrong," he said. Though there was no cricket to be played between April to September, it was a major threat to his career. Known for his guts and natural instinct to fight his way out, he decided to take the bull by its horns. He could not allow such a stigma to be attached to his name. Being Southern Punjab Cricket Association honorary sec-retary, Amarnath knew the modus operandi of the Board and he started making swift moves to counter de Mello.

To fight de Mello was not an easy task, as he was presi-dent of both the BCCI and Delhi & District Cricket Association (DDCA) and had high connections with politicians. Nonetheless, Amarnath decided to strike at de Mello on his own home turf — Delhi. DDCA Secretary Harjas Rai Malhotra was a good friend of Amarnath's and an ardent admirer. He too was not happy with de Mello's attitude and style of functioning. Finding an ally within the enemy camp, Amarnath devised a plan to remove de Mello from his post as DDCA president. With the help of Delhi cricketers and members of the Association, Malhotra called an emergency meeting, charging the president with autocratic behaviour and dictatorial functioning. Presuming this meeting to be nothing more than a small uprising of disgruntled mem-bers, de Mello decided to chair it and sort the problem out and, perhaps quell the uprising with a heavy hand. But before he could get a chance to speak, Malhotra moved a no-confidence motion against him, which was passed unanimously. Finding himself isolated, he had no choice but to resign. Amarnath had struck the first blow successfully. This victory demonstrated his influence and the hard time the Board president was about to face in the coming months.

With one vote in his pocket, he decided to contact other sympathetic but anti-de Mello associations in May and June. Cricket Association of Bengal (CAB) Honorary Secretary Pankaj Gupta too had a personal grudge against de Mello and this controversy gave him an opportunity to settle scores. CAB willingly took up Amarnath's cause against de Mello which meant an open revolt. They supported Amarnath against the injustice meted out and harm done to his reputation. Once this unflinching support of CAB was published in all the Calcutta newspapers, Associations like Assam, Bihar, Madras and others came out openly in Amarnath's favour. Some members, who were undecided till then, assured him of their support when the Board met in July to ratify the decision of suspension. By now, he had gathered enough votes to counter the threat of a ban.

With de Mello's charges published all over the country, Amarnath got down to collect all relevant papers to prepare for his defence. On May 6, 1949, the press approached him for his comments and he said, "I have not yet received the official copy from the Board, I have only seen the charges in the newspapers. I am not going to take it lying down. The country will soon know the other side of the picture and will then be in a position to judge and decide as to whether the charges framed against me are correct."

Going through the allegations and finding their own reputations tarnished, Gujarat Cricket Association Honorary Joint Secretary Nansha Thakore denied any truth in de Mello's charges of monetary gain. Then, on May 8, CAB revolted against de Mello for pressing frivolous charges against Amarnath and condemned the Board's action. In their opinion, this decision was highly irregular, arbitrary and improper to say the least. Pankaj Gupta, a former BCCI secretary described de Mello's allegation of purchasing P Sen's inclusion in the series at Rs 5,000 as indecent and regrettable. Assam Cricket Association Honorary Secretary B K Bose also came out in his support of Amarnath and stated, "India can hardly afford to lose the services of Amarnath in view of the present set up of Commonwealth cricket."

This response shook de Mello.

AMARNATH STRIKES BACK

Lala Amarnath had a sharp memory and he remembered several incidents, which led to this unpleasant episode. Anthony de Mello, he recalled, was a man with a huge ego, who had somehow become domineering but he (Amarnath) was a 'no yes man'. On a couple of occasions, he had offended the Board president with his candid replies. Refusing to accept de Mello's presumption that he was the Board had led to quite a few arguments. Amarnath did not agree with him on many issues, especially the revival of the communal Pentangular tournament. Unable to have his way there, de Mello tried to draw him into discussion several times about the selection of the Indian team but Amarnath's response was lukewarm. Every time this topic came up, he discouraged de Mello from getting into this domain. Frustrated, the Board president charged Amarnath with making disparaging remarks. Clearly, his vanity had been hurt that Amarnath did not accept him as the Board.

Just as de Mello used the media, especially in Bombay, to fight his battles, Amarnath decided to launch his attack through the same platform. On June 6, 1949, he called a press conference of sports journalists at the Broadway Hotel in Calcutta. At the outset, Amarnath said, "Believe me, I would never have told you what I am about to tell you today. But the fact is that Mr. de Mello has already made an international scandal of Indian cricket and India by steps he thought fit to take. Although, he claims he picked me from the gutter, he forgets I was captain of India. Any such action taken against an Indian captain for continued 'misbehaviour and indiscipline' reflects not on me, the humble Amarnath, but on the fair name of Indian cricket and India all over the world."

Then in a calm and composed manner, he read out his response to de Mello's allegations, along with his observations about the BCCI president.

Replying to the first charge regarding his decision not to captain or play for the State XI in Baroda, he stated that it was not a 'last-minute' decision. It rested not with him but with his employer, the Maharaja of Patiala. Quite sometime before the match, he was in correspondence with Baroda Cricket Association Honorary Secretary Karmarkar, who had been appointed, at de Mello's suggestion, as the assistant secretary of the Board in Bombay and was working under him. In course of that correspondence Amarnath had expressed not only his desire but also his keenness to captain the State XI. "I suggested that as I was captain of India, I might be permitted first-class travel, to which Karmarkar agreed. I also requested him to arrange for my leave from Patiala to enable me to play the match. In reply to Karmarkar's telegraphic request, inter alia, asking for my leave from my employer, the Military Secretary to the Maharaja of Patiala then sent the following reply by a telegram dated October 15th, 1948, to Karmarkar 'Your wire of 15th instant to His Highness Maharajadhiraj Stop Captain Rai Singh reaching Baroda 22 October Stop Regret inability to spare Captain Amarnath owing to trial matches in Patiala from 23rd.'

Elaborating further, he said, as the match between the State XI and the West Indians was scheduled to commence on October 23 and as Karmarkar had been posted with information of Maharaj of Patiala's inability to spare him in the telegram dated October 15, the decision was conveyed a full eight days before the match. Hence, the decision was neither last-minute nor Amarnath's. Under the circumstances, if, as de Mello alleged, that the tour started with an incident, he was absolutely unaware of his role in that.

As for the second charge of not being able to reach Delhi in time for net practice, Amarnath stated he was unavoidably delayed in reaching Delhi only on the morning of November 9 although he had planned to reach on the evening of November 7. Disappointed as he was, as captain of India, to lose the chance of conducting the nets personally before November 9, Amarnath said de Mello's charge that his late arrival deprived India of organised net practice was rather farfetched. He recalled how he almost missed the West Indies match at Patiala due to indisposition, but ultimately played, scoring 223 not out, on the last day of the match, i.e. November 6.

Apart from the strain of that long innings, as Southern Punjab Cricket Association secretary, he was required to attend to many details in connection with a big match in a place like Patiala. The match having finished on November 6, much as he had hoped to leave for Delhi the following day, he found it impossible to finish work as the West Indians left that afternoon and hence, he could leave for Delhi only on November 8 and conduct the nets personally the following morning.

Since he could not leave before November 8, he informed the local manager of the Indian team, K B Saxena, of his change of plan and late arrival and instructed Saxena to request Hazare, the vice-captain, to organise the nets in his absence. Amarnath pointed out that no Board official, including de Mello, had mentioned anything about this delay to him at that time.

Moving to the third charge, Amarnath agreed, in Delhi, he requested de Mello for additional 'bonus'. If by 'bonus' de Mello meant out-of-pocket expenses — on behalf of the team, it was absolutely untrue. However, Amarnath wondered how a request could be made threateningly, as de Mello put it. Amarnath then pointed out that for eight days out of pocket expenses, in a costly place like Delhi, a sum of Rs 5 per head per player was offered in the first instance and finally Rs 60 was granted to each player at Rs 7.50 per day. It was a paltry sum by any standard when compared with the consolidated sum of Rs 150 paid to each players during the four-day 'Tests' against the Australian Services team at certain centres. Since then, he argued, prices had soared higher and hence the demands were justified. Then, referring to de Mello's charge that he had not made the request on behalf of all the players but on his own, was absolutely untrue. That the majority of the team members made the request was obvious when all the players accepted the 'additional bonus' of Rs 60 each for a stay of eight days. Reverting to his request to de Mello for additional payment as a captain, Amarnath accepted that he made a request for additional expenses during the first Test at Delhi as only Rs 60 was ultimately paid to each player. At the end of the Test, all that de Mello very kindly sanctioned was an additional Rs 90. "In fact, Gentlemen, de Mello himself wrote my bill in his own handwriting with all the details, which included Rs 150 as pocket expense plus the railway fare, servant expenses while travelling by train and other incidental expenses. De Mello then instructed S C Nanda to pay this amount to me on November 15, 1948," Amarnath stated.

Making a special reference to this point, he stated that only during the first Test were any additional expenses given to him as captain. In all other Tests, he received the same amount of money as the other players and although he had to take the servant to all other tests except Madras, the servant expense had to be paid out of his own pocket. "The journey by train was long with little facilities. Only a berth, without any bedding, was provided. The servant's job was to make the journey comfortable by arranging food, making beds, etc., and packing the personal baggage at the time of disembarking the train," Amarnath recalled.

Continuing his defence, Amarnath said, "de Mello's expression of out-of-pocket expenses in entertaining friends in a Delhi hotel, appeared to be phrased so that it might convey the misleading impression that he was having a good time in Delhi at the Board's expense." In fact, the principle of granting out-of-pocket expenses to a captain, consistent with his status, not as a private individual, but as captain of India, has been conceded on our recent tours. Often, at home also, the incidental expenses of a captain were heavier than those of the players, and these expenses were accepted and paid by the Board, but the point was never raised.

Regarding the umpire incident, he accepted gracefully that there was a very minor incident in the Delhi Test, the likes of which the press knew was not uncommon in international cricket. "We were on the field and I was bowling when an appeal was made, which was turned down by umpire Naik at the bowler's end. I made a slight gesture of disappointment, which is not unnatural and unusual in cricket, which the umpire misunderstood, because at the end of that over, instead of handing my hat (which I take off for bowling) back to me, he threw it towards me. I tried to kick it up into my hands, as I would a cricket ball, but could not get hold of it properly. In the same action, I picked up the hat and put it on my head and forgot all about it. All this happened in a split second and indeed, a few people could have had noticed it, for no reference was made either by the Delhi Press or by the API or in the radio comments." Amarnath also said it was surprising that de Mello had to hang his head in shame since he himself had brought this incident to his notice. De Mello had then said, "It's alright, Naik had no business to throw the hat at you and treat an international captain in this manner."

Refuting the next charge, Amarnath stated that it was absolutely untrue that his decision not to captain the North Zone team was made at the last minute. The zonal tournament started in

Bombay on November 20 and North Zone was scheduled to play the first match from that date. As early as on November 13, when the Selection Committee of the board met in Delhi to choose the teams, Amarnath had indicated that it might not be possible for him to reach Bombay for the first match but if North Zone won that game, he would definitely be available for the final. Hence, his decision not to play the first match was not last minute as alleged. This fact was also confirmed by an API report from Bombay, dated November 19 that the North Zone team to play the next day would be led by Group Captain Jaswant Singh.

The Board president had alleged that Amarnath's decision not to captain North Zone in the tournament was 'last minute' but in making another charge, admitted that Amarnath promised him in Delhi that he would be 'watching' the zonal tournament. Amarnath brought this point to the attention of the press and proved that de Mello knew very well that he would not play the first match. "In fact, Mr. de Mello had accepted my suggestion that Group Captain Jaswant Singh be the Captain of the North Zone in my absence. Moreover, all the cricket that I missed was a day and a half out of a scheduled 10 days but Mr. de Mello found it fit to make this an issue," he said.

Then referring to the Board president's charge that he was not fit to play after a little injury to his foot at Poona, Amarnath said, "I strongly refuse to accept Mr. de Mello's presumption that if I have had an accident I must inform the Board president. As long as I inform the Board, unless you gentlemen of the Press feel as some do, that the Indian Board and he are synonymous." The pressmen burst out in laughter. "All I was concerned with was informing the Board officials, which I did immediately after my injury troubled me in Poona. First, I informed Board's Honorary Secretary M G Bhave in Poona. Mr. Bhave sent me to a doctor with Mr. Karmarkar as my escort. The doctor gave me the necessary medical aid and X-rayed my foot. A member of the Selection Committee, Mr. Dutta Ray, accompanied me from Poona to Bombay and on arrival at the CCI, Mr Dalal, local manager of the Indian team in Bombay was informed. Between Mr. Dalal and Mr. Dutta Ray, further medical aid was made available to me till about midnight. As for Mr. de Mello's charge that I was definitely unfit to play, he is certainly entitled to his personal opinion. But the attending doctor's advice was not against my playing and I was certain myself that I was fit enough to stand up to the strain. To attain complete fitness prior to the second Test at Bombay, I had done extensive training, which *The Times of India* reported, giving advice to other cricketers to follow my example. And, all of India knows, I fielded through the entire West Indies innings for two days and a part of the third, and never took a substitute. And, on the fifth and the last day of the match, I batted for about four hours to score 58 not out, when we successfully played for a draw and throughout the period, I had not taken a runner. And, all that in spite of Mr. de Mello's charge that I was definitely unfit to play in the second Test."

Rebutting the ninth charge, Amarnath said it was absolutely untrue that he made a demand. "I made a request to the Board president on behalf of the team and at the suggestion of the Selection Committee of the Board. As I have already told you, in connection with Mr. de Mello's charge No. 3, in Delhi, a request for a consolidated sum of Rs 150 each had been made, but Rs. 60 was sanctioned. This was discussed at the meeting of the Selection Committee in Bombay on November 30 and the Committee suggested that I, as captain, should approach him on the subject, which I did. Mr. H N Contractor, chairman of the Selection Committee, and honorary secretary of the CCI in charge of the Test match, also, I was told, spoke to him in favour of my request. Mr. de Mello sanctioned Rs 150 each to Test players. I leave it to you to judge that if the 'demand' was unreasonable, how could he grant it? Further, I believe all the other Test match centres were circularised by the Board, for payment of a consolidated sum of Rs 150 to each player, and all players accepted that sum. You will thus see that this sum of Rs 150 was sanctioned in response to the continuation of our request made in Delhi and this could not have been made on the sole consideration that players are required to be at the Test centres full two days before the match, as Mr. de Mello appears to emphasise in his charges. For you all know, ordinarily Test players always reach Test centres with two days in hand."

Responding to the charge of deliberate carelessness in not collecting the Indian team, Amarnath described it as totally untrue. Speaking frankly, he emphasised that he or any other self-respecting person would resent it. "Indeed, I am unable to accept his presumption that it is a duty of the captain to 'collect' the team for parties and receptions. It is an international practice, as also our own, that the team managers inform and 'collect' players for receptions, etc. Having said this, I would like to enlighten everyone regarding the Progressive Group's reception. Mr. de Mello casually mentioned to me during the zonal tournament about such a function but no official invitation ever reached me. As is the practice and convention everywhere, I, as captain, had not been consulted before accepting this engagement. Besides, I was confined to my room at that time (according to medical advice for complete rest, at least that day) with my foot injury and it was physically impossible for me to go and attend the party, far less collect the team even if I had so wished. And, I had also advised Mr. de Mello through a common friend, Berry Sarbadhikary, that it was impossible for me to go to the Progressive Group reception.

"As for the party given by HE Governor of Bombay to the players, as far as I remember they had been informed by Mr. Dalal (the local team manager in Bombay) and he had arranged for collective transport. I was further asked to go to the Government House with the team, which I did, especially as my foot was much better as a result of complete rest in the days preceding. All the players who were staying at the CCI went to the party and only a few Test players who live in Bombay and were not staying at the CCI did not go for reasons I am not aware of. Regarding my alleged inability and unwillingness to meet social commitments, the Australian tour was a grand social success." Then reminding the press, Amarnath said that at times the captains of West Indies and Australia or even England did not attend some social functions but no charges were ever framed against them. Since he had placed all the facts and the aspects to the questions before the press, it was for everyone to determine if he could be accused of deliberate carelessness and whether de Mello's charge came under the category of fair play.

Moving ahead, Amarnath denied that his behaviour was arrogant and rude in his room at CCI as stated by the Board president in his next charge. He clarified by stating that the expression 'arrogant and rude' behaviour was vague and not specific. "To the best of my recollection, after Mr. de Mello's arrival in my room and as two or three players were coming in,

Mr. Sarbadhikary left the room, followed shortly afterwards by Mr. Gupta, just as the informal meeting was about to start. After Mr. de Mello had rebuked Mr. Ghulam Ahmed for not turning up at the nets and Mr. Rege for his late arrival, he asked me how my foot was I replied 'I am not 100 per cent fit yet'. At this he flared up and accused me of not having informed the Board. I told him that this was not true. I had informed the Board Secretary Bhave in Poona and Mr. Dalal, the manager in Bombay, about my injury."

Replying to the next charge that he used rude or arrogant language at lunch on the first day of the second Test in Bombay, Amarnath denied and termed these allegations as rubbish. He said he had never used any arrogant or rude language with Mr. de Mello. "At the Progressive Group's reception, the Board President had made all earnest pleas in the presence of HE Raja Maharaj Singh, Governor of Bombay, for revival of the tournament in Bombay. The Governor remarked that I (Amarnath), as captain of India, might give my views. I strongly opposed revival of the Pentangular on communal lines. While conceding that the Pentangular in Bombay might prove to be a financial success even today, I asserted that its usefulness in developing cricket talent had gone with the division of the country. De Mello tried to impress upon His Excellency the value of the Pentangular by citing one instance. He told the Governor that during the visit of Woodfull and Ryder's teams, he (de Mello) had written to Lt Col C K Nayudu, requesting him to include Mr. V S Hazare in the Central Province and Berar team against the Australians, but Lt. Col Nayudu did not comply with his request. Thereafter de Mello played Hazare in the Rest team in the Pentangular, and he, through the Pentangular, practically unearthed a great cricketer of the stamp of Hazare. At that stage, de Mello mentioned the visit of Woodfull's team. As I was also in the conversation, I said Jack Ryder had come out to India with an Australian team and not Woodfull. Probably, these contradictions became the bone of contention," Amarnath said.

Coming to the so-called 'indisciplined speech' by him at the Bombay Cricket Association, Amarnath described it as absolutely untrue. As for the phrase 'open exposure of many controversial matters of Indian cricket', he categorically denied ever using these words, which de Mello sought to put in his mouth.

Answering the next charge, Amarnath did not contradict de Mello that he arrived at Calcutta only twenty-four hours before the third Test. Though guilty of arriving late, the delay was unforeseen and he could not avoid it. Then giving the reason, he said, "As I have already said, I was very much away from my family, being constantly on the move owing to the demands of cricket. I had therefore, planned, for once, to bring my wife, who was now much better, and my children down to Calcutta for the third Test. On my way to Calcutta, I was to have been joined by my family at Cawnpore (Kanpur). However, I found that my family could not leave till the next day. As I could not get anyone to escort my family the next day, I was compelled to stay back. From Cawnpore, however, I sent a message to the Cricket Association of Bengal honorary secretary, advising him of my unforeseen delay and requesting him to arrange for nets for the Test team on December 29 and 30." On arrival, Amarnath immediately checked that the team had had net practice on the 29th. Happy with the team's commitment, he was present at the nets on December 30 and saw to it that everything was in order.

Continuing with his defence, Amarnath said, "In 1947, I had a contract to play in the Lancashire League as a professional. There was a great prospect of my qualifying for the Sussex County CC to play as a professional on very good terms. Of these, I have documentary proof. On the other hand, there was the India tour of Australia in 1947–48 for which, if selected, I could not go, if I desired to fulfil my commitments in England. This difficult position troubled me considerably. Cricket was my main prop and the acceptance of the English contracts would establish me financially, of which I was in dire need, as the little property that I had in Lahore was threatened owing to the then impending partition. At the same time, my overwhelming desire was to play for India, if at all I could. Many lovers of Indian cricket, among my friends, however, advised me to remain in India. Somewhat undecided, I spoke to Mr. Pankaj Gupta and placed all my facts before him. Mr. Gupta was then the honorary secretary of the Board and he assured me that he would find out if there was any way in which I could be reimbursed partially for the loss that was to be sustained by me owing to the cancellation of the Lancashire contract and my inability to qualify for Sussex County as a professional. Mr. Gupta, I understand, spoke to Mr. de Mello in Bombay on the subject, some time early in 1947, and he caused a public appeal over his own signature to be issued in the Press through Homi Talyarkhan, then PRO of the Board."

Then referring to the Board meeting in Delhi on March 17, 1947 presided over by Mr. de Mello, in which he, as representative of Southern Punjab was also present, the Board had decided to help reimburse partially a certain amount for the cancellation of the Lancashire League contract through an appeal for him, taking into account that de Mello himself had received assurances from two associations at least, to the effect that they would be able to realise Rs 20,000 between themselves. A similar appeal was also proposed for Vinoo Mankad, if he agreed. The Board president had himself stated, if necessary, a sum of Rs 5,000 would be paid to him (Amarnath) from the Board's funds. De Mello was arranging a cricket match early in March 1948 between the Indian team then about to return from Australia and the Rest, under the auspices of the All India Industrial Exhibition at the Eden Gardens, Calcutta. In fact, at that time, he had himself suggested that on the occasion of the match, the Maharaja of Patiala, the Governor of West Bengal Dr B C Roy (premier of West Bengal) and himself (de Mello) would broadcast an appeal for raising funds for Mankad and Amarnath. "During the first Test against the West Indies in Delhi in November, (then CAB Secretary) Mr. Ghose told me that he would not perhaps be able to raise the promised sum (his quota of Rs 10,000), but now that I had become captain again, he would try and do his bit during the third Test in Calcutta and that he had already started collecting in a small way. I heard nothing more about it and the third Test was also over when I thought that the 'appeal' had gone astray once again," he said.

"During my stay in Calcutta, I made no mention of it to Mr. Ghose or anybody else. The day before I was to leave Calcutta, however, my wife and I received a telephonic invitation to a tea party at the residence of CAB President J C Mookerjee. On arrival, I found an informal social (but not secret by any means) party where a select few people were present, some of them I did not even know. I was taken by surprise when Mr. Mookerjee got up and started apologising for not having fulfilled a long standing commitment and said that since in spite of best efforts, the target of Rs 10,000 could not be reached, but only Rs 5,000 had been collected for a fund for me sponsored by CAB Secretary Mr. Ghose. They had decided to make a 'surprise presentation' at an informal meeting. Therefore, Mrs. Mookerjee, wife of CAB President, presented the purse to my wife. Making a connection between Mr. Sen's place in the Test team with my purse is rather sinister. How could Calcutta have 'bought' a place for Mr. Sen in all the Tests by the gift of a purse to me? I was, after all one selector in a committee of five."

De Mello, he said, could hardly take shelter behind the statement that he asked Pankaj Gupta about the purse at the Board meeting on April 10. "How did de Mello inquire in the first week of January from the Gujarat Cricket Association if they had given me any money?" he asked. Then, charging the Board president of playing a double game, Amarnath enquired why similar enquires were not made from the official body in Bengal before charging him of the crime he didn't commit? Talking about Mr. Sen, de Mello probably forgot that in his letter to the Maharaja of Patiala, dated January 20, 1948, he had apparently included Mr. Sen in the Indian side as the first wicket-keeper.

Denying the Board president's next charge, Amarnath stated it was absolutely untrue that he disregarded the Board by not replying to the under-noted letter dated January 8. He did reply to de Mello's letter of January 8 on January 14, a copy of which he had sent once again with his letter dated April 7 to him. He wondered why de Mello denied having received the letter of January 14. "It is my misfortune that this particular letter of mine was not received by Mr. de Mello, as he says, for if this letter had not been missing, the charge of my receiving money secretly in Calcutta would have lost much of its sting. The allegation of my receiving money in Ahmedabad was also answered in that letter. Under the circumstances this missing letter affected me considerably. De Mello never told me during the fifth Test in Bombay that this letter was missing."

Dismissing de Mello's allegation that he did not see him in relation to the Calcutta and Ahmedabad episodes, Amarnath stated that since he had replied to his queries in his letter dated January 14, the question of meeting him did not arise. About the charge that he did not sit with the team during the lunch,

Amarnath stated that he missed lunch only once or maybe twice during the Test at Bombay.

With regard to de Mello's charge that he made a reference to power politics at a lunch given in honour of the West Indies cricketers in Bombay on February 9, Amarnath said it was incorrect. "I did, however, give an interview to the United Press of India on February 11 in Bombay, after the final Test was over. Almost the entire interview dealt with the technical aspects of Test cricket and the appreciation of the West Indian cricketers."

Replying to de Mello's charge that he disregarded and insulted the Board by ignoring his letters, Amarnath said, "I did reply to Mr. de Mello's letter of January 8 on the 14th and his next letter of February 21 on April 7 which Mr. de Mello states he received on April 11, a day after the meeting chose to suspend me. The delay in replying to his letter was caused by various pre-occupations. My foot also had to be operated in Cawnpore and besides I was positive I had replied to his letter of January 8 on January 14, which would have served to inform him on the points he had raised."

On the next charge about his interview and the Board's intrigues, Amarnath emphatically denied that he granted any interview to the *National Herald* or authorised its editor or anyone else to publish any story quoting him. He said, "I possess conclusive documentary evidence to show that no interview could possibly have been given to the *National Herald* for publication on or about April 2. This will also be borne out by the fact as soon as my alleged interview to the *National Herald* came to my notice, I sent a registered letter acknowledgement due, dated April 4, to the editor, contradicting the statement that I had granted the interview. You will note that on April 4, when I denied having given the interview, I had no idea that there was any motion to suspend me on April 10. I thus acted in good faith in writing the letter of contradiction."

Reacting to the last charge that he spoke disparagingly to anyone about what transpired in the Selection Committee, Amarnath stated that, "de Mello often evinced keen interest in the proceedings of the Selection Committee with such questions as 'How on earth could so and so be chosen and how could so and so be dropped?' "My uniform reply was 'The selection committee did it, don't ask me'."

Then Amarnath cited an incident in May 1947 when de Mello accused Vijay Merchant of trying to get his own team to Australia by overtures to the other members of the Selection Committee. On May 15, 1947, Merchant challenged de Mello to prove such charges by an independent inquiry. If he were found not guilty, then de Mello should get out of the Board. Such allegations were found incorrect.

"Regarding the interview in Colombo I gave on my return from Australia when I spoke against Duleep Sinhji for his destructive criticism. I recall de Mello's dislike for Duleep Sinhji, whom he referred as 'that paid secretary of CCI'. Duleep Sinhji, at one stage, was tipped to be the Board president but preferred, due to reasons best known to him, the job at CCI. On my arrival a beaming de Mello congratulated me for the interview and even said 'Well done', in appreciation," Amarnath said.

Referring to his kindness and affection, Amarnath said de Mello seemed to have projected himself as a merciful godfather. "When the Maharaja of Patiala gave me a reward and leave to fulfil my commitment, how can de Mello claim he is responsible? When the Board appointed me vice-captain for the tour of Ceylon, de Mello takes credit. When he gives me two Autograph bats and a Lillywhite kit, it is as a token of his affection but when Bengal does something, it is different.

"As regards de Mello's claim that he was responsible for saving my career in the 1936 episode, I must clarify that it was actually the Nawab of Bhopal, the Maharaja of Patiala Bhupinder Singh, Sir John Beaumont, Dr. P Subbaroyan and Sir Sikander Hayat Khan who were instrumental in my getting exonerated. De Mello had been helpful in providing facilities only as the Board's honorary secretary in 1936. I am grateful to him but this cannot become the life-long investment for bullying, bluff and bluster. For all my life, I have had no greater benefactor than the sporting House of Patiala. Their Highnesses Maharaja-dhirajas of Patiala, Bhupinder Singh and Yadvindra Singh, who had always been kind, generous and affectionate to me are my chief benefactors. Known for their discipline, the Maharajas never spoke a single harsh word. Respect is earned and not demanded, de Mello could never understand this," Amarnath said.

Then making a dig at de Mello's indisciplined actions when he was the Board secretary, Amarnath said the Maharaja

Jamsaheb of Nawanagar had to resign as Board president in disgust due to to reasons mainly connected with de Mello's irresponsible conduct. The first being his inability to co-ordinate with the Board office in Delhi with the honorary secretary anywhere in India. For all the actions of the secretary, the Jamsaheb was held accountable.

De Mello's disregard for the Board president was so evident that he authorised the Rajputana Cricket Club to collect star players from different parts of India against Lord Tennyson's team in the Jamsaheb's absence and without his knowledge as he was away in Europe. Later, when the question of holding the fifth Test match at CCI, Bombay was proposed by the honorary secretary de Mello, the Jamsaheb wired back advising against such a move under the prevailing circumstances with the Ranji Trophy matches going on and the legitimate differences existing between the CCI and Hindu Gymkhana regarding seating arrangements. But the wilful de Mello, in spite of Jamsaheb's advice, continued having correspondence.

De Mello's self-proclaimed belief of I-am-the-Board was further exposed. In his zeal to claim as much publicity as possible, he crossed all limits. Not being satisfied with managing the Indian Board, he trod into the West Indies territory too. Without even bothering to consult the captain or the manager of the West Indies side touring India in 1948–49, he sent a cable to the West Indies Board in Jamaica, requesting the services of two more players in India. The captain and manager took strong opposition to de Mello's act and one player who was on his way to India, was stopped in London and recalled to the West Indies.

Having replied to all the charges with sincerity and documentary proofs, Amarnath also replied to the queries raised by the press. *The Nation* wrote on June 6: "Indian cricket has always suffered and is still suffering from 'continued misbehaviour'. In 1936, Vizzy accused Amarnath of misbehaviour. But, by his (Vizzy's) own confession, the Beaumont Committee fixed the guilt on him. Amarnath came back with renewed honour. Now, in 1949, de Mello has indicted Amarnath on this account. Lala has given his replies and we are sure that everyone will agree with us after going through Lala's replies that if ever anyone was guilty of 'continued misbehaviour' in Indian cricket, it is none other than Tony de Mello, the President of the Board of Cricket Control."

On July 8, 1949, de Mello returned from his European holiday. The feedback he received on his arrival was not encouraging and he could see for himself the changed scenario, which dismayed him no end. The change of heart worried him and he tried his best to win back his utterly confused flock, but to no avail. Finding his support base dwindling, de Mello tried both coercion and cajoling. Unfortunately, even this failed to get any positive response from the majority of the member Associations. Having lost his own domain Delhi unexpectedly, de Mello found it exceptionally hard to retain his crucial votes to fight a losing battle against Amarnath. To add to his woes, the sympathy wave swept across the Board in Amarnath's favour. It was a Catch-22 situation for de Mello. If, on popular demand, he agreed to revoke his earlier order of suspension against Amarnath, he was likely to be on a slippery turf and vulnerable. The chances were that his antagonist would go for the jugular and remove him from the post of president, too. But de Mello was no novice to Board politics. He had been a part of the BCCI since its inception in 1928–29 and it was unlikely that he would let go of the platform of power. He knew the BCCI better than anyone else, as also the chameleon character of its members. Hoping that they would switch their loyalty back to him sooner than later, de Mello continued with his efforts to teach Amarnath a lesson.

Despite all his connections and proximity with the Congress leaders, de Mello forgot that Amarnath was no ordinary person. He was a veteran of many battles and each time he had come out unscathed. If he could fight a battle against the British in 1936 and come out victorious, surely the Board president could not have thought himself to be more powerful than the British? To put his opponents in a quandary, Amarnath issued a powerful statement describing his suspension as a big mistake by the Board president and his followers. He threatened to fight this battle till eternity. Unable to restrain himself, de Mello took the bait and got embroiled in heated statements, much to Amarnath's joy. De Mello told the press at Bombay that: "Amarnath's statement is a veritable tissue of suppressions, mispresentations and invention. Amarnath has laboured hard like a mountain and brought forth a mouse."

Berry Sarbadhikary wrote in his column on June 11, 1949:

"The colossal length of Amarnath's reply running into 39 pages exposed the Board President in many ways and through his observations Amarnath in his serial replies to the chargesheet is likely to be greatly impressive and even to make him appear as 'Martyr' in many parts of India."

To fight this enormous battle against the powerful Board president, Amarnath reached Calcutta and consulted his friends and lawyers about his strategy. "The court of law remained the only place where you could get justice," advised his lawyers. On July 23, 1949, just a few days before the Board's Annual General Meeting, Amarnath played a masterstroke. He threatened to sue the BCCI for suspending him from playing any grade of cricket without giving him an adequate opportunity to defend and refute all the charges. This sensational news caused panic among the members of the Board.

Hardly had the effect of the news subsided, on July 27 he made his intentions clear by filing a defamation case at the Calcutta High Court against de Mello for a sum of Rs 1 lakh. Fighting his battle was the eminent lawyer from Calcutta, Niren De. The news reached Bombay in a flash, sending shockwaves through de Mello's supporters who were party to Amarnath's suspension. Immediately, certain member associations started sending messages of compromise, while others demanded a second look at the charges framed against Amarnath. Thunderstruck, the Board members were jittery. It was a huge amount to shell out in case the Board lost the proceedings in court. Soon, fingers started pointing at the president for taking this decision without consulting them or thinking of the consequences. The decision was neither unanimous nor were they consulted, lamented certain members of the Board. Having successfully created a division and confusion in de Mello's supporters' ranks, Amarnath found his battle becoming easier. These conflicting statements strengthened Amarnath's case and he received public sympathy. The lion of Punjab was roaring louder than before.

On July 31, 1949, the Board met at CCI in Bombay to discuss Amarnath's case. A huge crowd assembled outside the CCI and staged an "Amarnath Oay" and shouted slogans like 'Long live Lala', 'Tony must resign', 'Shame on the arch schemer, remove the unclean cleaner of cricket'. The press too came in a large numbers to witness the Board's stormy session involving two heavyweights. Like a shrewd captain and a cunning bowler, Amarnath sprang another surprise and checkmated the foxed Board members by sending his attorney Niren De on behalf of Southern Punjab Cricket Association (SPCA) to defend him against all the allegations.

The meeting had just commenced with de Mello in the chair, when Niren De walked in. All heads turned to him in surprise, as they were expecting Amarnath. Without wasting any time, Niren De clarified that he was representing SPCA by proxy and his client Lala Amarnath as his attorney. "I am holding this envelope with details of the defamation case against Mr. Anthony de Mello for Rs 1 lakh. Further, I am going to sue the Board in Madras (BCCI's office was in Madras then) for its involvement in suspending my client, Lala Amarnath. Unless and until, all charges against him are dropped, I will be left with no alternative but to approach the Court," he said.

There was shocked silence at this. Commotion swallowed the silence, first in whispers and later in high-pitched arguments. Some timorous members started pointing fingers at the chair for putting them in such a mess without explaining the repercussions. "The truth was hidden from us," said one. "We meant no harm to Amarnath," explained others. This volte-face was primarily related to the financial implications. They wanted an early compromise at all costs. No words of patience or encouragement could sooth the confused minds of several Board members. The disarray in de Mello's faithfuls amused Niren De no end.

Niren De had done his work swiftly and smartly. Observing the entire drama from a lawyer's perspective and sensing the situation favourable, he said, "Gentlemen, I can understand that you all need some time to think clearly and hopefully positively. When you all reach a decision, please be free to contact me." They wanted to thrash out the problem as soon as possible but they failed to reach an understanding, leading to a stalemate. The Board wanted Amarnath to apologise but Niren De insisted that the charges framed against his client be dropped first. Some members of the BCCI close to de Mello tried desperately to convince Niren De that unless Amarnath apologised, no retraction of the earlier order would be passed. The eminent lawyer had fought many battles in Court and none of the threats cut any ice. The meeting lasted for nine, nerve-wracking hours and finally the BCCI buckled. A compromise formula was agreed upon.

In a press release, the Board stated: "In view of the fact that the Board has been advised that the decision regarding Amarnath, taken by the Board in the extraordinary general meeting held in Bombay on April 10, 1949 is *ultra vires*, as no proper notice was served and no opportunity was given to him of being heard. The meetings in respect of the said matter as also any matter arising thereof or in relations thereto are expunged from the records of the Board.

"Amarnath hereby expresses his regret for allegations and conduct, if any, on his part against the Board or its President. All charges against Lala Amarnath are hereby withdrawn and whole matter is hereby dropped."

The reasons given were simple: No proper motive for the charges were attributed, Lala Amarnath was not given an opportunity to defend himself, insufficient notice was given to the members of the Board about the meeting.

Amarnath was in the hotel when his friends and admirers gave him the good news. There were celebrations in his camp in the Board as well as outside the CCI, where his ardent fans waited for hours to hear this good news. In a choked voice, Amarnath thanked everyone in a short message and said, "I am grateful to you. If I play again, it will be for the great support I got from Bengal and the media."

Having being exonerated again from all charges levelled against him, Lala Amarnath got ready to concentrate on his cricket, which was his first and only love in life. "I thanked God for being kind once more in my fight against the establishment and coming out unscathed."

NINE

COMEBACK TWO –
PAKISTAN'S TOUR OF INDIA

THE PERIOD between April 1949 and September 1952 had been quite turbulent and lacklustre as far as Lala Amarnath's cricket was concerned. His stand-off with the Board president forced the Selection Committee to change the Indian captain. First Vijay Merchant was appointed captain against the Commonwealth team and later Vijay Hazare led India against the MCC at home. Amarnath played a few games but opted out due to indifferent health. In the mid-1950s, a foot infection took a turn for the worse and he had to be operated upon at Kanpur. Feeling better after the operation, he replaced Frank Worrell (on the latter's recommendation) as a professional with Radcliffe Cricket Club in the Central Lancashire League for a season. Though he completed another successful season in England, the corn kept troubling him and he was operated on again, this time in England. Unfortunately, the result remained unsatisfactory. The forced long layoff gave his critics an opportunity to pronounce the end of his innings. They did not reckon with his determination as he was waiting for an appropriate opportunity to bounce back.

A complete break from active cricket did Amarnath a world of good. With his health returning to its peak and his instinct telling him that he would return to the team sooner than later, he spent all his energy towards his physical fitness at Chail or in Patiala. Amarnath informed the Board before the 1952 tour of England that he was fit and available. Since Merchant had retired, the captaincy choices were Amarnath, Hazare and Syed Mushtaq Ali. Hazare secured more votes and was nominated captain. During the Selection Committee meeting, Hazare (a co-opted member) impressed upon the other selectors not to include two senior colleagues (Amarnath and Mushtaq Ali) in the team, despite their vast experience of English conditions. He did not realise that their presence would have been of immense value to the others but personal differences prevailed over better sense.

Fred Trueman, the ruthless English fast bowler exposed the weak Indian batting. One particular batsman was so petrified of his pace that he prayed he would not have to face him. But the poor soul's prayers went unanswered. Trueman consumed him time and again. This led to a joke in English cricket circles that the Indians were so terrified at the sight of this fast bowler that an Indian batsman stopped Trueman a number of times when he was halfway through the run-up, requesting adjustment of the sightscreen. Frustrated, the umpire asked the batsman where exactly he wanted the screen placed. "Put it between the bowler and me," the batsman is said to have replied.

Battered and bruised, the Indian team returned home dejected and demoralised. This was not the team the Indian people wanted should face Pakistan which would be making its maiden trip to India. While the pro-Hazare lobby had its way for the England tour, the anti-Hazare lobby was keen to see him stripped off the post. With Amarnath already fit, some in the Board felt he was best suited to lead India. Being a product of Lahore and also good at speaking the same languages (Punjabi, Urdu and English) as a majority of the Pakistanis, he could counter all their moves. Like the team from across the border, Amarnath was equally determined and aggressive in his approach and style of playing cricket, they explained. Put to vote, Lala Amarnath squeezed past Vijay Hazare to lead India for the third time in an inaugural series. This shift of stance reflected the thinking of many in the Board, who had not forgotten the holocaust of Partition. For them, only Amarnath was capable of rising to the occasion and helping defeat their new rivals.

The inaugural Test was played at the Ferozshah Kotla ground in Delhi. The Kotla had not been a happy hunting ground for the home team in the past. It had not won a single Test on this ground and it was not a memory it cherished. Amarnath, at the helm of affairs, was keen to break this jinx. Since Test matches came to the city after long gaps, the atmosphere at the ground was both passionate and patriotic. The first president of the Republic of India, Dr. Rajendra Prasad inaugurated the match and wished both teams luck. This was an experience of a lifetime and a historic moment for the Pakistan players, as they were becoming another Test playing nation. Critics described them as underdogs against the well-established Indian line-up but Amarnath and his players knew the true strength of the touring side. It had rising stars in Fazal Mahmood and Hanif Mohammad and the experience of Abdul Hafeez Kardar, Amir Elahi and Nazar Mohammad to put up a good show. Moreover, many of them had played plenty of cricket as Indians before Partition. For all practical purposes, each knew the other's strengths and weaknesses.

Shrewd as the legendary Chanakya, Amarnath realised that this was his last chance to prove his critics wrong and keep his reputation as India's best captain intact. The strip at the Kotla was bald and the top layer a bit loose, a sure sign that it would assist the spinners. India won the toss and batted but lost Vinoo Mankad and Pankaj Roy early to Khan Mohammad. Wickets continued to tumble and at one stage a score of 250 seemed like a mirage, but Hemu Adhikari and Ghulam Ahmed rescued India from a perilous situation with a fine 109-run last-wicket stand to take India to 372. If the partnership warmed the hearts of millions of Indians glued to the radio, the sharp turn obtained by the Pakistan spinners caused Amarnath's eyes to light up with joy as he saw miseries for the visiting side.

Amarnath and Gulab Ramchand bowled tidy spells to the Pakistan opening pair, basically to remove the gloss. Once it was done, Amarnath introduced his spinners. The first delivery from Mankad turned viciously, making him grin from ear to ear. Obsessed with only one motive — victory — Amarnath marshalled his resources effectively. "It is a mind game," Amarnath always professed. This theory became evident when he applied an attacking field throughout Pakistan innings. Mankad and

Ghulam Ahmed bowled accurately and accounted for 18 wickets, the left-arm spinner capturing 13 scalps and the latter five to ensure an innings and 70 runs victory for India.

The team was besieged by congratulatory messages from the president, prime minister and other dignatories. *The Hindustan Times* wrote: "India's splendid victory in the Delhi Test is important not so much because it has boosted her cricket morale as for the new approach which Amarnath has introduced. The sight of an array of six, and at times seven, close-in fieldsmen almost at hand-shaking distance from the batsmen was something which had not hitherto been seen in Indian cricket. To say that Pakistan succumbed in the pitiless war of nerves would be but half-truth. It was the leadership of the highest calibre coupled with Mankad's amazing bowling feat."

Another critic described the bowling of Mankad and Ghulam Ahmed as a major factor in India's victory but lamented the intimidatory field placing by the Indian skipper. "Back in my hotel room, I looked at the various messages on the table and laughed loudly at my fate. It could only have been destiny which had taken me to this stage. Only a couple of months earlier, I had been the forgotten person in Indian cricket and now I was being hailed as saviour of Indian cricket," Amarnath recalled.

During the Test, the two teams were invited to the Rashtrapati Bhavan for a party. The players mingled and joked with each other, leaving the tension of the match behind at the ground. For a majority of the Pakistanis, it was a sort of homecoming, though officially they were in another country. But it did not matter, as most carried happy memories of India. The tourists utilised the tour to meet their old friends, cricketers and relatives who had stayed back in India. Smiles and tears were common to such reunions. "I could empathise with them and felt sad watching them becoming nostalgic when they embraced their dear ones," Amarnath said.

The victory at Delhi upset Amarnath's adversaries' calculations since the tide had turned the other way. Jealousy, intrigue and disloyalty were still prevalent in Indian cricket and they came out in the open during the second Test in Lucknow. The newly-built stadium opposite Chattar Manzil had everything but a proper turf wicket. It was surprising that Kanpur was overlooked and the United Provinces Cricket Association president,

Vizzy, favoured Lucknow. When Amarnath reached the centre a couple of days early, he found to his shock that a coir matting wicket was to be used. "Are we playing to our strength or that of our opponents?" he asked the local officials. The coir matting presented fear in the minds of players, especially from the West Zone. They were not accustomed to batting on matting and knew Fazal Mahmood would wreak havoc with his lethal leg-cutters. To minimise the effect, Amarnath got it replaced by the jute matting to cut down the pace, if not the bounce.

If Amarnath was busy making last-minute adjustments, his rivals were busy thinking up new ideas for his downfall. Hazare reported his inability to play after Delhi on health grounds and Adhikari cried off due to a thumb injury sustained at Amritsar before the first Test. Instead of resting, he played the Delhi Test and was on the field on all days, batting or fielding close-in. Amarnath was baffled at the fact that Adhikari had reported unfit for the Lucknow Test. Was it really the injury or the thought of facing Fazal Mahmood and other pace bowlers on a matting wicket, Amarnath wondered. He concluded it was definitely the latter. Then, Vinoo Mankad opted out with an injury to his middle finger. "I was not surprised as the reason lay somewhere else. The West was feeling insecure after our victory in the first Test, which meant extended life for me. Vinoo never complained or was inconvenienced when he bowled 24 overs on the trot and captured five wickets in the second innings in Delhi." Amarnath was furious but could do little at this stage.

The internal squabbles did great harm to the Indian camp even before the Test started. This development pleased the Pakistanis, as they saw a ray of hope after the withdrawal of players who had done so well in Delhi. The replacements available were no patch. Amarnath knew this but kept quiet and waited for fate to unfold the events. A day before the Test, Amarnath was himself down with high temperature and doctors diagnosed it as a touch of influenza. This news sent the selectors into a spin. The prospect of losing the captain as well spelt doom and misery for the team. But he put aside any doubts by declaring himself fit and available, though slightly weak. He told selectors Dutta Ray and Contractor, "India needs me and I'll never let my country down."

Many years later, Lala Amarnath stated, "The players who

opted out because India won under my captaincy, couldn't understand the mental trauma which had affected the displaced people due to Partition. I could because it had affected me. These people had only one goal in mind: how to harm my career, even if it involved the prestige of the country. No work or injury could be above national interest and dignity."

Expecting another victory, a large crowd came to witness the second Test. Soon cheers turned into jeers as one wicket after another tumbled. Fazal Mahmood relished bowling on the matting wicket and the Indian batsmen were clueless while facing him. Without its main batsmen, India found the replacements utterly inadequate to withstand the Pakistan attack and were bowled out for 106. In return, Pakistan faced no such threat early in the innings as they cruised to 63 before Ghulam Ahmed did the trick. Thereafter, India captured wickets but could not stop the flow of runs. Nazar Mohammad played a patient knock, which ensured a healthy lead for Pakistan. Amarnath, despite fever, bowled 40 overs and picked up two for 74 but Pakistan finished with 331 runs.

As Pakistan had gained a substantial lead, India was going to find it difficult to counter Fazal Mahmood and save the Test. True to Amarnath's fear, Fazal Mahmood again tore apart the fragile Indian batting, the exceptions being Amarnath (61 not out), Polly Umrigar (32) and D K Gaekwad (32). Amarnath faced Fazal Mahmood and the others with confidence and ease, reminiscent of his glorious past, when he cut and hooked the short-pitched deliveries. Stranded at the other end, he witnessed the defeat with despair. It was truly one man's destruction of India, with Fazal Mahmood capturing 12 wickets.

The sweet memories of Delhi seemed like a distant dream after India's poor show at Lucknow. The local college students found defeat difficult to digest and gave vent to their frustration and anger by surrounding the bus carrying the Indian players, shouting slogans and hurling vulgar abuses. Already upset by the defeat, Amarnath requested the police to make way for the transport but they just shrugged their shoulders. Unable to bear the sight of the petrified Indian players hiding under their seats to avoid the stones being hurled at them by the students, Amarnath grabbed a lathi from a policeman and charged towards the crowd, swinging it with all his strength. While avoiding the blow, a student fell and the others ran for cover. Soon, there was a stampede with an angry Amarnath chasing the large group of students and some cops joining in. Finally, the way was cleared for the team bus to leave.

Later, when the author toured England in 1973 as a member of the All India Schools team, with former Test star Vijay Manjrekar as manager, he recounted the incident. "If skipper (as Amarnath was addressed by many cricketers) had not been there, perhaps we would have been lynched by the unruly crowd that day." Only Amarnath could have done such a thing and got away with it.

Both teams had played hard cricket and even appreciated each others' performance. The relations between the players continued to be warm and cordial, despite poor relations between the two governments. After the Lucknow Test, Pakistan Radio aired stories meant to cause unnecessary tension in the minds of the listeners. A programme called *Qazi Ji* broadcast from Lahore repeatedly said that Pakistan had sent its cricket team to strengthen the relations between the two countries but the Indian public and especially the press was enraged at Pakistan's victory. It further alleged that the Indian players never applauded Pakistan's game. "It was a strange propaganda by Radio Pakistan, when their team was received in India with open arms and showered with utmost warmth and courtesy," Amarnath recalled.

The Third Test in Bombay became a crucial match for Amarnath, as the local press was after his blood and wanted him to be replaced as captain. After a few days' rest, the trio of Mankad, Hazare and Adhikari reported fit and were included for the Test. To strengthen the batting further, Amarnath requested the selectors to include Rusi Modi but they had reservations. Having learnt a bitter lesson at Lucknow, he wanted a player of Modi's class, calibre and dedication in the squad. Using all his influence, he convinced the selectors to include him. Before the Test, Amarnath discovered that certain players were going to under-perform. He called the team to his room on the eve of the Test match. "I placed a miniature national flag on the table in my room and directed each player to hold the tricolour with his hand and take a solemn oath of allegiance to uphold national prestige and honour at all costs. This move caught quite a few players off guard but everyone took the oath. Once done, they knew the consequences of letting the nation down. I was now satisfied that for the time being I had bound the Indian team into one unit to face Pakistan."

Having set his house in order, Amarnath embarked upon another mission to demoralise the tourists. He was remarkable at the game of nerves and always used this critical card when cornered. With the series level and the Bombay press after him, he invited a few journalists for an informal chat. There he predicted victory for India within three days. Next day, these remarks made headlines but not many took them seriously, including the Pakistanis, who had scored a convincing victory in Lucknow. Many critics dubbed Amarnath's outburst as one of his clever ploys to test the tourist's nerves and reaction.

The toss at Brabourne Stadium was of vital importance as he knew the wicket would have some moisture on the opening day and could be a deciding factor. He was desperate to field. "During my walk with Abdul Hafeez Kardar for (the) toss, I wanted to know the Pakistan captain's mind. I casually asked him what would he do if he won the toss? He looked at me with suspicion and said, 'What would you do?' Knowing Kardar's distrustful nature, I decided to tell the truth as I knew he would do just the opposite if he won the toss. After a little pause and feeling the turf, I said I would field. Pakistan won the toss and, as I had presumed, Kardar decided to bat first. I was thrilled at this decision and knew what awaited the touring side," Amarnath said.

Amarnath walked back into the dressing room with a broad smile and rubbed his palms in excitement. "Gentlemen, the marvellous circus is about to begin for everyone to enjoy," he said with conviction and authority. Walking ahead of his team briskly, he was like a hungry tiger waiting to pounce on its prey. To prove the Bombay press wrong for criticising his form and abilities both as a leader and a player, Amarnath took the new ball himself. What followed for the next two hours made the Pakistanis run to the dressing room and his critics run for cover. Off his short run-up and double-arm action, Amarnath produced one of his best bowling spells on Indian soil. The field placement for his bowling resembled a midfield conference. "For Hanif Mohammad, he arranged nine fielders to form a semi-circle around the batsman at a distance of only a few yards and a solitary cover fielder," wrote the *Bombay Sentinel*. The perplexed Pakistanis crumbled under such pressure tactics. Amarnath mesmerised all the batsmen with his immaculate line and length during the first session.

With only one fielder in the covers, Nazar Mohammad tried to force Amarnath's in-swinger on the up, only to find his stumps shattered. Kardar survived some anxious moments but could hardly meet the gaze of a grinning Indian captain as he too fell victim, caught in the leg trap while trying to drive him. A jubilant Amarnath was on song and enjoying his spell. Imtiaz hardly lasted two balls in the battle of nerves, perishing in a similar fashion, driving. The Pakistan captain realised his folly but it was too late. Hanif Mohammed held his end for sometime before Mankad bowled him with a quicker delivery. The crowd roared at the fall of every wicket and soon Masood was out to him and Mankad got rid of Wazir Ali to make Pakistan 60 for six. This session proved even better than Amarnath had anticipated. He bowled 13 overs for 19 runs and captured four wickets. Describing the Indian captain, famous radio commentator and journalist Sarbadhikary wrote: "Amarnath was a born exhibitor. He had a showmanship that would have been the envy of an advertising expert. When he strode to the field one could many a time see the end of 'the red handkerchief' peeping out of his pocket. With his graceful movements he was cynosure of all eyes on the field."

After lunch, the wicket eased and India found it difficult to break the partnership between Waqar Hussain (81) and Fazal Mahmood (33) as they took their team's score to 186. Amarnath failed to get his fifth wicket due to some poor catching. In one over, Fazal was dropped three times. The easiest of all the chances was missed by Umrigar, forcing Amarnath to remark: "My wife wouldn't have dropped that." A Bombay newspaper reported, "The redoubtable Pakistani side crumbled in just three and three quarters of an hour for a truly astonishing total and it was something in the nature of poetic justice that one of those mainly responsible for the debacle was Lala Amarnath."

This modest total was hardly daunting for the home side, which was in full strength. With the Brabourne strip playing easy, the Pakistan attack was sent on the leatherhunt. Hazare and Umrigar posted a century each on the second day. Writing in *Pakistan in Test Cricket*, Mukhatir Bhatti summarised the second day's play best: "Under the onslaught of the batsmen, our (Pakistani) fielders slackened. When India's lead had increased to 201, Amarnath applied closure. He was adventurous but he had weighed up the situation well — 'The Pakistan batsmen are tired as they have been on the field the whole day. The wicket is still playing well. Although there is more than two days' play left, there is a possibility of a draw if I carry on. Hence, the necessity of obtaining a couple of wickets this evening'." The move caught Kardar off-guard but Amarnath's critics felt the declaration was a bit premature and could be detrimental if India batted on the decaying surface on the last day. Amarnath never believed in taking any advice from anyone and none dared argue with his decision. His theory was simple. "Leaders make decisions and others follow their orders. The day followers make decisions, you don't need a leader. A puppet can do this job," he said. His observation of the opponents proved correct when the physically-exhausted and mentally-tired opening batsmen took strike in the dying moments and India scalped Nazar.

In the evening, the Governor of Bombay Sir Homi Modi invited the teams. The hot topic of discussion among the guests and the governor was Amarnath's declaration and whether India would achieve victory in next two days or if the Test would end in a draw. Those who spoke with Amarnath were convinced that it was a correct decision. Now the Pakistan camp at the party looked a worried lot at the prospect of losing the Test. The key to victory lay with him. An enthusiastic member of the Pakistani team approached Amarnath for his advice regarding the roller. He very respectfully asked him that if he (Amarnath) were in a similar situation which roller would he ask for the next morning. "This direct question stumped me for a while but knowing the psyche of these people, I decided to answer his question. 'I would take light roller tomorrow, if batting.' Hearing this, all the Pakistanis started laughing and one senior player said rather impudently, 'This is nothing new, we all know that' and they dispersed," Amarnath recalled.

Kardar opted for the heavy roller. Since there was no moisture underneath the soil, it crumbled. The result was disastrous. Mankad and Subhash Gupte spun the ball viciously to make life miserable for the Pakistani batsmen. Only Hanif played well and made a patient 96. After tea, Amarnath asked Ghulam Ahmed to wait in the pavilion and took Ramchand, the 12th man, to field at silly mid-off with instructions to stand as close to the batsman as possible. In the first over from Mankad, a delivery spun and cocked up to take the shoulder of Hanif's defensive bat and Ramchand took a catch. Having achieved the objective, Amarnath told him, "Ram, you have done your job, now you can go and relax in the pavilion." The spinners then ripped through the innings without a problem. India won the Test by 10 wickets and his prediction had come true.

The fourth Test in Madras was expected to be an exciting affair, with India trying to wrap up the series with another win and Pakistan trying hard to keep the series alive either with a victory or a draw. The pendulum swung to and fro till Pakistan's last pair came in to bat at 240 with less than half an hour to go. Amarnath told his team not to get the last pair out in the dying moments, as he feared that losing a wicket at this juncture would jeopardise the chances of a win for them. In the evening, the selectors expressed their unhappiness to Amarnath for under-bowling Mankad. Incensed at the accusation and other remarks about his captaincy, he allowed Mankad and other bowlers full opportunity to get the last wicket but it proved unsuccessful. They were all sent on a leatherhunt. Mankad and other spinners raised their hands and requested their skipper to do something. Lunch was taken with Pakistan at 344 for nine. The last pair had added 104 runs. The nervous selectors rushed to him in the dressing room and asked him to do something. Annoyed by their previous day's remarks, Amarnath said, "I think you gentlemen are satisfied with Vinoo and other bowlers' spells. Let me know how long you want me to keep them on." Taken aback, they pleaded with him to do whatever he felt was right.

After lunch, Amarnath took the second new ball and bowled Amir Elahi in his first over.

If there was excitement in the middle, then there was another unfolding in the corridors of the BCCI. The Board had decided to meet in Madras to select the captain and the other members of the team for India's maiden tour of the West Indies. Amarnath had got captaincy by a solitary vote against Hazare but this trend changed. The power to select the captain and the team was finally given to the selectors. Contractor and Ramaswamy had been singing different tunes which left only Dutta Ray in Amarnath's favour. Then came the news that Ramaswamy was likely to go to the West Indies as manager. He did not see eye-to-eye with Amarnath on various theories of captaincy. With a crucial Test match still going on, many in the Board felt that it would be an inappropriate time to announce the team or the captain for the tour in the middle of the series. But the selectors still held the meeting, raising doubts about their sincerity. Despite their best efforts to keep the minutes of the meeting confidential, the news of machinations pertaining to the composition of the team and the captain reached Amarnath.

The result of the Test hung undecided with rain forcing no play as India struggled at 175 for six. If there were no fireworks on the field, then many expected something special from him at the Board's dinner in honour of the teams at Madras Corporation Stadium. The gathering consisted of the Board president, high dignitaries, press and other important people. Amarnath, a great showman, loved such gatherings as it gave him an opportunity to enthrall the audience with his spicy speeches laced with numerous anecdotes. "Gentlemen, good evening. It has been a great privilege to lead India and also to represent the country for such a long time. Before coming to this function, I received a call from a journalist friend of mine from Delhi, conveying the good news of the West Indies tour, which I would like to share with everyone here. Gentlemen, my dear friend and compatriot Vijay Hazare has been nominated as captain of India for that tour. I congratulate him for this news and the appointment," he said.

The audience was stunned by this revelation. The pressmen scribbled all the details and waited for more bombshells. BCCI President J C Mookerjee, was bewildered by this exposure. He tried to control the excited press by repeatedly stating, "No! This is not true. How could you know the name of the captain when it is sealed in an envelope, right here," he said, patting his coat pocket. But the cat was out of the bag. Amarnath, however, continued with his speech. Then he expressed his desire to step down from the captaincy for the final Test in Calcutta to allow Hazare to lead the team before the tour. He also agreed to play under him and cooperate with him. The selectors and

Board officials requested Amarnath not to go by the rumours and instead concentrate and continue with his obligations as India's captain.

Though happy with this good news, Hazare was uncomfortable at the prospect of playing under him and failing in the last Test. If he accepted Amarnath's magnanimous gesture and led the team in Calcutta and lost the match, all hell would break loose. A couple of days before the Test, he decided to go for the third option — and withdrew from the team on health grounds. Hazare's absence turned out to be a blessing in disguise for a little known left-hander from Gujarat, Deepak Shodhan, who scored a century on debut. Since Amarnath had announced his desire not to lead and Hazare had abstained, he could not play under Mankad. Reluctantly, he played his last Test as captain and won the series 2–1. After the Test match, J C Mookerjee announced the team for the West Indies tour. Amarnath was neither the captain nor a member of the team. He promptly announced his retirement from international cricket.

Much later, he revealed the name of the person who was instrumental for his omission. He said that during the selection of the team for the tour of the West Indies, the selector and manager-designate Ramaswamy had opined that Lala Amarnath was too big for him and he would not be able to handle him on the tour.

TEN

MANAGING THE INDIAN TEAM ON PAKISTAN TOUR

AFTER BIDDING farewell to international cricket, Lala Amarnath decided he would be a part of the establishment to see that deserving cricketers got a fair chance and also help Indian cricket to progress. He had fought with the establishment for the cause of the cricketers, only to find himself in the dock. Cricket not only flowed in his blood but was also his lifeline. He wanted to give back what he had achieved through it and that was possible only if he were part of the establishment. He knew it was an uphill task but entry into the BCCI came easier than he had presumed. Being Southern Punjab Cricket Association honorary secretary, Amarnath received enormous support from all the members of the Board in becoming a national selector.

During his captaincy, he had not allowed personal likes and dislikes to affect a fair selection of the national team. Vijay Hazare was always a beneficiary despite their differences. A good performance by the team was of utmost importance to him. Hazare, on his part, due to reasons best known to himself never quite gave similar consideration to Amarnath. It was an open secret that Amarnath would have been an asset to the team in England but Hazare preferred defeat to having Amarnath on that tour.

With age catching up with him, Hazare's performance was hardly impressive as he averaged marginally over 19 runs per innings. The Selection Committee decided to replace him with Vinoo Mankad. The tour of Pakistan was of a special significance to the Board, not to speak of the government. They both wanted the tour to progress without any hitch. Many names were suggested for the manager's post but South Block and the Board unanimously accepted Amarnath as soon as his name was proposed. The main reasons were his familiarity with Lahore and its language, which made him popular with the masses.

The tour commenced from East Pakistan (now Bangladesh) where thousands turned up to watch the historic Test match in Dacca (now Dhaka). The contest was intense with the balance tilting this way or that but neither side capitalised on it and the game ended in a draw. If India failed in the first innings, the home team did likewise in its second knock. Overall, it was absorbing cricket, throwing up many ifs and buts. Though there was no extraordinary performance on either side, in the dying moments of the Test, Pakistan captain Abdul Hafeez Kardar made a mockery of the gentleman's game. Realising that a draw was inevitable, Hanif Mohammed bowled right-arm and left-arm in an over. It was perfectly legitimate but when he bowled under-arm, the umpire disallowed it and asked him to bowl over-arm. There was an argument between the two and Kardar intervened. Instead of reprimanding his player for the poor spirit displayed, he took off on the umpire for disallowing the delivery. As if this was not enough, the Pakistan captain gave Imtiaz, the Pakistan wicket keeper the ball to bowl the last over. Imtiaz removed his pads and kept them behind the umpire at his bowling end without any protest from the men in white. He completed the formalities by bowling six balls, with Kardar standing behind the stumps without pads but with the wicket-keeping gloves on. "It is unprecedented in the history of cricket that a Test match has been played in a street cricket manner," Amarnath wrote in his tour diary.

The inability to win the first Test and the argument with the umpire at the end of the match left Kardar frustrated and annoyed. During the dinner at East Pakistan Sports Federation, in an inebriated condition, he gave vent to his frustration in his speech when he started making digs at the Indian cricketers. He described the Indian cricketers as being afraid of fast bowling and of playing defensive cricket. Amarnath felt like leaving the function midway through the speech but his sense of duty prevented him from doing that. "The incident left a bad taste in the mouth and I wondered if winning against India was so important to the Pakistan captain that he was ready even to create a feeling of bad blood between the two teams. The tour was supposed to bridge the gap and bring two countries closer and not divide them further," he recalled.

On the evening of January 5, 1954, the Indian team left Dacca for Karachi aboard a Pakistan International Airlines flight, which was long but enjoyable. At 10 p.m., the lounge at the Karachi airport was packed with people to welcome the Indian team. As per the arrangements, the team reached Hotel Metropolo at 11 p.m. "I was shocked that there were insufficient rooms reserved for us and the hotel staff expressed its inability to help us. Finally, four players had to share a single room for the night. As if this shock was not enough, the hotel staff told us to vacate the rooms early the next day as these had been booked for someone else. Only my room was left with the team to be used as a cloak room," he recalled.

Putting aside these incidents, the Indians travelled from one city to another by train and played attractive cricket in the warm-up games to get as much practice as possible before the real Test began. The itinerary of the team was so tight that it reached Hyderabad (Sind) only on the morning of the match. "As our game was to start in a couple of hours, the team went to the Circuit House for a quick shower. To our surprise and dissatisfaction, we found there were no arrangements for warm water in such cold conditions. To add to our woes, there were no towels either," Amarnath said.

Realising the futility of arguing with the staff, Amarnath sent a local boy to buy fresh towels from the market. Half the team went to the ground without a bath or even a proper shave due to paucity of time. The uncompromising attitude of the local officials proved that the Indians were fighting battles off the field as well.

Not a day passed without a problem rearing its head. In Karachi, the collector was asked to provide a car to take a player for some checkup but he hesitated and asked Amarnath who would pay the fare. "I told him 'We (the Indian Board) have a contract with your Board that all medical arrangements would be provided by you'. Very casually, he said he would see what could be done and left. This attitude of indifference left a poor impression of the Pakistani official when our player required urgent medical treatment. With no help coming, I met the owner of the hotel, Mir Rasul Ahmed, who very promptly agreed to help and offered his personal car. He asked me to wait in the room but neither the car nor Mir Rasul showed up. Later, I came to know that the poor chap was sent for on an errand by the local authorities. Finally, I had to approach the deputy high commissioner of India, who with the help of the High Commission made necessary arrangements. This attitude made me realise that there was one single purpose — to break the spirit of the Indian team off the field so that it could tell on their performance on the field," Amarnath said. Unfortunately, it was all in vain. The Pakistanis were unaware that Amarnath was made of steel and that the Indian team was in safe hands.

If the arrangements at Hyderabad were bad, Bahawalpur was deplorable. The rooms at the venue of the second Test presented a picture out of some horror movie, with dust all over. It seemed as if the place had not been used for quite sometime. In the middle of the room was placed a hard bed but the wardrobe was missing. This meant, no place to hang the clothes. "At first, I thought that we had come to the wrong place but once it was confirmed that it was our official accommodation, it shocked me," Amarnath said. Unable to bear such ill treatment to the side any longer, Amarnath exploded in anger and threatened to boycott the Test and recommend terminating the tour. Realising the gravity of the situation, high-ranking officials apologised profusely and promised to do their best to make the Indian team's stay comfortable. Ultimately, a tolerable arrangement was made and India played the Test.

Pakistan was convinced that such treatment would sooner or later have its effect on the morale of the touring side. On the contrary, the Indians became more determined and decided not to allow such incidents to get the better of them. It was now unacceptable to lose to Pakistan as national pride was at stake.

Since the Test was played on coir matting, the pitch did not need any inspection, but there was something missing in the ground. After plenty of deliberation, Amarnath found that there was no boundary rope or line drawn. Instead, flags were pitched all round the ground. When he pointed out the mistake, the secretary said, "Oh! We forgot," and then got the marking of the boundary completed. India batted first and made a slow, modest 235, thanks to the half-centuries by Vijay Manjrekar, Gulab Ramchand and Naren Tamane. Pakistan, in return, started solidly but Polly Umrigar bowled a magic spell to curtail the home team from gaining a substantial lead and Pakistan declared their innings at 313 for nine. The Indian second innings fared much better with Pankaj Roy and Punjabi giving the side a good start and Manjrekar chipping in with another half-century.

Frustrated with the resolute Indian batting, Kardar became desperate. He took the second new ball and instructed his bowlers to aim at the bodies of the Indian batsmen. "Nine fielders, including the wicket-keeper were positioned on the leg-side and a solitary cover fielder making the eleventh man. Khan Mohammad and Mohammed Hussain bowled at least four bouncers on the coir matting aimed at the batsmen's body, similar to the Bodyline tactics adopted by England captain Douglas Jardine in Australia."

Surprisingly, the umpires watched the proceedings without interfering. Perhaps, they had been instructed by the officials to allow any tactics that Kardar felt necessary to achieve his goal of victory, even if it contravened the laws and the spirit of the game. "It is unfortunate that cricket is not played in the right spirit," Amarnath wrote in his tour diary. Despite these efforts, the match ended in a draw.

The third Test in Lahore brought smiles to the faces of all Indian batsmen as they were finally playing on a turf wicket. Since Lahore was Amarnath's erstwhile hometown, many of his admirers and friends came to meet him. Each meeting brought along memories of childhood and youth and loads of nostalgia. Nazar Mohammad also came one evening to pay his respects in the hotel. On seeing his old friend, Amarnath enquired, "Why aren't you playing cricket any more?"

In reply to this Nazar requested if he could recite a few couplets from Mirza Ghalib's poetry. Not knowing what to say, Amarnath said, "As you please." Nazar recited, *"Ishq nay Ghalib nikamma kar diya, warna hum bhi aadmi thay kaam kay* (Love made me hopeless, otherwise, I was a person of some worth). On re-turning from India, I met Noor Jahan (the famous actress and singer from Pakistan) at one of the parties. I was smitten by her looks and wanted to marry her but she refused. I followed her and called her regularly at her place but couldn't speak to her. One night I climbed to her second floor bedroom with the help of a pipe to speak to her. Seeing me in her room, she panicked and screamed. Six-foot tall Pathans, stationed for her security, came to her rescue. I knew if caught, they would beat me up without mercy. To avoid that beating, I jumped from the second floor but broke an arm and a leg. The injury forced me to give up cricket." Amarnath consoled his friend and termed the event as a hand of destiny.

The series exposed Kardar's and several of his team-mates' inferiority complex by their behaviour both on and off the field. The Pakistan captain had a number of arguments with Amarnath on the tour when he tried to run the Test match his way. Unable to forget these clashes, Kardar thought of teaching the Indian manager a lesson in Lahore. It was the wrong place to pick as Amarnath was treated with great respect in Lahore. Since he was coming back after a long gap, he was invited by his old friends for dinners and get-togethers. Hearing that Amarnath was attending these dinners alone, one evening Kardar arranged for three tall and well-built Pathans to accompany him.

As soon as Amarnath walked into the lobby of the hotel, he saw an inebriated Kardar walking menacingly towards him, closely followed by the Pathans. His instinct warned him of impending danger. Standing at eye level Kardar said, "You have been talking a lot. Now that you are in Pakistan let me see if you behave the same way." Without any provocation, Kardar tried to slap Amarnath with the back of his hand. Amarnath evaded the attack but Kardar managed to hit Amarnath's tie. Infuriated by this action, Amarnath realised attack was the best method of defence. He caught hold of Kardar by his collar and, before his escorts or anyone in the lobby could react, slapped him a number of times. This unexpected retaliation caught everyone by surprise and they intervened to separate the angry Amarnath from Kardar. Once done, the humiliated Pakistan captain was escorted to his room. In the lobby, the hotel staff and some Pakistani players present, along with the Pathans, profusely apologised to Amarnath for the ugly scene and blamed Kardar's condition for the incident.

Having tackled major problems, Amarnath faced another from within the team in Lahore before the third Test. As per his instructions, all the players were required to be in their rooms by 10 p.m. and leaving the premises after the restricted hours meant taking chances with the manager. Close to Hotel Faletti, where the Indians had been accommodated, was a place in Anarkali Bazaar where nautch girls performed the *mujra*. Amarnath kept a strict watch and checked each room personally at 11 p.m. On the first night, some players sneaked out to Anarkali Bazaar at midnight. But the secret could hardly be kept as word spread that Indian players were seen at a *mujra*. Amarnath was angry and felt cheated.

He was not the kind who would give up easily. As these players took a *tonga* (horse carriage) and bought *paan* (betel leaf) from the shop across the street from the hotel, Amarnath recruited two 'spies' to follow them. Spy no.1 was the *tongawala* and spy no. 2 was the *paanwala*. They were both promised a handsome reward if they helped catch these players red-handed. One evening, he was informed of his players' activities and followed them to the place of entertainment. Some of the Indian players sat inside, sprawled on the mattress and enjoying the dance like nawabs. As they sat with their back towards the entrance, they did not see Amarnath make his entry. When he said loudly, "Well done, my boys", those players literally froze. Without uttering another word, he left and so did the nocturnal birds. No words were exchanged the following day about the drama from the night before. Henceforth, none took another chance with him.

No one knew better than Amarnath that proper sleep was essential to rejuvenate the body just as much as overeating at lunch could have a devastating effect on a player's reflexes. During the matches, he would serve lunch to the players like a father but none complained. His commitment to the welfare of the team knew no bounds. For him, losing to Pakistan was an affront, which he could not digest.

There is an old saying that problems come uninvited. He realised that when he had plenty of problems on the tour. A very prominent member of the team from Bombay got involved with a girl named Begum Laghari in Lahore. Initially, Amarnath thought it was a casual fling, which would end soon. But it turned out to be much more. This player was seen constantly in this girl's company, leading to many embarrassing rumours. During the Lahore Test, he would often take out his hanky flamboyantly and wave at the pavilion where she sat. Begum Laghari would reciprocate the gesture with a smile. The situation became alarming. She even started calling him at Montgomery from Lahore. Once, just a few minutes before he went in to bat, he received a call and took it in a separate room. That evening, Amarnath decided to have a chat with that player in his room and seek an explanation. "To my surprise, this player had already made up his mind to marry her. Startled though I was, I still asked him, 'How could you marry her? Firstly, you are already married and secondly, she is a Muslim and you are a Hindu'. He said he was ready to change his religion," Amarnath recalled. No amount of dissuasion had any effect on his infatuated heart. After a long discussion, Amarnath convinced him that it would be improper to marry her while he represented India. If he wished to marry her, he was free to do what he deemed fit after the tour was over and he returned to India. He could then come back to Pakistan and fulfil his dream. Fortunately, the infatuation evaporated once the player returned to Bombay.

The Wagah border was opened for the Indian fans to watch the match at Lahore and cheer their team. To facilitate easy access, Indian fans were allowed to travel to and from Amritsar each day without any hindrance. The wicket was on the slower side, which made Indian spinners toil hard to achieve breakthroughs. Despite this handicap, Subhas Gupte bowled a marathon spell of 73 overs to claim five for 133 and not once did he falter in line or length. It was truly a magnificent display of concentration and the sign of a world class bowler. The Test hardly produced any spark except in the case of debutant Miran Bux, who bowled his deliveries bending his arm more often than keeping it straight. The teams played safe and the match ended in another draw.

From Lahore, the team travelled to Sialkot and then to the cooler climes of Rawalpindi to face a Services XI. Amarnath was doing a marvellous job as manager. With so many fixtures packed in the itinerary and quite a few players on the list of injured, skipper Vinoo Mankad and his deputy Polly Umrigar requested the manager to play this match. Amarnath accepted the offer and performed exceeding well at an age of forty-three scoring 45 and 54 not out and capturing three wickets to prove his immense capabilities. Finding their manager in good nick, Mankad and Umrigar requested him to play the fourth Test. Amused and slightly tickled, he thanked them for considering him good enough to play for India but declined the offer by saying, "If I had to continue playing Tests, I wouldn't have retired in 1952."

The fourth Test was played on a dusty wicket in Peshawar. One look at the wicket convinced Amarnath that India with its strong spin attack, was better placed. He predicted that India might decide the fate of the series in her favour here. Pakistan won the toss and batted first. Once the spinners, Mankad, Ghulam Ahmed and Gupte came on the scene, batting became difficult. Gupte bowled splendidly again and had another five-wicket haul to demolish the strong Pakistani batting for 188. Pakistan's advantage of winning the toss was lost. Initially, the Indian innings also didn't fare well as the openers fell within 44 runs. At this stage, Umrigar and Manjrekar defied the Pakistan attack to take India to 103 for two. Finding the game slipping from his grasp, Kardar resorted to the negative theory and asked Mahmood Hussain to bowl wide outside the leg stump of the batsmen with eight fielders and the wicket-keeper on the leg side. So wide were several deliveries that batsmen found it impossible to reach them or to make any contact. It was a pathetic display from the home side skipper, who in his speech in Dacca had boasted that Pakistan believed in playing attractive and positive cricket.

Amarnath wrote in his diary: "It is fun to note when the ball goes to mid-on, fielders throw it to the keeper, who in turn tosses it to the point fielder and then to the bowler. All this while the batsman stood ready to face the next delivery." The time-wasting tactics clearly demonstrated the desperation of the Pakistan team, especially Kardar. The prospect of losing to India in Pakistan haunted him. It seemed that Amarnath's prediction was coming true.

The Pakistan captain's spirit reached its lowest ebb when Manjrekar moved away from his stumps due to a movement behind the bowler's arm. Instead of stopping, Kardar released the ball and shattered the stumps. The excited bowler jumped with joy only to find the batsman standing firmly near his crease. He then appealed to the umpire who correctly declared the ball dead and negated the appeal. "It was in bad taste watching Kardar appealing for clean bowled," Amarnath wrote in his diary. "With each run scored, the Pakistan team invented new methods of wasting time. The cover fielder wanted a particular car parked outside the ground to be removed because of the glare. Having got that done, Imtiaz complained of finger pain and a doctor was summoned to check his injury. On both occasions, precious time was wasted. Still, the game had to start and it did with a few more tactics. At 186 for four, Khan Mohammad bowled to Umrigar batting on 99, so wide his leg stump that the embarrassed umpire had to reluctantly signal wide four runs. Polly soon completed a fine century. It was perhaps one of the best innings against such negative bowling."

India gained a lead of 57 runs with a day and a half remaining. On the fourth day, the ball was spinning viciously and Pakistan was reeling at 70 for four. At this point, victory seemed within sight. Suddenly, Mankad decided to go on the defensive when Masood launched an attack. Before this, the Indian captain had blundered early in the morning by offering the new and hard ball to Gupte instead of off-spinner Ghulam Ahmed, who had captured a vital wicket the previous evening. Going defensive meant removing psychological pressure off the rival. "By 1.45 pm, Pakistan had scored only 131 for four when India decided to open the field to save runs instead of going for the kill. Mankad was bowling with a lonely slip, deep cover, deep point, short third-man, deep mid-off, deep mid-on, deep mid-wicket, short fine-leg and a silly mid-on," Amarnath noted. It looked as though India, and not Pakistan, was trying to save the match. "On a turning track," wrote Amarnath, "India could have bowled out Pakistan twice in a day and a half but thanks to Mankad, Pakistan saved the Test." Shuffling his bowlers and playing on the defensive, Amarnath knew India was losing the advantage but Mankad had other ideas. In his desire to capture wickets himself, he kept Ghulam Ahmed away from the attack. The match petered out in a draw and

Amarnath was livid. He knew India had missed a golden opportunity of registering a convincing victory.

After the match, Amarnath asked Ghulam Ahmed as to why he had not bowled. Ghulam Ahmed told him that Mankad had asked him if he could bowl on the fourth day with his little finger still bruised. The off-spinner told him that he was okay and would not mind bowling. But Mankad replied, "Why take a chance? There is another Test to play." Poor Ghulam Ahmed did not bowl a single over on the fourth day of the Test, cooling his heels in the deep. "If he could field, then he could bowl, too," wrote Amarnath in his diary. Ghulam bowled for analysis of 13-9-9-1 in Pakistan's second innings compared to Mankad's 54 and Gupte's 35 overs each.

Happy that Pakistan did not lose the Test, the Rotary Club hosted a dinner for the teams. Unable to conceal his joy, Kardar boastfully challenged the Indians to win the last Test in Karachi. This remark was actually directed at Amarnath who had predicted an Indian victory in Peshawar but had not succeeded. Amarnath laughed heartily and dismissed Kardar's behaviour as childish.

After a gap of almost two weeks, the teams reached Karachi for the final battle. Realising his mistakes in Lahore and for the remarks at Peshawar, Kardar sent feelers to Amarnath to forget those incidents. Amarnath had known Kardar quite well since both had played for the united All India team in England in 1946 and accepted the Pakistan captain's invitation for tea. "I entered the room and occupied the sofa with my back towards the door," Amarnath recalled. "After a while, someone knocked on the door and entered and wished Kardar. He then said, 'Any instruction for tomorrow's game, skipper?' I turned my head to see who it was. The man was none other than Idris Baig, one of the umpires named for the last Test. 'What kind of an instruction do you want?' I said. Seeing me, Baig rushed out but the great plan to defeat India had been revealed. I looked at Kardar, who was visibly shaken. I bid him farewell and returned."

Late in the evening, after a great deal of deliberation, Amarnath summoned the Pakistan Board officials. By now word had already reached them of the *faux pas*. Amarnath conveyed in no uncertain terms that Baig would not be acceptable. If Pakistan insisted on retaining him, India would boycott the match. The officials tried to convince Amarnath that there had been some misunderstanding but he refused to budge. The officials panicked and tried looking for an alternate umpire but none seemed available at such short notice. It was almost past midnight and no solution was in sight. Finally, one official said jokingly, "We have one qualified first-class umpire — our selector Masood Salauddin — but you will not accept him." To everyone's delight and relief, Amarnath agreed and accepted him to officiate. This was probably the only instance in the history of world cricket where a home team selector officiated as umpire. Being a good judge of men, Amarnath knew that this selector would not be overawed by Kardar. "Salauddin gave Kardar out stumped when his individual score was 93. No other Pakistan umpire would have dared given him out," Amarnath recalled.

The newly-laid turf wicket played tricks from the word go. Some balls kept low while others sailed over the heads of the batsmen. It was a nightmarish experience for the batsmen. Pakistan could muster only 182 runs and India 145. It was a strip where batsmen danced to the wicket's tune rather than the bowler's abilities. It seemed that the match would be complete within three days. But the wicket suddenly started behaving like a sleeping beauty. Amarnath told the local officials and groundstaff, "I have played enough cricket in my life to know that no wicket can change its character so drastically as this one. Perhaps, it was ill and the local doctor improved its condition by giving a few doses in the night!" Realising their doctoring of the wicket lay exposed, without delay, the officials dispersed in all directions to avoid Amarnath. Batting was suddenly easy and Pakistan played a majority of the time to ensure another draw.

Amarnath was a happy man. To come back undefeated from Pakistan, against all odds, was a moral victory for India.

ELEVEN

POLITICS IN THE BCCI

I F CRICKET kept Lala Amarnath satisfied, life off the field was getting a bit frustrating. Like other riyasats (kingdoms), Patiala state after Partition merged into a larger state called Pepsu. With job prospects becoming bleak, he moved to Kanpur to assist his in-laws in their business but soon got bored. His heart lay in cricket, so he joined the Maharani Amrit Kaur Sports Scheme as director. Despite being away from Patiala, he remained Southern Punjab Cricket Association secretary. However, in 1958, he had not only resigned as Southern Punjab Cricket Association secretary but also severed his relations with Punjab cricket.

While attending a meeting of the Board, Northern Railway General Manager Karnail Singh asked him to join the Railways as a class one officer but on the condition that he would get the Railways affiliated to the BCCI. Amarnath did convince the Board to grant the Railways affiliation but realised that the Railways would not stick to its promise. At the Board's annual general meeting in 1960, the Railways also back-stabbed him by voting against him. Amarnath felt cheated.

Yet, his contribution to Indian cricket both as a player and an administrator remains unsurpassed. He had a sharp tongue but an open heart, ever ready to help deserving cricketers, irrespective of domicile. No doubt, he is remembered as a short-tempered person, but he did not carry a grouse after expressing his feelings. Amarnath was misunderstood most of the time. He was not a sycophant but an honest man with integrity. His refusal to be cowed down by his superiors led to controversies but his knowledge of the game and uncanny vision helped him to spot raw talent from various parts of the country.

In 1957, Amarnath went to Hyderabad to run a camp for prospective Indian cricketers while working for the Maharani Amrit Kaur Sports Scheme. The cream of Hyderabad talent had assembled there. One of the local officials whispered to Amarnath that Hyderabad had already produced a Test cricketer in the making. He was shown a lean boy. "So you are the cricketer everyone is talking about," Amarnath told him. "Let me also see your potential." Then he watched this cricketer in a torturous two and a half hour session. The youngster batted against four bowlers, including Amarnath, but missed the evening session and did not turn up the next day as well. When he did return, he complained of a back pain. Amarnath advised him various exercises to strengthen his back muscles and corrected a few minor faults. The cricketer was none other than M L Jaisimha.

Jaisimha not only served India for a long time but also became a role model for many cricketers, including Sunil Gavaskar. Another young cricketer who attended the camp was P R Mansingh, and later went on to become secretary of the Hyderabad Cricket Association. "Lalaji was about forty-six years old and we had two groups. The sessions would start with running and exercises before nets. Lalaji trained with the boys both in the morning and in the afternoon and also bowled in the nets. It was amazing to see him bowl holding two balls in his left hand and one in his right for bowling to avoid any delay. Each of his delivery was pitched at perfect length," remembered Mansingh.

Lala Amarnath's time as chairman of the Selection Committee was a period in which he tried to change the attitude of the selectors and get players to be chosen on merit and not because of their allegiance to a particular zone. For the only time in the annals of Indian cricket, the selectors' chairman played first-class cricket, hunted for talent and undertook coaching assignments all over the country. "I felt it easier to judge the potential of the players while being in their midst rather than watching the proceedings from the pavilion," he said.

The classic example of Budhi Kunderan speaks volumes of his farsightedness. Amarnath did not know the young cricketer personally but was impressed by his batting and wicket-keeping while he played for Western Railway in an inter-Railway match. Amarnath believed in the qualities he saw in Kunderan and congratulated him on his performance. Then, as chairman of selectors, he told Kunderan to visit the Board's official tailor. The puzzled youngster did not understand what Amarnath meant. Amarnath understood his dilemma and said, "You are selected. Go to the shop and give your measurement before I change my mind." Amarnath's clout in the Selection Committee can be seen from the fact that the other selectors accepted his inclusion and Kunderan played for India with distinction. He was probably the first cricketer to have played for India before figuring in a first-class match.

The selection of the right players gave him immense satisfaction. In 1958, when the West Indies toured India for the second time, the series produced ordinary performances from the Indians, resulting in quite a few controversial changes. The Selection Committee comprising Lala Amarnath (chairman), Dutta Ray from the east, L P Jai from the west and C Ramaswamy from the south was in total disarray. Much to his exasperation, the others tried to push their own favourites in the team. He had a tough time keeping them together on quite a few occasions. But at times, he also reacted like other people did. On quite a few earlier occasions, his brusque nature got Amarnath entangled in many an unwanted controversy with the establishment, but each time he came out unscathed. Now being part of the setup, he faced flak from within the Board for his uncompromising attitude while picking the Indian team. Every meeting was stormy and once an undeserving candidate was rejected, the interested selector complained of his inflexible attitude. On other occasions, if there was a deadlock over a particular player, he used a casting vote as 'chairman' to break it. All this led to quite a few heartburns.

At no stage did he promote an unsuitable cricketer from his state or try to hide any weakness of the players whose names he proposed. His was a frank and crystal clear opinion in case of a deadlock to ensure smooth functioning of the selection committee.

When the selectors met to nominate the captain, Jai and Ramaswamy favoured Polly Umrigar and later Pankaj Roy but Dutta Ray the selector did not agree with their views. Instead, he proposed the name of Ghulam Ahmed, the senior-most player with an excellent record. He had won the series against Commonwealth XI and proved his class as a fine off-spin bowler and a good captain. He was unanimously elected to lead India against New Zealand but, unfortunately, due to an injury and illness he could not fulfill his obligations after the first Test. Ramaswamy was not interested in Ghulam Ahmed's record and even objected to his inclusion in the team. Amarnath seconded Ghulam Ahmed's name to make it two against two. It was a deadlock. Amarnath then used the casting vote provided to the chairman for such occasions in Ghulam Ahmed's favour. Later this action became a bone of contention. "The situation demanded its use to settle the issue and moreover, it was meant to be used and not put in a picture frame and hung on the wall," he said.

The following day when the Selection Committee met to select the rest of the team, the question of the opening slot was raised. Much to the chairman's disbelief, Ramaswamy and Jai did not want Pankaj Roy in the team. Amarnath found it curious that the same selectors did a *volte face* in Roy's case. "Only yesterday they found him worthy of leading India and today, he cannot find a place in their team," Amarnath wrote in his diary. Amarnath objected to such inconsistent attitude and asked Dutta Ray for his views on the delicate issue. The Bengal selector strongly recommended Roy as he was India's premier opening batsman after Mankad. Once again a deadlock appeared, creating an unpleasant atmosphere. Unable to convince Jai and Ramaswamy that Roy was not suitable for captaincy but was a deserving opening batsman, Amarnath once again used casting vote in favour of Roy. This move proved Jai and Ramaswamy incorrect when Pankaj Roy was the most consistent Indian opener in the series.

A week before the first Test in Bombay, Ghulam Ahmed declared himself unfit due to a knee injury sustained in a match in Hyderabad. After all the efforts by Amarnath, it was an anti-climax. He cabled the BCCI assistant secretary suggesting Manohar Hardikar's name as a player to take Ghulam Amhed's place as off-spinner. But much to his displeasure, Bombay left-arm spinner Bapu Nadkarni's name appeared in the papers the next day.

Since no vice-captain had been decided at the Ahmedabad meeting and all the selectors returned to their respective zones, West Zone selector Jai made the unilateral decision of declaring Umrigar captain of India for the Bombay Test. The chairman or the other selectors were not even informed, let alone consulted. Two days before the match, another player dropped out because of illness. With the situation already volatile, Jai aggravated it further by now including Hardikar in the team. These actions tantamounted to bypassing the authority of the chairman and Amarnath was not amused.

He reached Bombay, hoping Jai would clarify the decisions before he himself reacted. Sensing fireworks, Jai avoided talking to Amarnth and the other selectors, preferring to be alone in the pavilion while his colleagues sat in a reserved Committee Box on all five days.

After the match was over, the selectors assembled to pick the team for the next Test at Kanpur. The atmosphere in the room was charged and required only a spark to explode. Jai, who was suffering from high blood pressure looked agitated as he walked into the room. At the very onset of the meeting, Amarnath questioned Jai's wisdom by not seeking chairman's permission before filling the vacancy of the captain. Jai adopted an aggressive attitude. He justified his actions by stating that it was within his jurisdiction to select anyone he wished, as he was the only selector available in Bombay. But Jai forgot that there was still time before the Test commenced. Amarnath objected to such an attitude and declared that such actions were unconstitutional. Moreover, he said that Jai had no power to take such an important decision alone and make it public as well. Having been caught on the wrong foot with no support coming from his colleagues, Jai found the situation too hot to handle. In a fit of anger, he picked up his papers, pushed his chair back with his legs and shouted, "Get lost!" before he left the room in a huff.

Knowing Amarnath's uncontrollable temper, Dutta Ray and Ramaswamy pacified him and severely criticised Jai's action. They requested him to ignore Jai's outburst. But they all felt very strongly against this display of arrogance and also his action of not informing the chairman before filling the vacancy. Though the last action was tantamount to an open revolt and disrespect to the chair, on his colleagues' request, Amarnath did not inform the Board president. It was a grave mistake on his part. Realising the gravity of the situation and the blunder committed, Jai wrote to the Board president, alleging that the chairman had used foul language during the meeting. To keep this delicate matter from blowing out of proportion, the BCCI president made an inquiry but found the charges untrue. The selectors and the captain Ghulam Ahmed vouched that the chairman used no such language.

Later, it became evident to everyone that Jai, a nominee of the Bombay Cricket Association, was desperate to display his loyalty to the state by selecting as many players as possible compared to Contractor (CCI nominee), even if it meant going about it the wrong way. "It was unfortunate that the Associations (Bombay vs CCI) dragged (the) Selection Committee into their dirty politics, in an effort to settle personal scores," Amarnath said. With Ghulam Ahmed reporting fit and no arguments in the selection of the team, everything fell in place. India dominated the Kanpur Test for two and a half days and Gupte produced another astonishing spell of nine for 102 runs but India enigmatically collapsed in the second innings to give the touring side its first victory.

This result brought pressure on both the captain and the selectors. Before selecting the team for the next Test, Dutta Ray and Ramaswamy approached Amarnath to forget the unpleasant episode in Bombay. Amarnath assured his colleagues that as far as he was concerned, the chapter was closed and forgotten. They felt if proper representation was given to all the zones, it would project the committee's good image. Immediately, Amarnath's concurrence was sent to the Board president, who too was anxious to bring about a re-conciliation between two former players. Regular correspondence between the Board president and Jai began. The Bombay selector remained adamant, not participating in the selection meetings or even resigning. Several reports appeared in the Bombay newspapers pointing fingers at Amarnath, holding him responsible for Jai's boycott and unhealthy atmosphere in the Selection Committee. Amarnath decided to ignore these articles in the interest of the game and the country's image as the West Indies team was still in India.

The third Test in Calcutta also went in favour of the West Indies as Wesley Hall and Roy Gilchrist ripped apart the Indian batting. The bowling too was not as effective as Gupte's 'rabbit', Rohan Kanhai, scored a double century. The Calcutta crowd was not amused by India's innocuous spirit. Ghulam Ahmed was ineffective with his bowling and he came in for special treatment. To add to his woes, the spectators also were critical of his leadership. This demoralised the Indian skipper and he resigned.

The loss of the captain and two defeats in a row forced selectors to meet at 10.30 p.m. to finalise the team for the fourth Test in Madras. Since Umrigar had led India successfully in the first Test in Ghulam Ahmed's absence, he became an obvious choice as captain. Then Ramaswamy proposed the name of A G Kripal Singh and C D Gopinath for the Madras Test. It was a smart move to get his players in the team on two accounts. First, India was struggling with its batting and required changes and second, the south had had no representation in the team. It seemed a fair request but in the same breath he dropped a bombshell by demanding Ghulam's exclusion from the team. It was harsh on the Hyderabad spinner, who, despite dislocating his bowling finger, tried his best. Dutta Ray furiously objected to such a lopsided suggestion. After a prolonged discussion, Kripal Singh was not considered as he was no patch on Ghulam Ahmed as an off-spinner, though he was a better batsman. A few days before the Test, Ghulam Ahmed conveyed his inability to play due to personal reasons.

To add to the confusion, Vijay Manjrekar reported unfit with an injury. Everything seemed to be turning topsy turvy in the Indian camp. With players falling out like dry autumn leaves, the BCCI honorary secretary approached Umrigar and conveyed the BCCI president's desire to accommodate Jasu Patel as off-spinner but Umrigar was impressed with P Sengupta and insisted that a batsman would be replaced only by another batsman. It was a house in total disarray where personal preference took precedence over the country's honour. The brief tiff between the Indian captain and the secretary created unnecessary complications and headache for the Selection Committee when Umrigar resigned after the Civic dinner on the eve of the Test. Panic-stricken Board officials requested him to reconsider his decision but he refused. Fortunately, Vinoo Mankad had been included in this Test after his dispute with the BCCI over his pay had been sorted out and he was approached to lead India. Chandu Borde was originally announced 12th man but made it to the side when Gopinath opted out because of injury. India lost this match and the series and with it, followed criticism of the Selection Committee. Critics blamed the panel for India's dismal performance whereas the fault lay with the players, who conveyed their inability to play at the last minute because of injury. Then, India fielded three captains in four Tests due to circumstances beyond the selectors' control.

As the last Test in Delhi was only of academic consequence, the Selection Committee took a bold decision to build a team for the future with an eye on the England tour and also find another captain. Jai had pushed his candidate in the beginning, Ramaswamy in Madras and now it was logical that Dutta Ray would do the same in the last Test and he did, when he proposed Mankad's name, hoping for a favourable response from the chairman. To his surprise, Amarnath rejected the proposal on the grounds that India needed a positive captain. He had observed Mankad closely during the Pakistan tour in 1954 and was dissatisfied. Amarnath, for the first time, proposed Ramchand's name, which Ramaswamy seconded but a sulking Dutta Ray took it as an affront and refused to accept it. Both Ramaswamy and he tried their best to convince him that there was nothing personal but failed. Unable to proceed further due to Dutta Ray's uncompromising attitude, a unanimous decision could not be reached on Ramchand. To make matters worse, Ramaswamy withdrew his support for Ramchand and asked for another name. But Dutta Ray stuck to his choice — "Vinoo or none." Since the discussion was leading nowhere, Amarnath proposed Hemu Adhikari's name. Ramaswamy agreed but again Dutta Ray would not budge. Ignoring him, Adhikari was nominated for the Delhi Test. This Test produced the best performance from the entire team and Adhikari did a reasonable job as captain.

The Delhi Test also resurrected Borde, whom all the selectors except Amarnath wanted to drop from the team due to poor form. Amarnath knew Borde was talented and wanted him to play. He tried to convince his colleagues that Borde may have struggled but it was a matter of time before he would be amongst the runs. But one selector felt that enough chances had been given to him already. Amarnath understood better than most the predicament of the players. After a great deal of argument, he convinced his colleagues to give Borde a chance in Delhi. Amarnath knew Borde's confidence was at its lowest ebb, hence, any advice could become counter-productive. Instead, he acted like a psychologist and boosted his morale by stating that he was a certainty for the England tour in the summer of 1959. "Play your natural game and enjoy batting," he told Borde. These words gave Borde's sagging confidence a great fillip, transformed his approach and he scored 109 in the first innings and 96 in the second. This exhibition gave tremendous satisfaction to Amarnath as he had just saved a cricketer's neck from the sacrificial altar. At no stage did he take any credit for prolonging Borde's career. As a matter of fact, he gave credit to Borde's temperament and will-power.

Despite being chairman of the Selection Committee, he donned his flannels whenever he found time to play the Ranji Trophy and there was never a dull moment. The matches between Railways and Services were keenly contested. The Services captain Adhikari knew this. He had learnt many aspects of captaincy watching Amarnath on the tour of Australia and thought himself at par with his former skipper. Since Adhikari could not play this important fixture, he instructed the stand-in captain to follow his instruction regarding 'the roller' very carefully. "If Amarnath takes the heavy roller, then opt for light or vice versa." Amarnath was amused when he heard of these instructions. To put his junior player in place, he did not opt for any roller, sending the confused Services captain scrambling for a phone for instructions in the middle of a match. Amarnath had a hearty laugh.

Amarnath did not have any time to take a breather when the Selection Committee assembled to pick an Indian team for the England tour. Since India had done badly, Ramaswamy thought it to be an appropriate time to seek his pound of flesh and tried to push his players into the team. When this failed, he started creating problems in the selection of players that he did not get along with. Being out-voted, he blamed Amarnath and depicted him as a fastidious dictator who rode roughshod over the others. "It was unfortunate to see him pushing his favourites and when I questioned their credentials, I was projected as a villain. I only had good intentions and the welfare of the country in my heart and this was the reason I objected when I felt a deserving player was missing the chance," Amarnath remembered.

The performance of the Indian players against the West Indies fell well below his expectations, which gave disgruntled members of the Board a chance to start a malicious campaign against his functioning. Bombay used the services of the local media, especially A F S Talyarkhan and V L Raman, to tarnish his image through a series of articles. The confidential discussions of the Selection Committee reached these people and they added their own flavour without bothering to ask him for his version. Plenty of fingers were pointed at Amarnath and he was made the scapegoat for playing with the image of the Indian captain. Yet, he kept quiet since the articles lacked substance or conviction. But soon, he realised the effect they were having on the public opinion. He called a press conference to put the facts before everyone to judge, whether he was guilty or innocent.

Giving his version to the press he said: "I did not wish to bring this issue of my controversy in public but the unprecedented statement of C Ramaswamy confronted me to the confidence of the sporting public, to first place my cards on the table. No doubt, it is in bad taste, but my reputation has been hammered by certain interested and frustrated critics, particularly A F S Talyarkhan and V L Raman. They are very famous for their integrity and knowledge of the game. Those who have studied the situation will realise that a lot of mud was thrown at me, of course, with selfish motives. This, unfortunately, came out at the time of selection of a manager, in which lots of top-ranking politicians were involved, taking personal interest and even making false propaganda against me. It is rather difficult to understand why suddenly a campaign started against me this year. As a matter of fact, I have been occupying the chair of the head of the Selection Committee for the last four years. If the team's defeat is my responsibility because we could not win a Test match against the West Indies, then let me say that India has won five Test matches so far since 1932. Two against

Pakistan (1952) under my captaincy, two against New Zealand under Umrigar (under my chairmanship) and one against MCC under Hazare."

The Selection Committee was hoping that their problem of finding a captain was over with Adhikari doing a reasonable job but Ramaswamy conveyed to Amarnath that Adhikari had expressed his inability to tour England. The decision surprised everyone but they could not force a player to play for the country. "We all agreed that India needed a young and dynamic leader to serve India's cause for years to come." Ramaswamy proposed Gaekwad's name, seconded by Dutta Ray. "Since the choice was of the majority, there was nothing I could do and I accepted their choice." According to tradition, in case of difference of opinion among the selectors, the captain became a co-opted member and his suggestions were accepted. Fourteen players were selected unanimously without any debate. When the discussion turned to picking an off-spinner, Dutta Ray proposed Ghulam Ahmed's name. Ramaswamy objected and threatened to leave the meeting if the Hyderabad spinner was considered. Amarnath tried to pacify the agitated Ramaswamy and showed him the letter Ghulam Ahmed had sent, offering his services in any capacity. It would be wise to include him, considering his potential and the conditions prevailing in England but Ramaswamy was in no mood to oblige. Unable to persuade him, Dutta Ray asked Gaekwad for his suggestion and the captain agreed with him and Amarnath. It was a different story that Ghulam Ahmed backed out yet again and sealed his fate forever. If Ramaswamy had acted obstinately, then Dutta Ray stuck to Milkha Singh when the choice fell between him and J M Ghorpade. To avoid any unpleasantness, Amarnath asked Gaekwad to once again give his frank opinion. The captain preferred Ghorpade and Ramaswamy seconded his name. Under these extraordinary circumstances, Amarnath had done a remarkable job and performed his duties without any malice or favour towards anyone. But he forgot that in trying to pursue the role of a referee, he had offended both his colleagues for not toeing their line at some time or the other.

Finding the situation favourable, some former players took pot shots at the ruling group, including Lala Amarnath and the Board president. These opportunists ran from pillar to post to eject him and others from their positions in the BCCI. The scenario resembled a contest for a seat to a Legislative Assembly where the end — and not the means — take precedence. Duleep Sinhji's critical articles against Amarnath in Australia led to his team boycotting him on the tour but at this moment Vizzy projected him as the sole maharaja of cricket, capable of improving cricket at all levels and fit to take over the reins of the Board as its president. Vijay Merchant too, canvassed hard for himself but received no positive response in his endeavour. It was a war of words fired to dislodge Amarnath. He retaliated in a similar manner, showing his opponents in poor light. Amarnath questioned Duleep Sinhji's contribution to Indian cricket and his reluctance to play for India in the early 1930s, which clearly demonstrated his lack of true patriotic feelings towards his motherland. Once this fact was brought to light, whatever little support he had garnered, vanished. Then directing a salvo at Merchant, he said, "Suddenly, Merchant has become an aggressive critic, though he was the most defensive batsman in his whole life." Merchant found Amarnath too strong to oppose, so instead decided to fight for the post of honorary secretary. But with no base in the Board, he could harness little support and finally withdrew from the contest.

With the selection formalities over, Amarnath was tipped to be the manager of the Indian team for the tour of England. Everyone agreed that he was tailor-made for the job because of his first hand knowledge of the conditions in England. Unfortunately, the series against West Indies had been disastrous. Since he headed the Selection Committee everyone blamed him. "My critics blamed me for everything. When the batting failed, the chairman was held responsible and when the bowlers did not strike, the chairman's intelligence came into question," he remarked. The Board was divided and Amarnath's adversaries proposed the name of a little-known North Zone player for the manager's post. This meant a contest whereas Amarnath wanted to be elected unanimously. Then came the disturbing news that some politicians had assured his antagonists that even if he romped home in the contest, he would be denied his passport. The Board politics had reached its nadir. Cornered but not defeated, he played a masterstroke and pulled the rug from under his rivals' feet when he proposed Fatehsinh Rao Gaekwad

— Maharaja of Baroda — as manager. It was a moral victory for him but India missed his experience and advice dearly when it was struggling in England.

The dismal performance in England made the Board realise its blunder of not sending him as manager. Amarnath retained his post as chairman with a thumping majority. He got busy preparing India to face Richie Benaud's team that was to tour India in 1959. The glorious moment came at Kanpur. Amarnath reached Kanpur a day before the game and saw some loose spots at the good length spot. Knowing the Australians' weakness against off-spin, he wanted Jasu Patel to play. Amarnath needed the captain's concurrence to include Patel in the team. He spoke to the India skipper Ramchand but received no positive reply. "Later in the evening, I called the Indian captain to my room and said, 'Ram, do you know that you have been nominated to lead India for only two Tests. I am sure you would like to continue as captain for the rest of the series'." The polite reminder was good enough and Ramchand agreed to Patel's inclusion.

When Australia batted, Amarnath was confounded as his trump card had proved ineffective. He realised Patel was bowling from the wrong end. Immediately, he sent a message across to the captain and Patel was brought from the other end. Patel was unplayable after this. He stunned the Australians and won the match singlehandedly, taking nine for 69 in the first innings and five for 55 in the second to give India her first victory against Australia. The entire nation rejoiced in this sweet victory and the president of India decorated Jasu Patel with the Padma Shri. Amarnath's intuition and analysis had paid rich dividends.

TWELVE

POLITICS & EXPERT IN MEDIA

C RICKET ALLOWED Lala Amarnath to rub shoulders with viceroys, governors-general, maharajas, Nawabs and politicians in his heyday. They discussed a variety of subjects, including cricket and politics. Like most Indians, he too presumed that the British Empire would last forever. But with each passing year, he noticed a rise in nationalism and its effect on the British. He had numerous opportunities to listen to intense political discussions between the viceroy and the royalty, emphasising their superiority and indispensibility. These deliberations always concluded on a sour note when the Congress and its leaders figured in the discussions. Amarnath was a great admirer of Mahatma Gandhi. He often wondered if a soft-spoken person like Gandhi could terrify Whitehall with his simple, yet effective, actions and policies, then anyone with a fraction of his ability could contribute towards the country's welfare. He hoped to join the Congress after his cricket playing days.

In the 1940s, when the Governor-General of India Lord Wavell asked Lala Amarnath to join the army with a promise that he would never be posted at the frontier, Amarnath politely declined the offer as cricket was more important to him. This inflexible attitude started changing after the Delhi Test in 1948 when he met Prime Minister Jawaharlal Nehru and admired his arresting personality. Although they exchanged just a few brief notes, Amarnath was floored by Nehru's remark, "We are both captains of India but in different fields. Yet, we carry the same burden!" With every meeting, whether it was with Maulana Abul Kalam Azad, Rajendra Prasad, C Rajagopalachari or Lal Bahadur Shastri, Amarnath's resolve to join politics firmed up. He knew that the British had used cricket to their advantage and this game could be of great assistance to him also if he were to join politics.

Rajagopalachari, or Rajaji as he was affectionately called, was an ardent fan of Amarnath and keen follower of cricket. A man of simple taste and lifestyle, he was one of the sharpest brains in Indian politics. After Gandhi, he was probably the most respected statesman both in India and Britain. It was not surprising that he became the first and the last Indian to hold the post of governor-general of India. Amarnath had known him for a long time. When he was governor of West Bengal, he advised Amarnath to become his aide-de-camp (ADC) but Amarnath declined due to his cricket commitments. After Rajaji assumed the important post in Delhi, Amarnath met him at a function at Governor-General House (now President's House). A slightly built man with a face that showed his wisdom, Rajaji wore a pair of dark glasses but behind them lay crystal clear vision and loads of cricket knowledge. The moment he met his favourite cricketer, he would discuss the common topic — cricket. "You would have been here as my ADC, if you had accepted my offer in Calcutta," Rajaji said.

"Sure, sir, but I wouldn't have continued as India's captain, either," said Amarnath, his reply making Rajaji burst into laughter. Then, looking at the Indian captain he said, "You don't get everything in life. What matters most is the satisfaction and contentment in one's profession. I can see that you have both in cricket. Good luck to you." The two remained friends till Rajaji passed away on December 25, 1972. Amarnath met him in Madras a couple of months before he died. A leading newspaper headlined the meeting as 'Raja of Politics meets Raja of Cricket'.

They discussed cricket and politics and at the time of taking leave, Rajaji patted Amarnath on his shoulder and said, "You took the right decision by sticking to cricket, otherwise India would have missed the Lala Amarnath we all know today." It was probably the best ever tribute showered on him and that too by a person as eminent as Rajaji.

In 1959, the Australians travelled to Lahore to play a Test against Pakistan and Amarnath was specially invited by the Pakistan Cricket Board to witness the match and exchange views regarding various schemes to promote cricket akin to the ones he had implemented in India. Amarnath emphasised private cricket tours because it served two purposes. One, the ordinary players got exposure and second, there would be regular contact between the people of the two nations. The Pakistan Board immediately grabbed the idea when they agreed to allow a private tour to take place April onwards for five weeks. To ensure the success of the tour, Amarnath involved Surjit Singh Majithia, a minister in Nehru's Cabinet and Maharaja of Baroda Fatehsinh Gaekwad in this venture. When he applied for government clearance, it came instantly. The team played matches under the banner of Indian Starlets at Sialkot, Lahore, Multan and Karachi. Wherever Amarnath went he was greeted with open arms and the tour was a grand success.

At Karachi, a gentleman met him in the hotel and re-quested Amarnath to carry a small gift for the prime minister, as a token of love from his admirers and people of Pakistan. Unsure and apprehensive of its contents, Amarnath cited customs restrictions and discouraged him but Nehru's fan would not take no for an answer. Amarnath had to give in. The gift was a table lamp made out of the best camel hide and decorated with gold motifs all over. On reaching Delhi, Amarnath sought an appointment with Nehru at Teen Murti Bhavan, his official residence. He remembered this meeting with the prime minister vividly. He said, "As I walked towards the majestic building, which was especially made by Lutyens for the British commander-in-chief of Indian forces, one of the members of the staff led me to the Green room directly op-posite the Prime Minister's Office. After a while, I was asked to proceed to meet him.

"It was a large room with a big oak-like study table in the middle of the room. The wooden panels of the walls were made of teak, rising to maybe, fifteen feet and well polished.

There were books all around neatly stacked in the cupboards and on one side hung a painting of Gandhi and Abdul Gaffar Khan. I noticed a radiant figure working under the light of a lamp with plenty of files on the desk and a small black iron trunk placed on his right, which intrigued me. Later, I was told that it was meant for highly classified documents. Dressed in a white *kurta*, waist coat and a Gandhi cap, Panditji looked up at me for a moment and smiled. He then gestured me to occupy a chair across the table. Making myself comfortable, I waited for him to finish writing. Out of respect and courtesy, I waited for the prime minister to commence the conversation. It started when Panditji asked about my trip to Pakistan.

'It was very pleasant and fruitful,' I replied.

'What was the general feeling of the people towards India?'

'Sir, they remember you very much and were friendly to us.'

"Panditji kept asking me questions and I tried to keep pace with him. All along he kept writing something on the files or kept flipping pages but at no stage did our conversation pause. Then, suddenly Panditji narrated his wonderful experiences at Peshawar, Muree, Lahore and many other places. I was mesmerised by his personality and tremendous control over his mind, as he kept writing and talking simultaneously. A phone interrupted our discussion. I was designated to be with him for ten minutes but forty minutes had passed. After a brief chat on the phone, Panditji extended his warm but firm hand to me and bid good-bye. Before I left the room, he said smilingly, 'Do call me if you need anything.' I thanked him for his valuable time and left the room.

"As I walked back to the reception, his Private Secretary Muthia quizzed 'What took you so long? You were supposed to be back within ten minutes.' When I stated that it was personal, he laughed and refused to believe me. He then said, 'You know, the prime minister is very particular about time, even ambassadors don't get an extra minute. He has a habit of looking at his wrist watch when they overstay — a reminder to the visitor that the time is over. You, Lalaji, were with him for forty minutes! Unbelievable!'"

After this meeting, Amarnath made up his mind to join the Congress. Punjab Chief Minister Pratap Singh Kairon was a fan of his and he wanted to promote sports in his state. He called Amarnath over for breakfast in Chandigarh to discuss a sports policy for Punjab. During the meeting, Amarnath expressed his inclination towards politics. "Are you serious?" Kairon asked him. Amarnath replied in the affirmative. "First, change your western dress. These suits and hats will not get you anywhere," the chief minister remarked. "I will speak to Panditji on my next trip and I assure you a nomination to the Rajya Sabha (Upper House of Parliament)."

On his return to Delhi, Amarnath ordered dozens of khadi kurta-pyjamas and waist coats. All his Marks & Spencer suits were packed away. Attired in his new outfit, he looked like a Congressman. Word quickly spread that he was joining politics. Suddenly he was hobnobbing with various Congressmen, with the topic having changed from cricket to politics. But destiny had something else in store for him. Kairon was assassinated on his way to Chandigarh from Delhi. It shocked Amarnath as his route to the Rajya Sabha evaporated. He then thought of meeting the prime minister but the after effects of war with China had made things difficult. By then, Amarnath had begun to lose interest in politics.

In September 1964, a telephone call was received at home. Prime Minister Lal Bhadur Shastri desired that his sons be taught cricket personally by Amarnath and to discuss coaching modalities he must report at the PMO in South Block. Since it was just a telephone call, Amarnath presumed it to be a crank call and did not respond. The next day, an officer from the PMO arrived in an official car with a message that he was required at the PM's residence immediately. Amarnath hurriedly changed and accompanied the messenger in the official car.

The following morning, he ordered his sons — Surender, Mohinder and Rajender — to get ready to meet the prime minister's sons. They reached the Railway Stadium, which was walking distance from their house and waited for them. A white Ambassador car came with a police escort and three young boys emerged. All of them wore white khadi shirts, khaki trousers and sandals. They were introduced to Amarnath as Anil, Sunil and Ashok by a staff member of the PMO. After a brief chat, these boys were instructed to report the following day in proper cricket gear. The trio followed instructions and their coaching commenced. Hardly had the coaching picked up pace when security became a problem at the multi-purpose stadium. Shastri was keen to continue with the coaching, hence Amarnath was again summoned to the prime minister's residence to find a solution. Amarnath found the prime minister immensely interested in cricket. He inspected the adjoining house, 10 Janpath and had a cement strip laid there for uninterrupted coaching. On several occasions, the prime minister would come and watch the sessions.

The relations between the two families grew and the Amarnath boys were at the prime minister's house practically every day. One day, his eldest son Hari discovered that Amarnath had been very keen to join politics. Then the Indo-Pakistan war broke out in 1965. There were no more surprise visits by the prime minister at the nets as he was busy working overtime for a settlement with Pakistan and making preparations for talks in Tashkent. The day he was leaving for Tashkent, the Amarnaths also went to Palam Airport to bid him farewell. As the prime minister walked towards the waiting aircraft where Hari Shastri and Amarnath were standing, Shastri told him, "Hari told me that you are interested in joining the Congress. If only I had known earlier I would have done the needful. But don't worry, on my return, I'll create a new portfolio for you, minister for sports." Sadly, he never returned to India after signing the Indo-Pak agreement with Gen. Ayub Khan. He died of a cardiac arrest in Tashkent. Amarnath took this disaster as the hand of destiny preventing him from joining politics.

JOURNALIST & EXPERT COMMENTATOR

Between 1960 and 1965, Lala Amarnath was not involved with cricket in any capacity but he missed the cricketing atmosphere. Journalism was last on his list of priorities as he did not savour the thought of sitting and watching the match for the entire day and then using his pen to dissect the day's proceedings. Amarnath did not appreciate those journalists who only had a theoretical knowledge of the game but commented on cricketers' mistakes. "It is easy to give advice but very difficult to rectify the mistakes," he always said. He also lamented the intrusion of certain people who were biased, corrupt and had little knowledge of the game. At the same time, he admired Arthur Mailey, Jack Fingleton, K N Prabhu, John Arlott and other honest journalists for their critical analyses.

Amarnath had admirers from all walks of life and Frank Moraes was one of them. Moraes had been Amarnath's fan for a long time. The 1969 Indian calendar was busy with the New Zealand and Australian tours. Frank Moraes was now the editor-in-chief of the *Indian Express* and wanted to increase the circulation of the newspaper by providing something new to the readers. Cricket captivated him and he wanted the series to realise this objective. In one of his meetings with Floraes (a journalist), Moraes sought his help in finding a suitable cricketer to cover the series. Floraes proposed Amarnath's name and a meeting was arranged. Amarnath disliked the dreary reporting and insisted on writing his personal views which Moraes readily accepted. The new column was called 'Expert comments by Lala Amarnath'. It was an instant hit. He was elated with this success. He worked hard for his columns, getting them typed by the secretaries of his friends, and personally dispatched the reports to the newspaper. His column became so popular that at times important portions from his articles were lifted and used with some changes in other newspapers. Amarnath laughed, "Even here we have healthy competition!" From then on, he dispatched his articles much after local journalists had reported their stories to avoid duplication.

The Indian Express became Amarnath's springboard in becoming a journalist and soon other leading newspapers started approaching him during the home series. He was in circulation again. Both players and readers appreciated his frank remarks. Certain phrases like 'bowled lock, stock and barrel' as well as 'catches win matches' became synonymous with him. He continued giving his expert opinion on the radio and in his columns but he was getting bored with them. This problem was solved with the advent of television. It was a medium that covered the length and breadth of the country live and allowed him to build his reputation as an authority on cricket. Television exposed the inadequacy of those commentators who had no knowledge of the game but had got away with it on radio. Amarnath relished his new role, drawing upon his vast knowledge and experience to make predictions about the outcome of the matches. The line *"Lalaji, aap ka kya khayal hai* (What do you have to say, Lalaji)?" became famous. In Hyderabad, India was struggling to save the match against New Zealand when a fellow-commentator asked Amarnath how could India save the match. Amarnath looked at the clear blue sky and replied, "Only rain can save India." After a while, a patch of dark clouds blew over the ground and opened up, forcing the match to be abandoned. The commentator asked him, "Are you a soothsayer also?"

"No, I'm a patriot!"

In 1978, the Indo-Pak series was being revived after a gap of eighteen years in accordance with the policy of the Janata Party to bring the people of the two countries closer through cricket. It was a special occasion for both countries, as they possessed the world's best players between themselves. India had Bishan Singh Bedi, E A S Prasanna, B S Chandrashekhar and S Venkatraghvan to counter the batting of Zaheer Abbas, Mushtaq Mohammed, Asif Iqbal and Mudassar Nazar. Pakistan had great pace bowlers in Imran Khan and Sarfaraz Nawaz to check the blades of Sunil Gavaskar, G R Viswanath and the Amarnath brothers, Surender and Mohinder.

Since the series was to be telecast, Lala Amarnath was hopeful that he would be covering it for the Indian channel. Doordarshan dilly-dallied in making a decision. At the same time Pakistan President Gen Zia-ul-Haq ordered PTV (Pakistan Television) to seek the services of Amarnath as its expert. Amarnath accepted the offer. Hearing this, the Ministry of Information and Broadcasting sent frantic requests and apologised for the *faux pas* but Amarnath had already committed himself and so he declined. He was not in good health but the prospect of meeting his old friends prompted him to accept this offer. Despite a tight schedule, Amarnath had time for his friends and admirers. He had captured the hearts of everyone, whether on TV as an expert or as a product of Lahore speaking the same language.

The euphoria in both countries was unbelievable. The atmosphere of distrust had evaporated and the gates of Wagah border were opened once more for Indian fans to cross over to follow their heroes. Fatehsinh Rao Gaekwad of Baroda was manager and Bedi was the captain of the team. A large crowd at

Lahore airport received the team. Many of them wanted to have a glimpse of Amarnath's sons. Surender and Mohinder recall, "People asked us if our father was also coming. When we replied in the affirmative, they were very excited. It was amazing to see these people still remembering dad and holding him in such high esteem, even after a gap of almost two decades."

When the grand old man of sixty-seven years disembarked from the aircraft, he was accorded a tumultuous welcome befitting his association with Lahore. Thousands came to get a glimpse of this proud son of Lahore from a different era. The new generation also came in large numbers with their elders to see the man who had left an enormous impression on their elders with his exploits. The reception at the airport touched Amarnath and he was unable to express his happiness in words to his friends and well-wishers. For an emotional Amarnath, it was a sort of homecoming, similar to the one accorded to him when he scored his test century in 1933–34. The difference was that he now belonged to another country.

The new assignment began and ended on a happy and friendly note. He made many new friends on this tour and on top of the list was the Pakistan president, who became his fervent admirer after spending a hilarious half-hour listening to his anecdotes, instead of a five-minute courtesy call. The president always sent new year greetings to Amarnath thereafter.

The Indian team returned to Pakistan in 1983 and once again Doordarshan adopted its usual tactics and skipped Amarnath. Gen Zia-ul-Haq requested Amarnath again to assist PTV as an 'expert'. Sunil Gavaskar led the Indian team and Fatehsinh Rao Gaekwad was its manager. Amarnath too flew with the team to be there in time for the Test matches. On reaching Lahore, the Indian team moved to the terminal building in a coach, while Gaekwad and Amarnath discussed something at the tarmac. A black limousine halted near the aircraft and seeing it, Gaekwad bid him goodbye and moved towards the limousine. A tall Pathan emerged from the car and opened the passenger door. When Gaekwad tried to get in, the Pathan stopped him and said, "Sir, this is not for you. The car has been sent specially for Lala saheb."

The friendship between the Pakistan president and Amarnath was revived once more. During a break from commentary, Amarnath spent time with the president in the pavilion cracking jokes and narrating hilarious experiences from his life. That evening in Lahore, the president invited the teams for dinner. It was a big gathering consisting of high dignitaries; important personalities; the media from both sides. The president welcomed the Indian team and in the same breath spoke of the wonderful time he had with the man he called Lala Saheb. Then he said, "I would like to share some of the finest moments of the afternoon with everyone present if it is okay with Lala Saheb." Amarnath was busy talking with some people at the table. He did not hear the president who repeated the request. A high ranking military officer rushed to Amarnath and requested him to respond to the *Sadr-e-Riyasat*. Amarnath slowly got up from his chair, raised his right hand and announced, "Mr. President, you have my permission."

It was a treat to see the expression on the faces of the Pakistani officials present at the venue. "No one in Pakistan could have got away with replying so casually to the president as skipper did," recalled *Press Trust of India* correspondent Jagannadha Rao. The evening was memorable with General Zia-ul-Haq in his element enchanting everyone with his lucid speech and sumptuous dinner.

The party finished late in the night and they took a cab to the hotel. On the way Amarnath cracked jokes and spoke of his days in Lahore. On reaching the hotel, Rao reached out for his wallet to pay the fare but Amarnath held his arm, *"Chote nahi dete* (Youngsters don't pay)." Amarnath then asked the driver in the local dialect *'Beta kinnay paise ho gaye* (What is the fare, son)?"

The driver, aged around forty, replied, *"Assey paise nahi lawangey towadey toh* (I will not take money from you)."

"Why?" asked Amarnath.

"Tussi toh Lahore di shaan ho (You are the pride of Lahore)," replied the cab driver.

Rao was impressed. "I have never ever seen such genuine respect for any cricketer anywhere in the world, as skipper commanded in Pakistan. This driver couldn't have seen him play but yes, he must have heard all the stories of his exploits on the cricket field. If you went shopping with skipper, you did not pay anything. The skipper was truly charismatic."

THIRTEEN

THE FAMILY MAN

IT WOULD not be incorrect to say that Papa's first and last love was cricket. His dedication to cricket, at times, made Mom jealous of this sport, which took precedence over her, too. She would often tease him saying though she had been given the status of a wife through matrimony, in reality he was married to cricket with his heart and soul. He lived for cricket till the end, first through his own efforts and later through his sons.

His travelling was drastically reduced after he relinquished his responsibilities at the BCCI. With much time at his disposal, he turned his attention towards his family. It was a large family of seven children. The first three were daughters, followed by three sons and again a daughter. Bimla, the first-born, was the apple of his eye. She took liberties with Papa, even picking his pocket. Known for his short temper, he was gentle and loving with his children. Despite that, Kamla and Alka were petrified of his personality, hence hardly exchanged any words with him, though he encouraged them. They would route all their demands through Bimla. And he doted on the youngest — Dolly.

Papa's obsession with cricket was passed on to the sons very early in their childhood. He took upon himself the responsibility of planning the cricket careers of his two elder sons Tom and Jim

(English pet names given to Surender and Mohinder in keeping with the Patiala tradition).

His old cricket rivalry with Delhi and District Cricket Association President Ram Prakash Mehra meant that his talented sons would not get a break in the capital. With precious time wasted in Delhi, Papa summoned the Punjab Cricket Association (PCA) Secretary H R Mohla for a discussion. He wanted PCA to assure him that his sons would be given a fair opportunity in Punjab. This opportunity was godsend for Mohla, who wanted to build Punjab cricket but did not have sufficient talent.

In 1963, Surender and Mohinder were sent to a boarding school in Jalandhar to make their careers in cricket. Education became secondary as these youngsters showed immense potential in the game. Encouraged by their results on the field, Amarnath pushed them to achieve the ultimate. He knew that cricket demanded total attention and dedication and any dilution in their pursuit would be detrimental to his sons' careers. He instructed the school and the PCA to allow his sons every opportunity to pursue cricket without any hindrance. If Papa was uncompromising with them on the field, as a father he ensured they didn't miss home. Several players owed their careers to him and they requested him to allow them to repay their gratitude by taking care of his sons when they were in Jalandhar.

During summer, under a scorching sun, when the two brothers were playing matches, homemade food and *lassi* were provided to them. If they became homesick, many families would step forward to fill the vacuum. "I missed my sons like any other father would do but their careers were more important," he said. Instructions were also left at the Burlton Park cricket ground to allow these two boys net practice throughout the season. "The love and affection which we received from so many families and cricketers showed how much respect people had for Papa," Mohinder says.

Whenever there was a lull in cricket in Jalandhar, Papa called his sons back to Delhi. He missed them but would not admit this openly. I think we were very fortunate that Papa had enough time for us and he utilised it for our benefit. All of us learned skills of cricket at our bungalow at Panchkuian Road (New Delhi) which was spread over an acre. Being a genius in cricket, he taught us the basics at home. The vast open space was fully utilised to allow us to have an experience of different conditions and learn the finer points of the game under his watchful eyes.

Papa knew that each one has to be different. Otherwise, there was bound to be competition among us, which he didn't want. Though Surender was an attractive right-hand batsman, he converted him to a left-handed batsman when he was around eight years of age. He was forced to take a left-hander's stance and lift the bat with one hand only. There were two reasons behind the move. One, he didn't want competition amongst his sons and secondly, he felt left-handers had a distinct advantage against most bowlers.

Surender still remembers the problems he faced when he was being converted to a left-hander. "There used to be a sharp pain in my arm but I never complained. I knew Papa had my best interests at heart," he recalls. "As a child, it was constantly drilled into me that he (Papa) had a dream that one day I would emulate him and make him proud. Papa's advice was simple. 'If you have to succeed, then practise hard and sincerely,' he said. This remained our guiding philosophy throughout our careers."

My own memories of Papa are very pleasant. For us, he was a guide, friend, philosopher, father and guru rolled into one. In 1966, West Indies came to India under Gary Sobers. Papa was approached by All India Radio to commentate on the Test match in Calcutta. Papa always felt strongly that if one watched the game in true perspective, one would learn something worthwhile. Keeping this in mind, he took me along on a forty-eight-hour train trip to Howrah. I remember watching the match from the old single-storey, wooden pavilion along with both teams. While the large Bengali crowd inside and outside the stadium was thrilled by Lala Amarnath's spicy comments, a tussle between the police and the spectators temporarily halted the match as the crowd spilled close to the boundary. Some officials of the Cricket Association of Bengal (CAB) had sold more tickets than the ground capacity. Sobers was keen to continue as his team was in a good position but the commotion prevented him from doing so. After a brief halt, the contest commenced.

At that very moment, an enthusiastic spectator ran onto the field to shake hands with the players. Some police personnel were in hot pursuit. Before the poor chap could do what he intended to, he was slapped and dragged away from the field amid loud jeering from the stands. Suddenly, all hell broke loose when the spectators pulled the bamboo poles supporting the temporary canopies and jumped onto the ground, chasing the policemen themselves. There was total chaos as the sides fought a pitched battle. The mob even torched the stands.

The shocked and disoriented players ran for their lives. Fearing injury to me, Papa pushed his way through the agitated mob and rescued me. We huddled in the dining hall in the pavilion along with the teams. Soon, the situation became alarming as a few canisters of tear gas burst next to us. The smoke from the burning stands and the roof of the pavilion along with the tear-gas stung our eyes and made breathing difficult. Seeing tears rolling down my cheeks, Papa sprinkled cold water on my eyes but to no avail. While all the people around us were terrified, I knew Papa would ensure I would not be harmed. Through thousands of agitating fans, he took me away from the ground to safety.

Not many know that behind the veil of an angry man stood a very simple person, generous to the core of his heart, helping people. Later, when he developed an interest in horticulture, the caring heart became apparent while he tended his plants. He often showed us how to handle fragile flowers. In the summers, he would lift hundreds of flowerpots (weighing about ten kg each) and moved them to cooler areas under the trees each day. "They are like babies needing tender care and affection," he would often say. No wonder, our home was always decked up with the best flowers, mainly due to Papa's obsession and supervision. In the winters, he would get up as early as 4 a.m. to water the plants with a portable water sprinkler. The can weighed around twenty kg and he appeared to lift it that many times effortlessly. Then, he would feed and play with his six Alsatian dogs.

When it came to cricket, his eyes would light up and he loved watching us play and always encouraged us to do well. If he lost his temper, it was probably because he wanted us to be better than the others. "Being an Amarnath, you will face many hurdles in your life but never give up in despair," he would often say. Whenever Papa was in town and available, he discussed only cricket with us. Like obedient students, all three of us would listen to each word of advice and then try to implement that through hard work during net practice. It was always refreshing, talking to him and sipping hot tea in winters, cup after cup made either by Mom or my sisters.

These discourses enlightened us and gave us an insight into all departments of the game, very early in life. "Never think you are inferior to a bowler, when facing him in any situation," he would repeatedly tell us. Being the youngest and his favourite, I would always question his wisdom. "What if I am a bowler?" I would ask. Instead of getting angry, he would tap my head with his strong knuckles. Watching my pained expression, Tom and Jim would cover their faces with their hands and giggle while Papa would have a hearty laugh. "Listen to the theory first before butting in," he would then say. A little later, the smile would return and he would answer my query. "If you are a bowler, be prepared to be hit and once you overcome this fear, you will be in a position to formalise your method of attack."

After a brief pause, he would then take up the most interesting subject, and that was captaincy. "Everyone loves it as it gives one a sense of pride and authority. Like wicket-keeping, this is also a very difficult job. Your head will always be on the altar, awaiting one grave mistake and it is chopped off instantly. It is important to lead from the front and set an example. There is no harm in listening to the suggestions of your colleagues but not to advice. Once the captain starts following advice, his days are numbered. Leaders are born and not made," he would say. He would then look at us for our reactions and all of us would nod our heads in the affirmative.

Finding us involved, he would continue with the other aspects of leadership. "It is the captain's prime duty to be good in reading the wicket and formulating his strategy accordingly. If he is confused, then he is like the blind, who need no help when the path is straight and smooth but topple when it is uneven and crisscross. His decisions make or mar the game," he emphasised.

As kids, all of us were made to play under the blistering sun of May, June and July. I remember Papa would sit under the *pipul* tree and watch us sweat it out but Mom would often fear that we would have a sunstroke. Unmindful of her pleas,

Papa was determined to make his sons rough and tough. Then, he would give us the example of kundan jewellery which is produced under intense heat and when it is ready, it sparkles. Every word of his was ultimate and our interest reached the level of maniacs. Once, we nearly fainted in the heat but wouldn't leave the ground till he called us to quit. We saw his eyes moist with emotion and he tightly embraced us and in a cracked voice said, "I have done my duty and now it is up to destiny to give you your rewards."

If summer cricket was tough, then winter was no better. He knew why Indians struggled when they played abroad. To get us used to playing in different conditions, he divided the large area at home into three zones and monitored our progress. In the winters, the green lawns were covered with morning dew and he insisted that we batted, bowled and fielded in these conditions. At 6.30 a.m., we would be pulled out from our cozy beds to the freezing winter temperature of Delhi to acclimatise. The instructions were to play with bare feet and none of us dared question his wisdom. To get us accustomed to use the bat, no gloves or pads were allowed. Soon, the hard cricket ball would become soggy and skid off the grass. Gripping it was a problem we faced while bowling or fielding. It was tough cricket all the way. Any lapse of concentration during batting resulted in excruciating pain after a blow on the shin by the hard ball. Papa would be puffing his pipe or smoking his cigars under the garden umbrella as he watched us for hours on end.

Papa always believed in the practicals and we were moved to the side driveway, with a tennis ball. The instructions were simple to the bowlers, hit the deck and make the batsman hop or play cut or hook shots. We played these shots for hours and he appreciated the correct execution of these strokes with a smile and if we played the rising delivery casually and got out, he would lose his cool and remind us, "You don't get another chance in the match, my boy."

Unlike today, there were no movie cameras available to assist us. Hence, after the session, we were moved to the verandah to stand in front of a six-foot tall mirror, the one he had used, to allow us to see for ourselves the mistakes we committed. No wonder, all of us played the hook with ease. Mohinder scored many runs and even got out while hooking, but Papa never stopped him from playing it. "You don't stop playing a shot which gives you runs and also because some jokers discourage you or criticise you in their articles."

Indian conditions produced many great spinners and this factor was not ignored either. To master spin, we were asked to play in the courtyard at the back. This area was especially reserved for the ladies of the house to relax and enjoy the winter sunshine privately but he laid the ground-rules. It was dusty and about twenty yards all around. We bowled spin, the ball turning at sharp angles. With no protective gear or abdominal guards, at times we would get hit in the more delicate parts of our bodies. We would be in pain but could not rub the area since there were ladies present there. He would understand our predicament and laugh out aloud. *"Sheran dey putr rub nahi kardey* (Lion cubs don't rub the painful area)." We realised how handy and useful such early coaching was much later in our careers. Papa was far-sighted and simple in imparting the lessons. It was a great experience and fun interacting with him. He was our Dronacharya, indeed!

We grew up on the stories of his exploits in the Lancashire League. For him, playing in the League was the ultimate test of skills. He wanted all of us to play in England as professional cricketers, which we did with distinction for a long time. Papa had a good but subtle sense of humour and he would warn us of the problems we would face as professionals. "When you play as a professional, many girls would seek your company. Go and enjoy but be in bed early on Fridays so that your performance does not suffer the following day. Once you realise and understand the value of yourself as a cricketer, you will succeed in life, too."

When all of us started playing regularly in the Leagues in England, we would ask Mom and Papa what they needed from England. Mom was always content with her Indian dress and attar (perfume). But Papa always wanted English pipes and tobacco. Since Marks & Spencer suits fit him the best, they were on the top of the list along with a matching tie and a hat. In case he forgot to mention his Italian shoes, he would mail us an impression of his foot so we would buy the correct size. We always asked him once more before we returned to India if he had forgotten anything. "Have I marked my collar size for C&A shirts?" Papa loved to dress well and we had always seen him that way even at home. It was customary for us to call him from England and keep him posted about our performances. In case our performance fell below his expectations, he would remark, "Concentrate on the game and not on the dames!"

Many had seen him in Western clothes but hardly anyone knew that he could recite *shabads* from Guru Granth Sahib or understand classical music. During his time, it was mandatory to know ballroom dancing. Not knowing the steps, he took special dancing classes in London from a lady called Betty. We had never seen Papa dancing in his black tailcoat and dancing shoes but he often showed us the steps. When he was in a good mood, he would switch on BBC Radio and wait for the right music to play and then hold Mom's hand and dance a few steps but being shy, she would go pink with embarrassment.

Papa followed our cricket progress very closely. In 1972, he received a telegram from Siddartha Shankar Ray, requesting him to send his sons to play a charity match at Calcutta for the flood victims in Bengal. As this was for a good cause, he enquired from Surender and Mohinder, who were representing Guru Nanak Dev University (GNDU) in the Rohinton Baria Trophy, if they could play this match. The brothers sought the team manager's permission. As GNDU's next match was against a weak team, the permission was granted. Surender and Mohinder played the match in Calcutta but their university team unfortunately lost the match. Fearing action against him, the manager blamed the Amarnath brothers. Instead of giving the youngsters a chance to explain, the GNDU vice-chancellor made the harsh decision of rusticating them. It shocked them. With his sons' careers at stake, Papa approached the vice-chancellor and explained everything and requested him not to harm his sons' careers but he would not budge. The meeting ended on a rather sour note when the vice-chancellor declared, "No one on this earth can make me change my mind or my decision." Papa had been very patient but the parting remark infuriated him. "Till now, I had been acting as Surender and Mohinder's father but from now, you will deal with Lala Amarnath," he said as he left the office.

On his return to Delhi, he called Ray and explained every-thing. Meanwhile, a frustrated journalist from the *Indian Express* reported the news of the rustication and derived pleasure from it. The case was referred to the then prime minister, Indira Gandhi, who directed the Ministry of Education to act immediately. When the vice- chancellor was ordered to revoke his decision, he had no option but to accept it meekly. Having secured justice for his sons, Lala Amarnath moved Mohinder from Amritsar to join Khalsa College in Delhi University.

This change brought glory and success to the family when both my brothers represented India with distinction. I remember waking up early one morning to the high volume of the radio commentary which Papa had tuned in to. I joined him and was excited to hear that Tom (Surender) was batting at 90. When Tom hit a six to complete his century, Papa could not control his emotions, tears of joy rolled down his cheeks and he pressed my hand. For him, it meant a lot as his son had suffered at the hands of those who could not harm him during his own play-ing days but were trying to hurt him through his sons. When Surender got out at 124, Papa was very annoyed. As a father he was thrilled, but he kept reminding me of the difficult path ahead for my brothers. Papa was a man of few words but each of his words had some message.

Having been brought up in a male-dominated society, he hardly expressed his emotions in public. On the Pakistan tour in 1978, Jimmy (Mohinder) was hit on the skull, ducking into a bouncer from Imran Khan, and collapsed, Papa was in the com-mentator's box. He was watching his son writhing in pain but controlled his emotions and worst fears. To everyone's surprise, he did not leave his position. Instead, he explained Jimmy's poor technique for this mishap. But in a father's heart there was a genuine concern and he was longing to be beside his injured son. He held himself back as showing emotions at that stage meant a weak heart. In the evening, the worried father called on his son and was relieved to see him chatting with his elder brother. *"Zyada tey nai laggee* (You are not badly hurt, are you?)" he asked his battered son. "Don't duck. Your technique for that is incorrect. Stick to hooking." Getting assurance from the best hooker of his time, Mohinder played the hook shot against all Pakistan pace bowlers, much to Papa's delight. "Papa always made it a point to spend his evenings with me and Surender during the Test matches," Jimmy told me. "Every detail of the match was discussed. When we didn't do well, he would ask us to overcome the fear of failure and raise our spirits by narrating his experiences and how he overcame hurdles. He knew the mind of a player better than anyone else. His advice and presence boosted our confidence immensely."

Injuries are part and parcel of the game, Papa would often tell us. In 1979, Mohinder was making another comeback. Helmets were still not in vogue or readily available in India. A bare-headed Mohinder was batting against Nottinghamshire. While attempting a hook shot against Richard Hadlee on a green top, he was hit on the head again and this time the injury looked more serious as he lay motionless on the ground. All India Radio personnel conveyed this news to us. Worried, Papa tried to reach him over telephone but it took an eternity to get through. Unable to hold himself back, he asked me to take him to the AIR office and after a few anxious hours, we were able to get news of Jimmy's welfare.

Satisfied that he was awake and talking, he thanked the AIR staff profusely for the help. On our way back, he kept talking to himself and wondering what could have gone wrong. Then he asked me to stop the car. Getting out of the car on a busy pavement in Connaught Place, he held his walking stick as if he were gripping a bat and took the stance and played the hook shot. Everyone around wondered what the old man was upto. But he didn't care about the public attention. Satisfied that he had reached the right conclusion, he got back into the car and asked me to call up Jimmy and remind him the correct position and the hook shot he had just played. It was amazing that he could pinpoint the cause of a mishap thousands of miles away.

Cricket was his lifeline but at the same time he never neglected other joys of life. He loved wearing the best of clothes, the company of beautiful women and enjoyed delicious meals. No wonder, Mom would often say his heart lay in his stomach! All those who had an opportunity to sit and listen to his fascinating tales would vouch that time flew by without anyone realising it. He had a tremendous ability to draw the attention of his audience and captivate the listeners. If cricket anecdotes held the guests' interest, then tales of his close encounters with the supernatural too made everyone sit on the edge of their seats.

I still remember listening to one such experience. Papa had moved into an old house in Jowria di patti in Sherawala Gate, Patiala, since his official residence was being renovated. One evening, while ascending the stairs to the bedroom, he felt someone was following him. He turned back but found no one. Before he could reach the last step, he saw a large arm reaching out for him. He screamed in fear. Later that night, he became terribly sick and even threw up blood. He kept the lights on through the night. The following day, when he went to make his enquiries, his neighbour could not believe that Mum and Papa had spent a night in that house. "No one has ever stayed more than an hour in the evening in this place. I am surprised you didn't know that the landlady of the house had committed suicide and her soul haunts the place," the neighbour told Papa.

Having heard the story, Papa decided to stay put. Since Thursday is considered auspicious for *puja* (prayer), Papa drew a big circle of a hundred candles at the spot where the arm had tried to reach him and prayed. "I couldn't believe my eyes when I saw a *ghagra* (long gathered skirt) rise from within the circle of lit candles to about three feet, vanish and then reappear. We stayed in that house for two months but candles and lamps were lit every Thursday," he said. I remember this story being narrated umpteen times to his friends and goose pimples would dot the bodies of all those who heard him. Once, while listening to this incident, a friend of his from south India nearly fainted, when a mouse in the room accidentally knocked his glass over from the side table breaking it with an astounding crash to pierce the pindrop silence. The captivated friend almost collapsed in his chair with fear. This was the kind of effect he had on the gathering whenever he narrated an experience — mesmerising.

Unknowingly, Papa always seemed to move into places which were considered haunted. He remembered his domestic help Mainga Ram running down the terrace of his home at Anardana Chowk in Patiala, with fear writ large on his face, complaining of bodies being ferried from left to the right. Presuming it to be a bad dream, Papa ordered the other servant, Hardum, to sleep on the terrace. He too came down shrieking and narrated the same sequence. Fearing for his family, the following day Papa moved out.

If he seemingly had close encounters with the dead, he once met an angel in the hills of Chail during his Sunday training. "I was on my way back from Kandhaghat when I noticed a beautiful girl on the upper path smiling at me. Her face was glowing and she gestured me to come closer. Just as I ran to catch up with her, unknown to me a huge boulder was hurtling down towards the spot where I was standing. I was saved by a whisker. Just as I turned around to thank her for saving my life, she had disappeared. I searched high and low but she seemed to have vanished into thin air. I was convinced she had appeared to save my life."

Apart from being a master chef, Papa also had an enormous appetite. Once, the famous Asian wrestling champion Chandgi Ram visited our place with a big watermelon that weighed five kg. Looking at the wrestler and the watermelon, Papa asked him, "Is it for me or for us? If it is for us, it is too little." He then sent his servant to buy ten kg more. They consumed the entire fruit and topped it with a big glass of *lassi*. At the age of sixty-plus, Papa was perfectly fine but the big wrestler was down and out for the next two days with an upset stomach.

Much later in life, recollecting the Indian team's tour of Pakistan in 1983 he said, "While I was ascending the stairs in the Gaddafi Stadium at Lahore, a section of the crowd shouted, 'Look, Mohinder's father has arrived.' It made me so happy that on the 1978 tour Mohinder was recognised as my son and he had now overtaken my reputation." After yet another successful comeback by Jimmy, Papa warned him of the impending danger ahead from the umpires. He cautioned him to avoid getting hit on the pads as the Pakistan cricketers felt that he was the major threat to them and umpires had joined hands with them. This observation came true in the following Test when Jimmy was adjudged lbw to a pre-planned move.

With age catching up and his physical exercises reduced, he suffered from diabetes and other ailments. In 1985, he suffered a massive heart attack and I took him to the Ram Manohar Lohia hospital. News of his critical condition spread through TV, radio and the newspapers. He was struggling for his life. Soon, VIPs including Rajiv Gandhi, P V Narasimha Rao and other leaders made a beeline to enquire about his health. Speaking to us about his favourite star 'Lala Amarnath', Narasimha Rao told us how he would travel all the way from his native village to watch him play in Madras. He only stayed at the ground as long as Papa was batting or bowling. Then, looking at Mohinder he said, "You and Surender combined together are not half as good as your father was!" We all agreed, as he was not the first person to make such comments.

Miraculously, Papa survived this ordeal and came out victorious. Once he stabilised, he was shifted to a nursing home where an old journalist friend of his, R Sriman, went to meet him. "Amar, what happened?" he asked. In his characteristic style, Papa replied, "I went up to heavens and met God. He was surprised to see me and said 'Oh! It is you! Sorry, you have a few more years to bother your friends' and I was promptly sent back!"

This lease of life brought him more recognition from different parts of the world. The CBFS in Sharjah presented him with a substantial purse. The Government of India, which had wanted to honour him with the Padma Shri (and Indian civil decoration) in 1960 — he declined, stating that every Indian male was a 'Shri' — decorated him with the Padma Bhushan. In 1991, Prime Minister Chandra Shekhar's office called to tell him that he had been recommended for the Padma Bhushan and his consent was needed. He accepted the award. Our home was flooded with messages from all over the country. Madhavrao Scindia drove down to the Amarnath residence to congratulate him. When he conveyed his wishes, Amarnath stated matter-of-factly, "It should have come much earlier." He received the award from an old admirer, President R Venkataraman.

Not to be left behind, the Delhi government also decided to honour him at a function. With Amarnath in demand, many in the Board felt that they too should do something to show their appreciation for his services to Indian cricket. He was nominated to receive the first award instituted in the memory of C K Nayudu. After receiving the award, Amarnath thanked the BCCI, especially the Board President I S Bindra and N K P Salve, for the gesture. Bindra was also instrumental in naming the main gate of the Punjab Cricket Association Stadium in Mohali near Chandigarh as the Lala Amarnath Gate.

"I have lived my life to the full. There is nothing more I could have desired to achieve. I think I can go and meet God," he said one day after receiving all possible rewards and recognition. In the early hours of August 5, 2000, at the age of eighty-nine, he passed away peacefully in his sleep. The legend was no more but his aura will always remain.

LALA AMARNATH'S CAREER STATISTICS
Up to 1960 (incomplete data)

	Batting						Bowling		
	inn	no	hs	runs	100's	ave	runs	wkts	ave
Ranji Trophy	57	2	155*	2,162	6	39.36	2,764	190	14.54**
Tests	40	4	118	878	1	24.38	1,481	45	32.91
'Tests'–unofficial	21	0	123	691	2	32.90	287	11	26.09
Pentangulars	17	1	241	705	1	44.06	349	12	29.08
TOURS									
England 1936	20	1	130	613	3	32.26	668	32	20.87
England 1946	30	3	106	731	2	27.07	1,173	43	27.47
Pakistan 1954	2	1	54*	99	-	99.00	86	3	28.66
Australia 1947–48	13	2	228*	1,072	5	92.90	487	17	28.64
Visiting sides	30	7	223*	1,320	6	57.39	745	22	33.86
Zonal tournament	5	1	49	94	-	23.66	267	14	19.07
Other first-class	4	0	262	402	1	100.50	222	6	37.00
Total	**238**	**22**	**262**	**8,767**	**27**	**40.58**	**8,529**	**395**	**21.59**

*Not out
**Amarnath still heads the list of Ranji Trophy averages of all-time bowlers who have taken 100 or more wickets in the tournament.

TEST AGGREGATE AGAINST EACH COUNTRY

	Batting					Bowling				
	inn	no	hs	runs	ave	overs	mo	runs	wkts	ave
v. England in E.	5	0	50	69	13.80	137	50	330	13	25.38
in India	10	1	118	270	30.00	158	44	320	7	45.71
Total	15	1	118	339	24.21	295	94	650	20	32.50
v. Australia	10	0	46	140	14.00	126	23	366	13	28.15
v. West Indies	10	2	62	294	36.75	96	20	263	3	87.66
v. Pakistan	5	1	61*	105	26.25	127.5	60	202	9	22.44
Total	40	4	118	878	24.38	644.5	197	1,481	45	32.91

Note: Lala Amarnath still holds the World record of longest interval between two Test appearances — 12 years & 160 days as well as longest career spanning 19 years for India.
Against England in England and against Australia, he led the bowling averages and had also captured the highest number of wickets for India.
Overs v. Australia consisted of 8-balls an over. In all, he bowled 4,121 balls in all Tests.

AGGREGATE SCORES ABROAD

	Batting					Bowling		
	inn	no	hs	runs	ave	runs	wkts	ave
In Ceylon	2	0	30	46	23.00	18	0	-
In England	55	4	130	1,413	27.70	2,171	88	24.67
In Australia	23	3	228*	1162	58.10	853	30	28.43
In Pakistan	2	1	54*	99	99.00	86	3	28.66
Total	82	8	228*	2,720	36.75	3,128	123	25.43

Note: Against Australia he led the batting averages and was second in the bowling averages.

5 or more Wickets in an Innings in Test
5-118 v England at Lord's, 1946
5-96 v. England, at Manchester, 1946
Ranji Trophy
7-30	Patiala v Services, 1956–57
7-37	S Punjab v UP, 1936–37
7-39	Patiala v E Punjab, 1957–58
7-60	S Punjab v UP, 1935–36
7-70	Railways v Delhi, 1958–59
6-25	S Punjab v NWF Provinces, 1937–38
6-32	Railways v Jammu & Kashmir, 1960–61
6-36	S Punjab v NWF Provinces, 1938-39
6-95	S Punjab v N India, 1946–47
6-110	Patiala v Services, 1957–58
5-22	S Punjab v NWF Provinces, 1939–40
5-29	Punjab v N India, 1943–44
5-32	Punjab v N India, 1945–46
5-42	Gujarat v Saurashtra, 1952–53

Tours
6-29	Middlesex, at Lord's 1936

Centuries in first-class Cricket
109	S Punjab v MCC, at Amritsar, 1933–34
118	India v England, at Bombay 1933-34
144	Moin-ud-Dowla's XI v Ryder's Australian team, at Secunderabad, 1935–36
114*	India v Northamptonshire, at Northampton, 1936
130 & 107	India v Essex, a Brentwood, 1936
109*	Patiala v Lord Tennyson's Team, at Patiala, 1937–38
121	Moin-ud-Dowla's XI v Lord Tennyson's team, at Secunderabad, 1937–38
123	India v Lord Tennyson's team (III 'Test'), at Calcutta, 1937–38
241	Hindus v Rest, at Bombay, 1938
103	S Punjab v Rajputana, at Ajmere, 1939–40
105	S Punjab v Delhi, at Patiala, 1940–41
148	S Punjab v Delhi, at Delhi, 1943–44
133	S Punjab v N India, at Patiala, 1945–46
113	India v Australian Services XI (III 'Test'), at Madras, 1945
163	Princes ' XI v Australian Services XI at Delhi, 1945
104*	India v Glamorgan, at Cardiff, 1946
106	India v Sussex, at Hove, 1946
262	India-in-England v Rest of India, at, Calcutta, 1946–47
144	India v South Australia, at Adelaide, 1947–48
228*	India v Victoria, at Melbourne, 1947–48
172*	India v Queensland, at Brisbane, 1947–48
171	India v Tasmania, at Hobart, 1947–48
135	India v Tasmania, at Launceston, 1947–48
223*	North Zone v West Indies, at Patiala, 1948–49
155*	S Punjab v E Punjab, at Patiala, 1951–52
110	S Punjab v Services, at Delhi, 1951–52

Note: Of the 27 centuries 4 have been over 200, 10 have been scored abroad, 8 against the Australians and 5 on his 'home' ground–Patiala.

Partnerships over 100 Runs
In Tests
186 for 3rd wicket with C K Nayudu v England, 1933–34
144* for 4th wicket with V S Hazare v West Indies, 1948–49

In Ranji Trophy

196 for 2nd wicket with Murrawat Hussain, for S Punjab v Delhi, 1943–44

128 for 2nd wicket with Omprakash, for SPunjab v N India 1945–46

119 for 5th wicket with K Rai Singh for S Punjab v N India, 1946–47

135 for 5th wicket with H H Patiala for S Punjab v N India, 1951–52

143 for 2nd wicket with Abdul Rehman for S Punjab v NWFP 1938–39

110 for 5th wicket with Azmat Hyat for S Punjab v Rajputana, 1939–40

171 for 6th wicket with Prithviraj for S Punjab v Services, 1951–52

In Pentangulars: (For Hindus)

197 for 5th wicket with V M Merchant v Rest, 1938

197 for 6th wicket with L P Jai, v Rest, 1938

102 for 2nd with V Mankad, v Europeans, 1939

On Tours:

England, 1936

113 for 8th wicket with S N Banerjee v Essex, at Brentwood, England, 1946

*143 for 2nd wicket with V M Merchant v Northamptonshire, at Northampton

219 for 3rd wicket with Nawab of Pataudi, v Sussex, at Hove

Australia, 1947–48

176 for 7th wicket with C T Sarwate, v S Australia, at Adelaide

*175 for 6th wicket with v Mankad v S Australia, at Adelaide

107 for 4th wicket with C T Sarwate, v Victoria, at Melbourne

153 for 8th wicket with C S Nayudu, v Victoria, at Melbourne

104 for 6th wicket with H R Adhikari, v Queensland, at Brisbane

255 for 3rd wicket with V S Hazare, v Tasmania, at Hobart

253 for 2nd wicket with C T Sarwate, v Tasmania, at Launceston

Against Visiting Sides

134 for 4th wicket with Yuvraj (later HH of Patiala), S Punjab v M C C 1933–34

178 for 4th wicket with Mohammed Hussain, Moin-ud-Dowla's XI, v Ryder's team, 1935–36

150 for 5th wicket D R Havewala, Maharaja of Patiala's XI v Lord Tennyson's team, 1937–38

172 for 3rd wicket with S Mushtaq Ali Princes' XI v Australian Services, 1945

112 for 7th wicket with Balbir Chand, North Zone v West Indies, 1948–49

Other First Class Matches

410 for 3rd wicket with R S Modi, for India-in-England v Rest of India, at Calcutta, 1946–47

---

* Unfinished partnerships

Statistics compiled by Anandji Dossa

INDEX

OTHER CRICKET BOOKS FROM SPORTSBOOKS

George Lohmann – Pioneer Professional
Keith Booth
Lohmann had a better average and strike rate than any other bowler in Test cricket. Tragically his life was cut short at the age of 36 due to pulmonary tuberculosis. Surrey scorer Keith Booth examines the life of one of the county's greatest cricketers.
ISBN 9781899807 50 5
PRICE £18.99
Hardback
Published May 2007

Encyclopedia of World Cricket
Roy Morgan
A truly comprehensive encyclopedia of world cricket. In the past, books like this have concentrated on the Test-playing nations but this looks at the game all over the world, including the non-Test-playing countries and the women's game. It details all the international and domestic competitions and is a must for every cricket fan's bookshelf.
ISBN 9781899807 51 2
PRICE £17.99
Paperback
Pagination 400
Published June 2007

Local Heroes
John Shawcroft
The story of the Derbyshire team which won cricket's county championship in 1936, the only time the club has finished first. What was remarkable was that all its members were drawn from the Derbyshire coalfields.
The book was shortlisted for the Cricket Society's 2007 Book of the Year award.
"This is a very good cricket book... enthralling narrative... fine contextualising sentences... recommended". Association of Cricket Statisticians
ISBN 1899807 35 7
Price £14.99
Paperback
Published May 2006

Colin Blythe - lament for a legend
Chris Scoble
Blythe was the most famous England cricketer to be killed in the First World War. "Historians with a tragedian's bent will... swoon over Christopher Scoble's poignant, near perfect biography," said the Guardian's Frank Keating
ISBN 1899807 31 4
Price £16.99
Hardback
Published May 2005